CHILDREN'S PARTICIPATION:
The Theory and Practice of Involving Young Citizens in Community Development and Environmental Care

CHILDREN'S PARTICIPATION:
The Theory and Practice of Involving Young Citizens in Community Development and Environmental Care

By Roger A. Hart

With contributions by:
Maria Fernanda Espinosa
Selim Iltus
Raymond Lorenzo

United Nations Children's Fund

Earthscan Publications Ltd, London

First published in the UK in 1997 by
Earthscan Publications Limited

Reprinted 1999

A catalogue record for this book is available from the British Library

ISBN: 1 85383 322 3

Page design by S&W Design
Typesetting by PCS Mapping & DTP, Newcastle upon Tyne

For comments or further information on this and other UNICEF concerns please contact:
Division of Communication
UNICEF
3 UN Plaza
New York, NY 10017 USA
Email: pubdoc@unicef.org
World Wide Web: http://www.unicef.org

Printed and bound by Biddles Ltd, Guildford and King's Lynn

Cover design by Andrew Corbett
Cover photo @ The Environment Centre, Edinburgh

Cover photo: The square metre cornfield has enabled thousands of children to plant and manage their own mini-farms, regardless of whether they live in rural or urban areas. This is one of the programmes introduced to schoolteachers, children's and youth organizations, and community groups by the Environmental Centre in Edinburgh, Scotland.

For a full list of publications please contact:
Earthscan Publications Limited
120 Pentonville Road
London N1 9JN
Tel: (0171) 278 0433
Fax: (0171) 278 1142
Email: earthinfo@earthscan.co.uk
World Wide Web: http://www.earthscan.co.uk

Earthscan is an editorially independent subsidiary of Kogan Page Limited and publishes in association with the WWF-UK and the International Institute for Environment and Development.

The material in this book has been commissioned by the United Nations Children's Fund (UNICEF). The contents of this book are the responsibility of the authors and do not necessarily reflect the policies or the views of UNICEF.

Contents

Part II Children's Participation in Practice

Chapter 5 Action Research with Children   91

Chapter 6 Environmental Planning, Design, and Construction by Children   108

Chapter 7 Environmental Management   119

Preface

This book was commissioned by two separate units of the United Nations Children's Fund (UNICEF), the former Environment Section (now part of the Water, Environment and Sanitation Cluster) of UNICEF headquarters in New York and the Children's Rights Section of the International Child Development Centre of UNICEF in Florence, Italy. It is an attempt to further the prospects for marriage of these two concerns of growing international importance: the environment, as now expressed by the international movement for sustainable development, and children's rights, as reflected in the United Nations Convention on the Rights of the Child. It is designed to serve two audiences. For those who are concerned with sustainable development, but have not worked with children, it is an introduction to children's participation and its effectiveness in community-based environmental planning and management; I hope it will be useful to both governmental and non-governmental agencies involved in environment and development work. For educators, community leaders and others who already understand children's capacities but would like to know more practically about how to involve them in community development and environmental projects, it offers organizing principles and methods.

For a number of reasons, this is not designed as a 'cookbook' style manual; participation must be a dynamic constructive process, with the score being built, like jazz, as a programme proceeds. Furthermore, this book is intended to be of use in different cultures. There is no universal model of how children should participate in society. I recognise this problem by including examples of children's participation from a diversity of cultures and social classes. Extracting from these, it has been possible to identify some useful principles about the processes that have worked for different groups and a range of techniques that have been found to be effective.

The book focuses on childhood and early adolescence, to about fourteen years of age, rather than upon the older teenage years, even though the Convention on the Rights of the Child (CRC) defines the child as any person under 18 years of age. Most children in the world have either formally or informally entered the workforce by 15 years of age and are intellectually able to understand environmental issues on a par with adults. For them, many of the existing guidelines for involving adults in environmental and community projects are relevant. In contrast, this book is particularly concerned with the special developmental issues to consider when involving children and adolescents. Nevertheless, many of those who work with older teenagers might also find it useful, for I certainly found many valuable ideas from programmes with these age groups.

This publication concentrates on the conceptual issues, processes and methods for authentically involving children in research, planning, design, management and monitoring of the environment. While many case studies are provided, there is no attempt to be comprehensive in describing all of the specific kinds of direct actions children can carry out to improve the environment. There are hundreds of publications on how children can recycle, garden, build solar ovens, be selective in their shopping behaviour and so on. Instead this book looks more critically at the processes of working with children so that we can engage them in more genuinely participatory ways.

Inevitably, the book reflects the biases of an English author living in the United States, but it draws equally from examples from the Southern Hemisphere, particularly South America. Children's community participation seems to be developing more in some of the emerging democracies than in the self-proclaimed well-established democracies of the North. More important than any North–South differences, though, are the great contrasts within all countries between those who do and those who do not recognize the capacities and desires of children to play a meaningful role in the development of their communities and in the care of the environment.

My thinking on children's participation began with Robin Moore in 1979. Together with a small team of graduate students and high school students we produced a series of newsletters on children's participation for the International Year of the Child. Some time later, Mary Racelis, then responsible for Women's Development and Community Participation at UNICEF, saw the potential of children's participation in community development and asked me to visit Sri Lanka and Colombia, South America, where there were some interesting initiatives. But it was the Convention on the Rights of the Child, with its visionary articles on children's participation, which provided the context for the commissioning of a book on the subject. Following my consultations with organizations for poor and working children in Kenya, India, the Philippines and Brazil, for the UNICEF International Child Development Centre (ICDC) the director of the Urban Child Program, Cristina Blanc, concluded that a handbook of methods for children's participation should be produced. This fit well with the Child Rights initiative of the Director of ICDC, Jim Himes. An international survey of children's participation projects was launched in collaboration with Malfrid

Flekkoy of Norway, who was then a visiting scholar at ICDC. The task of producing a handbook on children's participation was enormous, but Deepak Bajracharya, Chief of the recently formed Environment Section of UNICEF, suggested that it might usefully focus on environmental projects. The writing was carried out with the close support of the Environment Section of the New York Headquarters of UNICEF and with much encouragement from other UNICEF inter-sectoral sections: Social Mobilization and Communication, Urban, Children in Especially Difficult Circumstances, Development Education, and the NGO Liaison Office.

Three people were so helpful in preparing sections of this book that I have listed them as contributing authors. Maria Fernanda Espinosa, ecologist, social scientist and poet, helped a great deal with many sections, and was my support throughout the long process. She also offered her personal accounts of the Program of Working Children in Ecuador where she had worked as an environmental advisor. The second contributing author is Selim Iltus, Co-Director of the Children's Environments Research Group. Selim is an architect and environmental psychologist with multiple talents. It is not possible to think of any of my own work in New York separately from him. Ray Lorenzo, a planner from Perugia, Italy has been a friend and colleague for 20 years and has worked continuously with children in environmental projects for all of this time. I was fortunate to have his help in writing sections on children's futures and collage-making by children, as well as his fascinating case studies of work with WWF in the south of Italy. Special thanks also go to Jeff Bishop, expert on community participation in the United Kingdom, who should have been a co-author had funds allowed it.

Alison King, also of the Children's Environments Research Group, joined with Selim Iltus in producing the graphics and provided valuable editorial assistance throughout the writing.

A large number of people around the world have assisted by contributing material to the book or through their critical commentary on an early draft. I will attempt to recognize most of these generous people here by simply listing them, although some spent many hours helping me: Eileen Adams, Deepak Bajracharya, Sherry Bartlett, Christina Blanc, Annie Brody, Jo Boyden, Rex Curry, Louise Chawla, Vicky Colbert, Fabio Dallape, Ximena de la Barra, Mark Francis, Tony Gibson, Muriel Glasgow, Nora Godwin, David Goldenberg, Clare Hanbury, Ray Harris, Randy Hester, Tony Hewitt, Jim Himes, Heather Jarvis, David Kritt, Margarita Marina de Botero, Sarah McCrum, Kavitha Mediratta, Dianna Mitlin, Robin Moore, Janet Nelson, Marjorie Newman-Williams, Dolores Padilla, Carlos Pagliarini, Tom Price, Joan Schine, Michael Schwab, Jason Schwartzman, Jac Smit, Clay Smith, Surabhi Splain, Lucy Trapnell, Fred Wood, David Woolcombe, and Mike Zamm.

Finally, my friend David Satterthwaite helped me bring the book to fruition through his critical commentary and his enthusiastic support. The team he introduced me to at Earthscan, Jonathan Sinclair Wilson, Rowan Davies and Jo O'Driscoll, were very supportive and patient in helping me pull together all of the many disparate pieces of this collection.

This Preface ignores the hundreds of people I have met in situ, doing innovative work in South America, India, Kenya, Niger, Sri Lanka and the Philippines. As a writer learning from people working in low-income communities it is difficult to know if one can return something equal to what one takes. When this book reaches you, I hope you recognize your work in my writing, and feel that your generosity has served others a little through these words.

Figure 1:
A nine-year-old girl managing ducks in the Brazilian Amazon. Rosetta lives on the banks of the Tapajós River in the Brazilian Amazon. Like most girls in most countries of the Southern Hemisphere, she has a great deal of work and responsibility in managing the domestic environment. Regular visits by Projeto Saude y Allegre (the Health and Happiness Project) bring training, primary health care, and primary environmental care to her and her friends in a creative way. A boatload of volunteer workers dressed as clowns come ashore to teach the children about how to use the diversity of natural resources around their village and the nutritional and health values of these resources. This community, like so many colonist communities in the Amazon, has lost the knowledge possessed by the indigenous Indian communities, and this mobile circus is one creative way of introducing some of the principles of sustainable development into the community. © Roger Hart.

For those many people I did not meet who are carrying out authentic participatory projects with children, I hope you will let me know of them.*

Roger Hart
New York
May 1996

* Children's Environments Research Group
City University of New York
Graduate School and University Center
33 West 42nd Street
New York, NY 10036 USA

PART

1

INTRODUCTION AND CONCEPTUAL ISSUES

Introduction

Children of the 1990s have entered the world at a point in history when many nations are radically reassessing their use of natural resources and the role of citizens in managing the environment. At the same time almost all countries of the world have signed the United Nations Convention on the Rights of the Child (CRC), leading them to rethink the extent to which children have the right and responsibility to be involved in shaping their own futures and the futures of their communities.[1] I have written this book in the belief that the most sound approach to development lies in the establishment of a citizenry that understands, and cares about, the management of the environment and which can operate in a highly participatory manner in democratic communities. Children's environmental education needs to be brought into line with the principles and practices of local community participation in all countries and with all communities.

Only through direct participation can children develop a genuine appreciation of democracy and a sense of their own competence and responsibility to participate. The planning, design, monitoring, and management of the physical environment is an ideal domain for the practice of children's participation; it seems to be clearer for children to see and understand than many social problems. Furthermore, people's relationship to nature is the greatest issue facing the world at the turn of the century. All over the world, young people are becoming enthusiastically involved in environmental action. Unfortunately, children's great energies can also be manipulated by the social issue of the moment, and this is often true of the environmental movement, which is replete with examples of children involved in large-scale, highly superficial, short-term actions to 'save the earth'. This book is written with the conviction that all children can play a valuable and lasting role, but only if their participation is taken seriously and planned with recognition of their developing competencies and unique strengths. Too many children are naively parroting clichés from someone else's environmental agenda about environments entirely removed from their own experience. We need children to become highly reflective, even critical, participants in environmental issues in their own communities. We need them to think as well as act locally while also being aware of global issues.

THE ENVIRONMENT BECOMES THE CONCERN OF ALL COMMUNITIES

The 'environmental movement' that began at the end of the 1960s in North America and Europe remained for more than 25 years a largely middle-class movement of the industrialized countries. Finally it is maturing into a movement with central relevance to all communities, rich and poor, in both hemispheres. With this maturation comes the need for new institutional alliances and new roles for citizens and thus for children. A brief introduction to some of the changes in perspective on the environment that are beginning to occur, particularly in the countries of the 'South' or the Third World, is necessary as a background to a full understanding of why community-based sustainable

[1] The UN Convention on the Rights of the Child describes 'children' as all people up to, and including, 18 years of age. This book focusses on those 14 years of age or younger. For clarity of discussion, this book uses the following arbitrary divisions: 'preschool children' (under 6 years), 'young children' (6 to 9 years), 'older children' (9 to 12 years) and 'adolescents' (12 to 14 years). See UNICEF (1990).

[2] It was difficult to come to terms with the confusing array of options for describing differences between groups of countries. Any of the terms seems to oversimplify the enormous differences with any one region and in so doing to set up an unrealistic contrast between them. Nevertheless, communication requires us to use categories in order to make generalizations which then can be qualified. In much of the text I have chosen to use the North/South terminology rather than First, Second and Third worlds or Developed and Developing, because all of these alternatives imply a continuum of development on which the South should advance toward the North. The North/South terminology has come to be used by many NGOs because it simply seems to express a grouping of countries that are different. It remains for the writer to articulate how they are different and to avoid oversimplification and overgeneralization by surrounding these categories with a richer debate.

[3] See the journal *Streetwise*, Bishop, Adams, and Kean (1992) and Ball and Ball (1973) for an overview of this movement in the United Kingdom, and the journal *Children's Environments* for examples in the USA.

development and children's involvement in this is so important.[2]

Transcending 'Green' in the Environmental Movement

Following the ecological principle that the entire planet is an interdependent system, we understand that the environment is everything and that we are each part of one another's environment. For this reason, this book attempts to recognize all types of environmental problems. Unfortunately, the term 'the environment', as discussed by the environmental movement and environmental education curricula, is commonly not so broad. The first step, then, in any environmental programme or conversation is to consider how the term environment is being used. The major distinction is between those who speak primarily of the natural environment and natural resources, and those whose emphasis is the built environment. The emphasis of the environmental movement and of most environmental education programmes has been upon the natural environment. Related to this, environmental education in most countries has been seen as the task of educating the public about nature conservation or how to protect the natural environment from damaging human actions. There are, however, other groups of professionals who educate children about, and lead them to be involved in, environmental settings with little or no attention to the natural environment.

In Europe and North America the largest of the environmental education and action groups outside the nature-oriented environmentalists are the urban planners and designers, the community organizers, and a wide diversity of urban activists who have been concerned with improving the built environment for human beings.[3] A subgroup of these includes those architects, artists, and others who have been concerned primarily with improving children's awareness of and concern for the visual properties of the environment, usually the built environment. Similarly, in the developing countries there are thousands of organi-

zations that work with communities, sometimes involving children, on the improvement of people's living conditions through education and participation, but commonly with little or no relationship to the concerns for the natural environment or the environmental movement. In recent years there have been some excellent books documenting the environmental conditions of poor children and their families and the kinds of programmes needed to address them (Boyden and Holden, 1991; Enew and Milne, 1989; Hardoy et al, 1992; Blanc, 1994; Satterthwaite et al, 1996). In urban areas this work has included many of the environmental concerns of urban activists in the industrialized countries, such as housing and transportation, but with a much greater emphasis on issues of health and nutrition in relation to human survival.

These two major professional groups, one oriented towards the natural environment and the other towards the human environment, have had little to do with each other, yet they are both concerned with the physical environment. The reason for this is largely one of social class. The nature-oriented environmental movement has, until very recently, drawn its members largely from the middle and upper classes. They have not felt that housing, adequate parks, municipal services, opportunities to earn a living, and so on were appropriate questions to be considered by environmentalists or environmental educators. Even in rural areas, where people make their living from the natural environment, the integration of environmental issues with issues of human survival and development – employment, education, health, and nutrition – has begun only recently.

Environmentalists have made the expression 'only one earth' a popular cliché and insist that we look at it in its entirety, but most environmental educators remain fixated only on the earth's green parts. In addition to the class bias discussed above, much of this is a result of the separation of academic fields and professional practice into the natural and the social sciences. While it is of course necessary to focus on particular parts, or ecosystems, of this entirety at different times, this book adopts the perspective that it is not acceptable for environmental awareness programmes to ignore the built or living environments of people, and particularly the poor, even when environmental educators and animators may be quite right in saying that they are addressing critical environmental issues that affect us all, regardless of social class. In the past few years there has been a growth of what is being called the 'environmental justice' movement in the United States. This is an important development, for it is bringing social class into the concerns of the environmental movement by investigating and acting upon social inequity in the improvement of environmental quality. Unfortunately, so far this movement is adopting the agenda of the 'environmental movement', with its exclusion of housing and the living environments of the poor. Thus the items on the agenda remain the same – for example, air pollution, toxic waste disposal – though now there is a concern with the unfair distribution of environmental contamination in the backyards of the poor. In Latin America a similar movement, called *seguridad ecologica* ('ecological safety'), has taken an important step further. Garbage recycling, for example, which was a concern of the middle classes, has now grown in some countries to include not only the improved management of solid waste in low income areas but also the livelihood and working conditions of the garbage recyclers.[4] Now that the environmental movement wishes to incorporate all social classes, it is necessary for environmentalists and human development professionals of all kinds to begin to work together so that the total environment becomes the concern of environmental education. For these reasons, the examples of children's environmental projects in this book include the environments of people as well as whales, housing as well as forests.

The Concept of Sustainable Development

In 1987 the World Commission on Environment and Development, commonly called the Bruntland Commission, announced to the world a strategy for the future that they felt would simultaneously offer development and the eradication of poverty while also rescuing the earth from its perilous path of degradation.[5] The strategy, called *sustainable development*, was defined as 'development that meets the needs of the present without compromising the ability of future generations to meet their own needs.' For so long the environmental movement had spoken of 'conservation' without referring to development. Even the 1970 World Conference on the Environment in Stockholm focused on cleaning up the environment and conserving natural resources with little attention to issues of poverty. The report of the Brundtland Commission led to the UN Conference on Environment and Development in Rio de Janeiro in 1992, a momentous event commonly called the Earth Summit.[6] This time, the poor nations insisted that the agenda include development as well as the environment. If the countries of the North wanted the South to reduce their destruction of the environment, then the North was going to have to pay. The less industrialized countries were already saddled with enormous debts to the Northern Hemisphere and could not accept another constraint on their ability to address poverty at home. The conference had to address head on the issue of human survival. Economic growth and environmental care would now need to be considered hand in hand.

Unfortunately, the phrase 'sustainable development' has already been so used and abused to legitimize all kind of policies and decisions that the reader should not see this phrase as some kind of magic key. It is a useful term but, as with any social construct, children, and youth, should be ready to be critical of it. First, there is a genuine confusion over the meaning of the term *sustainable*.[7] In this book I use the term to imply 'ecological sustainability'. This preserves the original intention of the Brundtland Commission, who wished to stress that the ecological integrity of the environment must be maintained in order to guarantee its value to future generations. In

4 Pacheco (1992).

5 See World Commission on Environment and Development (1987). The World Commission on Environment and Development was conceived by the United Nations under the chairmanship of the former Prime Minister of Norway, Gro Harlem Bruntland, and so the book *Our Common Future* is sometimes called 'The Bruntland Report'.

6 Keating (1994).

7 See Hardoy et al. (1993) and Satterthwaite et al. (1996).

[8] For a discussion of the different motivational bases for environmental caring see Hart and Chawla (1982), or Chawla and Hart (1988).

[9] For a critique of the concept of sustainable development, see Escobar (1995) and Redclift (1987).

[10] Korten (1990).

this sense it is fundamental to any other kind of sustainability: social, cultural, programme, or project sustainability, which are other uses to which the term has already been put. I agree with Hardoy et al. (1993) and Satterthwaite et al (1996) that 'social sustainability' and 'cultural sustainability' are extremely important contexts for the achievement of ecological sustainability, but that they should not be allowed to confuse the fundamental importance of ecological sustainability in the phrase 'sustainable development'. Ironically, many people already use the phrase to refer to development, meaning that it is growth (capitalist market expansion), not ecological integrity, that must be sustained!

A second major problem with the concept of sustainable development is that it seems to accept a given definition of nature as being important only inasmuch as it serves human interest. The concept describes ecological sustainability as that which guarantees the needs of future generations of human beings, seemingly giving no recognition to the other possible motivators for people's care for nature, namely the value of nature itself.[8] It would be a mistake for children to be introduced to the concept of sustainable development in such a way that they are encouraged to believe that the sole concern is the utility of the earth's resources for humankind.

If we cannot continue to use natural resources as we have and we are no longer going to ignore the plight of the poor, then there will need to be radical changes in the distribution of resources and particularly changes in the lifestyle of those who will most use nature's capital, the people of the industrialized countries.[9] The question, then, is who will be the planners and managers of these resources? This book has been written on the assumption that resources have to be managed at the local level despite world trends to remove environmental management decisions to even more distant places. The sustainable development movement must then fundamentally address the control of resources: resource redistribution and decentralization in decision making.

The Need for Strong Local Democracy

For too long the word *development* has been equated simply with the word *growth* – growth in economic output or increase in industrialization. There is a thriving movement towards an alternative, more 'people-centred' vision of development. Box 1 offers a concise summary comparison by David Korten of those who hold a 'growth-centred' vision of development with his own 'assumptions of fact' concerning a more people-centred vision of development.[10] This comparison leads to a set of principles of people-centred development that merge the concept of sustainable development with issues of social justice and equity in the distribution of resources and inclusiveness in decision making. The first priority in the use of the earth's resources is to allow all people an opportunity to produce a basic livelihood for themselves and their families. Furthermore, every individual should have the right to be a productive, contributing member of family, community, and society. To achieve this, the control of productive assets should be broadly distributed within society, and local economies should be diversified and reasonably self-reliant in producing for their basic needs. While decision making should be as close to the level of individual, family, and community as possible, he recognizes that local decisions should reflect a global perspective and should accept the rights and responsibilities of global citizenship.

To achieve this vision, nations will need to make numerous structural changes to their economies. The emphasis will need to be upon using local resources to meet the needs of local populations, even though the market could demand a higher price for export products from these areas. Changes will be needed that will allow communities to take greater control of their own resources and will require difficult reforms in the use of water resources in most countries. National investment will need to be focused on strengthening smaller and intermediate scales of production, which use resources

---

Box 1: The Growth-Centred Vision of Development in Contrast to a People-Centred Vision

Assumptions of the Growth-Centred Vision of Development

- The earth's physical resources are for all practical purposes inexhaustible. (The explicit argument is made that somehow science will come up with suitable substitutes for any resource that becomes exhausted or prohibitively expensive to recover.)
- The environment has a virtually infinite ability to absorb waste.
- Poverty is simply the result of inadequate growth, which in turn results in inadequate capital investment.
- The international markets in which a country is competing are freely competitive, without subsidies or restraints that give competitors from some countries an advantage over others.
- Foreign borrowing is used for productive capital investments that will generate exchange for repayment.
- Those workers who are displaced from agriculture or other resource-based occupations, such as fishing, by productivity-enhancing investments will be readily absorbed in industrial employment in urban centres.
- Market forces will automatically distribute market benefits.

Assumptions of the People-Centred Approach to Development

- The earth's physical resources are finite.
- The productive and recycling capacity of ecological systems can be enhanced through human intervention, but this enhancement cannot exceed certain natural limits.
- Governments by nature give priority to the interests of those who control power.
- Political and economic power are closely linked in that the possession of either increases the holder's ability to exercise the other.
- Markets are important allocation mechanisms, but all markets are imperfect and, by their nature, give to the wants of the rich over the needs of the poor.
- Just, sustainable, and inclusive communities are the essential foundation of a just, sustainable, and inclusive global system.
- Diversified local economies that give priority, in the allocation of available resources, to meeting the basic needs of community members increase the security of individual communities and the resilience of the larger national and global economies.
- When the people control the local environmental resources on which their own and their children's lives depend, they are more likely than absentee owners to exercise responsible stewardship.

From Korten (1990), pp 42–3, 68–9.

---

in a sustainable manner, rather than upon large-scale export production.

These kinds of economic change are not the subject of this book. The focus is instead upon the human changes that will be necessary for a people-centred vision to take hold and for the world to achieve an international economy made up of multitudes of interrelated, local, sustainable economic units. This involves the building of strong local democracies.[11]

Great changes will be needed in the way the public

[11] See Aronowitz and Dhaliwal (1994) and Barber (1995).

[12] Korten (1990, pp. 114–32) discusses at length the development of NGOs that have transcended the stage of local empowerment and are now working on his 'third generation' of voluntary action, which he calls 'sustainable systems development'. These go beyond individual communities to develop policies and institutions at all levels which will foster and strengthen greater community control over resources. These NGOs are not only devoted to fostering in the public the kinds of empowerments proposed in his book but are also working to help coalesce these self-initiating and self-managing local groups. The fourth generation of NGO development must be at the level of a global movement for people-centred development. While Korten is not able to identify many NGOs that are operating at this level, he can point to the power of people's movements in driving social change in thinking and acting on the environment, women's issues, peace, and population.

[13] The case study of street and working children of Olongapo in the Philippines is described more fully in Blanc (1994).

thinks of development and its own role in it. For this to happen, children now need to be investigating their own communities in ways that will heighten their awareness of the need for a people-centred approach to development. At the same time, through their community research and action, children will develop a sense of shared responsibility and skills that will enable them to continue to participate as adults and to recognize the importance of their participation in local, national, and even global environmental decisions. This fundamental democratization of children is the most important aspect of their participation in the environment of their communities, more than the particular impact of any of their projects. *Development*, most fundamentally, is the process by which individuals and communities are able to increase their capacities to use resources, and to improve the quality of their lives, in an equitable manner.

It may seem naive to assume that local-level participation of communities will be sufficient to achieve development. Surely local power structures will resist any attempt by local communities to establish a fundamental reorganization of the distribution and use of resources no matter how well based it may be on ecological principles and principles of social justice. These local power structures are supported by national and international systems that are too well established for any local empowerment programme to modify. If one follows this logic in such a linear way, would it not be naive and irresponsible to suggest to children and youth that they can help make a difference?

The answer is that one needs to think of young people's involvement as a democratizing experience. We should always be honest with children so that, as they confront barriers in their genuine pursuit of understanding through research and action, they come to understand the nature of those barriers. In this way they can become the possessors of the knowledge that extends beyond their own local community. In subsequent sections of this book, examples are provided of how children's local projects can be linked with one another so that children can begin to understand some

of the issues that extend beyond their community and how people all over the world at the local level are struggling with some of the same barriers to change. Many NGOs around the world are already supporting local action by simultaneously working with local and national governments to achieve system changes that are more responsive to local initiatives.[12] It is this kind of coordinated NGO initiative that has enabled the Philippines to be so progressive in its work with children. Following the collapse of the Marcos regime the new mayor of the city of Olongapo, next to an American navy base, was able to support a network of NGOs in their efforts to empower the street children. Whereas in the past the streets were swept clean periodically by police, and children were even placed in cells with adults, now they were treated as citizens and given a chance to work together in peer groups of working children's associations to improve their lives as market vendors, porters, plastic bag sellers, and washers of jeeps.[13]

The Concept of Primary Environmental Care

The 1972 United Nations Human Environment conference in Stockholm recognized the importance of environmental education and citizen environmental action, but it clearly saw this as being achieved entirely through top-down environmental education leading to social mobilization: 'directed towards the general public, particularly the ordinary citizen, with a view to educating him as to the simple steps he might take, within his means, to manage and control his environment' (Recommendation No. 96). While there have been benefits from this kind of educational approach, it is time for a deeper, more grounded involvement of citizens with the environment.

It seems that the Rio de Janeiro conference initiative is spawning the development of more participatory approaches to environmental problems, at least in the countries of the South. As a follow-up to the UN Conference on Environment and Development in Rio, for example, UNICEF proposed an approach to environmental sustainability that accords with the participatory approach described above.[14] The following is extracted from the UNICEF Executive Board Summary of 'Children, Environment and Sustainable Development: UNICEF Response to Agenda 21':

... UNICEF advocates 'primary environmental care', a community-based approach to meeting basic needs through the empowerment of local communities, while ensuring the protection and optimal utilization of natural resources within the community. Priority should be given to the most vulnerable – especially children, women and the very poor – who are threatened by drought and desertification, urban poverty and the destruction of tropical forests and fragile mountain ecosystems. Environmental education should be promoted to encourage the active participation of women and children, to enhance their life skills and adaptability, and to enable them to attain a sustainable livelihood. (UNICEF 1993, p. 1). See also UNICEF 1992a, 1992b, 1993a and 1993b.

The kind of environmental education called for here by UNICEF is very different from that being practised and taught in our communities and schools today. There is a burden of responsibility on international agencies and NGOs to find ways to form alliances at the local level between schools, community organizations, and local government agencies in order to involve children with the larger community of adults in the improvement and on-going monitoring of their environments.

To be globally successful, the concept of sustainable development must promote public involvement in environmental management at the local level. This will come only from a citizenry that feels truly involved in its own local community, not one that simply responds to universal environmental dicta passed on by the media regarding what constitutes universal ecologically good behaviour. Building from modest local bases of community-based research and action offers the best hope for

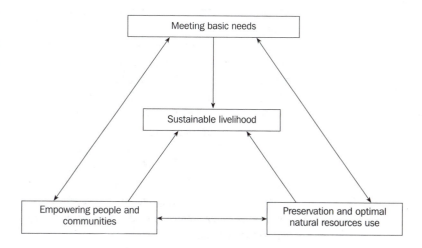

Figure 2:
The concept of primary environmental care (from Bajracharya 1994)

Figure 3:
The provision of safe drinking water, close by so that children are not burdened by the heavy labour of carrying it, is a priority of primary environmental care for all communities. Boys add potable water they have fetched from a protected source to a drum used for the neighbourhood water supply in Guayaquil, Ecuador.
© UNICEF, by Bernard P Wolff.

[14] UNICEF (1992); Bajracharya (1994, 1995); Taylor-Ide and Taylor (1995).

achieving the global participation of citizens in solving environmental problems.

Environmental education must be radically reconceived in order to be seen as fundamental to the residents of communities from all social classes in all countries. We need programmes based on the identification and investigation of problems by residents themselves, with 'action research' as the dominant methodology. There is of course a central place for the teaching of environmental science – 'ecology', as it is often called – but this should at first be directly related to the local environment. Environmental education from this perspective is intrinsically tied to community development in general.

What, then, is the meaning of *primary* in the phrase 'primary environmental care'? The answer will be different for different communities. Partnership is needed: the identification and diagnosis of local issues by community residents, in dialogue with environmental professionals, and collaboration in the solving of these problems. The residents of any community know best what many of the environmental priorities and problems of their community are. On the other hand, environmental scientists and health professionals are often better prepared to identify what parts of the environment are most at risk from human action and what parts of the environment are most seriously affecting the health of a community. But, many environmental problems cannot be fully addressed by a local community. They are either too large and require outside action by a larger agency, or they are too interdependent and require collaboration between communities.

The first step in all environmental education and action programmes must be the identification of problems by residents themselves. This is particularly difficult at this time because the mass media have done such a good job of bringing to the attention of much of the world's population the importance of environmental problems and a select list of actions that residents should carry out to improve the environment. Many of the problems in any community are, of course, neither visible nor identifiable by the community alone. There is certainly a role for environmental scientists to bring such awareness to all communities, but then these problems need to be seen in the context of the communities' mapping out and prioritizing of their total set of problems, including those that are relatively unique to them. It enables the abstract scientific knowledge of environmental problems that has been generalized from other environments to be confronted by the detailed and specific indigenous environmental knowledge of the residents of a particular community.[15] In this way, the identification and analysis of environmental problems is sensitive to the particular characteristics of local settings and the solutions to these problems are carried out in ways that are appropriate for the particular culture.

CHILDREN'S RIGHTS AND RESPONSIBILITIES

The UN Convention on the Rights of the Child (CRC)

In 1989 the United Nations adopted a document with extraordinary implications for how children should be perceived and treated. The United Nations Convention on the Rights of the Child (CRC) is a set of universal standards for the protection and development of children, which, at the time of writing, has been ratified by over 170 nations.

Because many countries have extended 'childhood' by keeping children in school, the child in the CRC refers to 'every human being under the age of 18 years unless, under the law applicable to the child, majority is attained earlier.' In addition to articles that guarantee children's rights to survival, proper development, and protection from abuse and exploitation, the CRC also has a series of 'participation articles'. These are designed in part to guarantee further children's protection as individuals with rights rather than possessions by stating that children should know about their rights and be able to voice them, but they are also visionary articles which recognize children as developing citizens. They are a challenge to all nations, for certainly none fully complies with all of them. Specifically how and at what age children are socialized by their families and communities to participate fully in society varies enormously according to the culture and is not something that can be universally mandated. It is therefore fitting that the role of the family is stressed in Article 5 of the CRC:

> States Parties shall respect the responsibilities, rights, and duties of parents or, where applicable, the members of the extended family or community as provided for by local custom, legal guardians or other persons legally responsible for the child, to provide, in a manner consistent with the evolving capabilities of the child, appropriate direction and guidance in the exercise by the child of the rights recognised in the present Convention.

Many would argue that on the question of protection of children this is too strong a statement and that in many cases children need to be protected from their families. This issue is taken up by the CRC and is now being fought out through the establishment of new legal statutes in many countries. But this book is about children's civic participation, not their defence and participation in legal proceedings. Nevertheless, for the participation articles, it is true that, if children are to be encouraged to participate more, we need to work also with their parents, who themselves may not have had opportunities to participate in society.

Although the CRC is meant to serve as a standard for the establishment of both a legal and a moral code concerning children in each nation, it will take a long time in most countries before we see broad changes in attitudes toward children's participation in civic life. In the meantime, the CRC can serve as a valuable instru-

Figure 4:
Children's rights demonstration in Quito, Ecuador.
© UNICEF Ecuador.

ment of persuasion for those persons wishing to promote the idea of children as independent, thinking subjects capable and deserving of a greater degree of participation. Many will argue that children need to be protected so that they can have a childhood. Precisely how to balance children's needs for physical and psychological protection with their participatory rights remains a complex issue that many nations are now begining to face in light of the CRC, which they have ratified. If this process is done in an informed and sensitive way, children's participation in each culture will look different. I have attempted to extract in Box 2 those sections on the CRC that I think are most relevant to the issue of children's participation. I strongly recommend that readers obtain a copy of the CRC, either through their own government or through the offices of UNICEF in their country.[16]

Beyond Child Protection: Children as Protagonists of their Own Rights

The CRC offers two complementary views of children: less powerful and less competent than adults and therefore in need of certain kinds of protection, and oppressed

[16] See UNICEF-UK/Save the Children (1990) for an excellent four-volume series for guidance on introducing the CRC.

Box 2: Children's Participation as Recognized in the UN Convention on the Rights of the Child

The first four articles listed below focus most exclusively on the right to participate. An additional four are given because they are also explicit in their recognition of the importance of maximizing children's involvement according to their capacities. The headings are by the author.

Freedom of Expression
Article 12
1) States Parties shall assure to the child who is capable of forming his or her own views the right to express those views freely in all matters affecting the child, the views of the child being given due weight in accordance with the age and maturity of the child.

2) For this purpose, the child shall in particular be provided the opportunity to be heard in any judicial and administrative proceedings affecting the child, either directly, or though a representative or an appropriate body, in a manner consistent with the procedural rules of national law.

Article 13
1) The child shall have the right to freedom of expression; this right shall include freedom to seek, receive and impart information and ideas of all kinds, regardless of frontiers, either orally, in writing or in print, in the form of art, or through any other media of the child's choice.

2) The exercise of this right may be subject to certain restriction, but these shall only be such as are provided by law and are necessary:

a) For respect of the rights and reputations of others; or

b) For the protection of national security or of public order (ordre public), or of public health and morals.

Freedom of Thought, Conscience, and Religion
Article 14
1) States Parties shall respect the right of the child to freedom of thought, conscience and religion.

2) States Parties shall respect the rights and duties of the parents and, when applicable, legal guardians, to provide direction to the child in the exercise of his or her right in a manner consistent with the evolving capacities of the child.

3) Freedom to manifest one's religion or beliefs may be subject only to such implications as are prescribed by law and are necessary to protect public safety, order, health or morals, or the fundamental right and freedoms of others.

Freedom of Assembly
Article 15
1) States Parties recognise the rights of the child to freedom of association and freedom of peaceful assembly.

2) No restrictions may be placed on the exercise of these rights other than those imposed in conformity with the law and which are necessary in a democratic society in the interests of national security or public safety, public order (ordre public), the protection of public health or morals or the protection of the rights and freedoms of others.

Access to Information
Article 17
States Parties recognise the important function performed by the mass media and shall ensure that the child has access to information and material from a diversity of national and international sources, especially those aimed at the promotion of his or her social, spiritual and moral well-being and physical and mental health. To this end, States Parties shall:

a) Encourage the mass media to disseminate information and material of social and cultural benefit to the child and in accordance with the spirit of article 29;

b) Encourage international cooperation in the production, exchange and dissemination of such information and material from a diversity of cultural, national and international sources;

c) Encourage the production and dissemination of children's books;

d) Encourage the mass media to have particular regard to the linguistic needs of the child who belongs to a minority group or who is indigenous;

e) Encourage the development of appropriate guidelines for the protection of the child from information and material injurious to his or her well-being, bearing in mind the provisions of articles 13 and 18.

Special Support for Disabled Children
Article 23
1) States Parties recognise that a mentally or physically disabled children should enjoy a full and decent life in conditions which ensure dignity, promote self-reliance and facilitate the child's active participation in the community.

Education for Personal Fulfilment and Responsible Citizenship
Article 29
1) States Parties agree that the education of the child shall be directed to:

a) The development of the child's personality, talents and mental and physical abilities to their fullest potential;

b) The development of respect for human rights and fundamental freedoms, and for the principles enshrined in the Charter of the United Nations;

c) The development of respect for the child's parents, his or her own cultural identity, language and values, for the national values of the country in which the child is living, the country from which he or she may originate, and for civilisations different from his or her own;

d) The preparation of the child for responsible life in a free society, in the spirit of understanding, peace, tolerance, equality of sexes, and friendship among all peoples, ethnic, national and religious groups and persons of indigenous origin;

e) The development of respect for the natural environment.

[17] Boyden (1991); Cussianovich (1994).

> *2) No part of the present article or article 28 shall be construed so as to interfere with the liberty of individuals and bodies to establish and direct educational institutions, subject always to the observance of the principles set forth in paragraph 1 of the present article and to the requirements that the education given in such institutions shall conform to such minimum standards as may be laid down by the State.*
>
> ### Play and Participation in Cultural and Artistic Life
> #### Article 31
> *1) States Parties recognise the right of the child to rest and leisure, to engage in play and recreational activities appropriate to the age of the child and to participate freely in cultural life and the arts.*
>
> *2) States Parties shall respect and promote the right of the child to participate fully in cultural and artistic life and shall encourage the provision of appropriate and equal opportunities for cultural, artistic, recreational and leisure activity.*

or constrained and hence needing more opportunities for self-determination. It is also believed that giving children more of a voice in their own self-determination will improve the protective aspects of the CRC. See Blanc (1994) for examples in five countries of how the CRC is relevant to the improvement of urban children living in difficult circumstances.

Probably the most dramatic impact of the participatory articles of the CRC is the way they are being used in some countries by people working with children who live, or at least work, on the street. Article 32 of the CRC spells out the importance of protecting children from economic exploitation and harmful work. However, according to some of those who work with these children, the CRC gave no specific recognition to the 'child of the street' and put too much faith in the family as the guarantor of children's rights.[17] For example, Alajandro Cussianovich, who works with working children in Lima, Peru, complains that the wealth of research reports on the conditions of street and work-

Figure 5:
Much work by children is clearly exploitative and children need to be protected from it. This boy is being used as cheap labour on a cotton plantation in Nicaragua.
© UNICEF/Maria Morrison.

ing children in many countries 'have still not broken the paradigm of the child as a private individual, protected, or overprotected, or not protected at all, by the private castles of the family.'[18] Cussianovich argues that 'protectionism' still dominates the conception of work with children throughout the world, yet is still ineffective in helping the masses of children who work at a very young age or are abused, neglected, or even involved in warfare. It is because of this failure, he argues, that a new social movement is emerging from protection to 'protagonism'. The conclusion that many of the child's rights promoters have reached is that the best protection and guarantee for the development of childhood is 'self-protection'.

The NGOs who work with street and working children, particularly in Latin America and the Philippines, have helped children read and interpret the CRC as a way of empowering them in the struggle to improve their lives. These street workers, or 'promoters' as they are often called in Latin America, see themselves as offering a supportive role for the children as they learn to be their own protagonists. It is ironic that in many countries the principles of the CRC are better known by children who are illiterate and who live primarily on the streets, beyond the influence of their families, than by those who are well off and live within the homes of intact families.[19] Sadly, this is not also true of the millions of working children who are hidden even from the street workers, trapped inside factories and mines or in domestic slavery inside homes. It is particularly difficult to promote children's rights to education and participation in those very poor families who rely on the income of their children's labour in the short term and who themselves lack basic human rights. A special section of this book is reserved for a discussion of working with these groups of children.

The Under-Recognized Potential of Children

When children's energies are recognized, they are almost always in the form of 'social mobilization' rather

Figure 6: Children's work needs to be seen in the context of the culture, the family, and a child's knowledge and aspirations before knowing whether or not it is exploitive. Here, girls in a village in Cambodia are pumping water for their families. © UNICEF/5690/Mainichi/Shinichi Asabe.

than participation. Social mobilization involves the activation of people to carry out a predetermined agenda. The great value of participation over social mobilization for all ages, of course, is that it fosters the long-term development of citizenship and, more specifically, a sense of local responsibility, rather than simply providing a short-term solution to a community problem through the use of free labour.

While there is a growing involvement of children in environmental issues, it is often not grounded in their own daily lives. It has become common, for example, for children to speak at national and international environmental conferences, sometimes with great emotion, about national and global issues, but with little apparent knowledge of their own communities and with no accounts of personal experiences. One cannot help but

[18] NGO Committee on UNICEF (1994), p. 29.

[19] An excellent series of booklets on the CRC for teachers and facilitators working with children is available from UNICEF UK/Save the Children (1990). For a practical introduction to the CRC for children, see Fountain (1995). The video 'Raised Voices' (1993), also by UNICEF, is a good introduction for children and adults to children's right to have a voice.

Figure 7:
Even communities that believe in community participation commonly underestimate the competence of children. When I ask village or neighbourhood leaders about children's participation, I am commonly met with blankness even when their own photographs of building a new well or drainage system show me that their children were centrally involved in carrying out the project. They have simply taken this involvement for granted and not found ways to build upon it. From the earliest ages children are observing the work of their community and looking for ways to exercise their competence through involvement.
© UNICEF.

feel that these children are parroting the messages of the media and of environmental education programmes. If we thought more carefully about children's involvement in these events, we would not pretend that any child selected by adults could represent other children. Children should be elected by other children to attend conferences as their representatives, to express issues identified, investigated, and discussed with these other children at the local level.

National and international conferences are not ideal settings for children's genuine participation. They are mentioned here only to highlight the need to convince politicians and NGOs to treat children's participation seriously at the local level. Many politicians may appear moved by children's testimonies at conferences, but few of them bring children's perspectives into their

own agencies or, even more important, encourage children's participation in environmental planning and management issues in their own communities.

We need fewer trite examples of children speaking or singing about how they are the future or how they alone best understand global environmental problems, and more models that genuinely recognize the untapped competencies of children to play a significant role in community-based sustainable development, particularly when collaborating with adults.

Parental Resistance to Children's Rights

It remains to be seen how successful those who work with children can be in promoting within families, both rich and poor, the conception of children's rights. Families are often highly authoritarian structures. Many parents fear that 'children's rights' implies a loss of control over children, who, they think, already have too much freedom. This is a misreading of the CRC, which does not call for a collapse in the teaching of discipline or responsibility to others. Neither does it seek to remove the rights of parents to make the final decisions, but it calls for a transparency of action and an openness to listen and to communicate with children according to their maximum capacity. The debate about children's rights can be expected to rage for many years because it involves a fundamental change in a culture and how a culture reproduces itself.[20] As the debate rages, inevitably arguments become simplified and polarized. It does not help to speak of 'equal rights' for children in the sense of power to make decisions equal to that of their parents or other overseeing adults.[21] Clearly, children start out life dependent upon the caring decisions of adults. Ideally, the family and other institutions gradually increase children's ability to act as their own agents, while recognizing that making more and more decisions themselves is necessary to their development as mature adults.

Confusion commonly seems to revolve around the meaning of authority. The granting of children's rights

[20] Alston (1994).

[21] See Purdy (1992).

should not undermine the legitimate authority of parents and other child caregivers; the purpose is to challenge arbitrary authority.[22] Some Western child development theorists and child-rearing guides for parents make this distinction through the use of the terms 'authoritarian' versus 'authoritative' supervision of children.[23] Parents and others need to recognize children's right to appeal decisions concerning their lives and they should be able to explain why these are wise decisions; it is not enough to say that this is 'the law'.[24] According to this perspective, adults must be able to justify their exercise of authority to their children as soon as children are capable of understanding. But this is a Western perspective on child rearing, and a recent one at that, which still is not shared by a large proportion of parents. There are enormous differences in cultural understandings around the world in what is an acceptable kind of authority to exercise with children, and more specifically with girls and boys respectively, and these will not change quickly. It surely cannot be questioned, however, that in all cultures there is a need for serious reflection on this issue, and the CRC is a superb base document for this reflection.

THE DEVELOPMENT OF CHILDREN'S ENVIRONMENTAL KNOWLEDGE, CONCERN, AND ACTION

Children and teenagers play an important role in the 'environmental movements' of many industrialized countries. Unfortunately, it is often not clear how much this is a fashion which will fade, like the environmental education fad of the early 1970s in the United States. Why is it that children in recent years have become the most fervent supporters of environmental action? Perhaps it is because since 1970 many schoolchildren have experienced a great deal of environmental education which serves as a valuable source of information about environmental problems. Add to this the influence of the media, and in particular the voices of popular musicians and actors. Also, children are more receptive to change and less integrated into the exist-

ing economic system and social order. They do not yet see the many barriers that might prevent change from being achieved. Even if these explanations alone could account for the fervour of many children for the movement, these pathways to concern seem inadequate to establish the kind of deep, lasting caring for the natural world that will be needed.

The Roots of Environmental Knowledge and Concern In Children

How do people develop a deep and lasting concern for the natural environment? This is an important question for anyone who believes that a concerned and informed citizenry is central to the healthy stewardship of the earth. Unfortunately, there is remarkably little theory or research on this question. There is a large literature on environmental education practices, but we know very little about how and why children develop a concern for environmental issues.[25] Many people still seem to believe that goodness comes to children who simply have contact with nature. It is hard for a Western urban dweller to discuss this without enormous bias, for the entire culture and its literature is saturated with romantic notions of a special relationship of children with nature.[26] Regrettably, there is very little discussion of children and nature from anthropology to correct this and so the following comments must be read with that bias in mind.

Paramount among the conceptual issues that cloud the area is the notion that children are 'closer' to nature. Poets often try to capture the loss of self-consciousness of children and their fresh, full experience of nature. While it seems to be true that there is a greater immersion in sensory perception in childhood, this does not necessarily mean that a child has a closer, more caring relationship to nature. One of the great theorists of child development, Piaget, observed from his research with young children in Switzerland that they were both closer to, and further from, nature.[27] They are closer perceptually because they are physically closer and less mediated in their

22 Matthews (1994).

23 Baumrind (1971); Maccoby and Martin (1983), pp. 41–9.

24 Matthews (1994), p. 79.

25 While there are multitudes of poems and stories that refer to children's special relationship with nature, there are very few theoretical discussions. See Cobb (1977) and reviews by Hart and Chawla (1982) and Chawla and Hart (1988) and Nabhan and Trimble (1994).

26 Hart and Chawla (1982); Chawla and Hart (1988); Ward (1988); Chawla (1994).

27 Piaget (1954, 1960, 1963); see also Sugarman (1987).

Figure 8:
'... an important aspect of pre-adolescent children's relationship to the natural world is that they are innately curious about it and struggle to understand their relationship to it as part of their desire to understand the meaning of life.'
© Roger Hart.

[28] See Wilson's 'biophilia hypothesis' for a related discussion; Wilson (1984); Kellert and Wilson (1993).

[29] Though very old, the reader is referred to a fascinating study of the spontaneous biological questions of young children, revealing how much more interest they have in animals than in plants (Isaacs, 1930).

[30] Carson (1984).

[31] Chawla (1986); Hart and Chawla (1982); Chawla and Hart (1988).

[32] Hart (1987); Nabham and Trimble (1994); also see *Children's Changing Access to Public Space*, special issue of *Children's Environments*, Vol. 9, No. 2, (1992) for data on children's reduced spatial range in the industrialized countries.

response to things, but they are further conceptually because they think everything is made *for* people, even the clouds, lakes, and mountains. Interestingly, Piaget also describes a phenomenon that could form roots for children of a different kind of relationship to nature as adults: 'animism', the tendency to find intention and consciousness in things, including those that are inanimate. The most famous of Piaget's accounts is of a child who gathers pebbles together so that they will not feel lonely. This is the kind of thinking that we label 'irrational' and rub out of children as quickly as possibe and yet this less differentiated perspective on the human and non-human attributes may have the potential to serve as a base for a different vector in the development of human caring for the non-human world.

There are probably other aspects of children's rela-

tionship to nature that differ from those of adults and could lead children to play an essential role in establishing new approaches to the care of the environment. I believe that an important aspect of pre-adolescent children's relationship to the natural world is that they are innately curious about it and struggle to understand their relationship to it as part of their desire to understand the meaning of life.[28] It is this existential kind of urge which I think is at the root of children's deep interest in animals.[29] We need to find ways of building upon the empathy that children often feel with animals and extending it to a larger interest in, and concern for, the total environment; to cultivate what Rachel Carson called the 'sense of wonder'.[30] But can children develop such an interest in, and affection for, nature in general? From an analysis of autobiographies, there is reason to believe that they can, but that to do so they need to empathise with it and this requires unmediated contact.[31]

We canot rely entirely upon an environmental education that reduces the complexity of ecosystems in an analytic way and presents it in texts or films (or even in single field trips), and then expect children mentally to reconstruct this beautiful complexity. Neither can we rely upon field trips or environmental action projects to compensate totally for this lack of an experience of place in childhood. We should feed children's natural desire to contact nature's diversity with free access to an area of limited size over an extended period of time, for it is only by intimately knowing the wonder of nature's complexity in a particular place that one can fully appreciate the immense beauty of the planet as a whole. It is ironic that the electronic media are enabling children to have greater understanding of the earth and of global environmental issues at a time when the geographic mobility of many children in the North and in urban areas of the South is becoming more constricted due to parents' fears, and they have little everyday, spontaneous contact with the natural world.[32]

Anyone who has seen children stoning crabs on a beach or burning cigarettes into frogs knows that contact with nature alone is not sufficient for a child to develop understanding of, and a caring relationship for, the natural world. The role of adults is also crucial. Opportunity for a rich diversity of direct experiences with the natural world alongside adults who are informed and caring about the natural world is ideal.[33] Without this, children will be left to construct meaning from a confusing and contradictory array of secondary sources.[34] Presumably the particular orientations to nature held by the significant adults in their world will also be important. Adults in the USA have been found to have very different orientations to nature from one another – from those based on consumption and utility for people to the more ecocentric ideologies, where human development needs are balanced with the demands of ecological sustainability.[35] We need to find ways for children to observe, imitate, talk with, and walk alongside adults who actively demonstrate knowledge of, and caring for, the environment.

In the less industrialized countries of the South, the situation is very different. Many families still live on the land, and from a very early age children work with their parents to produce a living from it.[36] Unfortunately, we know remarkably little about how these children think about the environment because anthropologists rarely engage in research with them. Cindi Katz, a geographer, has illustrated the great amount of environmental knowledge possessed by children in an agricultural village in the Sudan, including their knowledge of conservation practices and how to make a living from the land. More important, she has documented how this knowledge changes as a village is transformed from a subsistence economy, where children are exposed to a wide diversity of crops and agricultural practices, to a cash economy with only one or two types of crop.[37]

When families of countries of the South are led by a variety of forces to leave the land for an urban life, there is an enormous disruption in children's informal learning about the environment. While this is often a staged process from rural area to small town before moving to a large city, survival is usually no longer directly related to work with the land or with animals.

Most of the villagers living in Piqatuba in the Brazilian Amazon, described in Chapter 7, have lost the great knowledge of the environment of their Indian ancestors. The traditional tools of their parents and grandparents are displayed on the walls of their homes with almost as much understanding of their use as ploughshares are displayed on the walls of an English pub. The interesting difference with the Brazilian case study is the sense of the animators of the 'Health and Happiness Project' that these families can regain an understanding of how to live from the land in a sustainable manner. The biggest question is, as in so many parts of the world: will their children want to stay on the land or will they be pulled by the attractions of city life? Young people in many countries look down on agricultural occupations as inferior, even when life in the city for new migrants is commonly one of comparative degradation. Surely the mass media, with their images of the good life, all produced by urbanites, are partly to blame. Children are not presented with realistic images of their life options. As the world's development agencies race to make every child in the world literate by the year 2000, it should be a priority to have the content of their education be related to their futures. Children should be able to see alternative pathways to making a living, with realistic images of where they are leading, and these choices should include the opportunity to be involved in the sustainable development of rural communities offering a reasonable living from the land. Too often, schools in rural areas present agriculture as the low-status option remaining to children who are unable to leave for the cities. We need progressive approaches to the development of local livelihoods, with school curricula building upon rather than turning their backs on the traditional agricultural and environmental knowledge of communities.

The foregoing analysis suggests that, for urban children everywhere, we should be providing regular opportunities for the everyday enjoyment of natural environments close to home—wild commonlands, gardens, ponds, city farms, or schoolgrounds, ideally with interested

[33] Tanner (1980).

[34] Isaacs (1928).

[35] Kellert (1981).

[36] Rogoff et al. (1976).

[37] Katz (1986a, 1986b).

[38] Hart (1978); Moore (1986); Nabhan and Trimble (1994).

[39] Froebel (1887, originally 1826); Dewey (1960, originally 1900 and 1902), 1963; Piaget (1963, originally 1947).

[40] Hart and Chawla (1982).

[41] See Leopold (1966); Berry (1987); Orr (1992).

and informed adults nearby.[38] As they develop they should also have gradually expanding opportunities to be directly involved in developing these places and caring for them.

The Value of Environmental Action in Education

Most environmental educators recognize that a substantial part of an educational programme, particularly for pre-adolescent children, should involve some kind of direct action on the environment. Unfortunately, educators usually assign children to work on environmental projects rather than involving them in identifying problems themselves and collaborating with them in finding solutions. This is founded, I believe, in a restricted notion of the value of children's actions in environmental learning. Educators, if asked why actions by children are important to their environmental learning, commonly answer that such direct experiences are necessary for the understanding of pre-adolescent children. This concept goes back as far as the early educational philosophy of Froebel and extends through the writings of Dewey and Piaget. But children's actions with environments have importance beyond the purely cognitive.[39] I have argued that there is considerable theoretical reason to believe that concern for the environment is based on an affection that can come only from autonomous, unmediated contact with it.[40] This analysis of the roots of environmental concern has many implications for social policy, but a central one is surely the need for schools to allow young children to play regularly in as diverse a natural setting as possible surrounding the school and to be given gradually increasing opportunities to care for that setting.

For older children and adolescents to feel that they are playing a useful role in environmental improvement, it is not always necessary that they physically change the environment. One of the most effective roles they can play is to conduct research on the quality of the environment and communicate their findings to the larger community, including community leaders, planners, and politicians. Such research is frequently of much greater value to a community than some minor physical improvement. As long as the children feel that adults will listen to their conclusions and engage in a dialogue, the benefits to their sense of belonging to their community will be great.

There is an ideological aspect to the issue of children's involvement in environmental actions. Not all environmentalists believe it is necessary for all citizens to develop an active, responsible relationship to their environment to deal with the world's environmental problems. Many believe that it is necessary only that the general public be conscious of the importance of the issues so that politicians and technocrats can solve environmental problems through the improved application of scientific knowledge and technology. For them, environmental education in the form of classroom learning and the development of an abstract understanding of ecology would be adequate. In marked contrast, there are those, like myself, who see changed styles of living, the fostering of earth stewardship in everyone, and a more decentralized participatory democracy as essential.[41] They see that community environmental management for sustainable development must come from the multitudinous actions of individuals. This calls not only for the development of a personal knowledge of the natural world, leading to affection, but also for the skills of resourcefulness, cooperation, and more generally of community building that can come only from practising these skills in real environmental projects.

Local Knowledge as the Priority

The frequently used dictum 'Think globally, act locally' seems inadequate as a guide to the effective and responsible actions of citizens. It was designed during the first environmental movement in the Northern Hemisphere in the 1970s and has generally been interpreted to mean that environmentalists know what the problems are and the role of citizens is to carry out local actions while being aware of global consequences. This top-down conception of citizen involvement needs to be replaced with one that recognizes the importance of individuals thinking locally, too; citizens need critically to evaluate their local environment and how it is being used and abused as a result of both local and global factors before acting on it. This may lead citizens to conclude that the solution to a local environmental problem lies beyond changes in their own environmental actions and requires them to network with other groups or to raise environmental awareness and mobilize others, including those in positions of power. In short, they may also need to act more globally, too! But this global concern will be better grounded than many of the expressions of concern one now hears from children of the industrialized countries.

No matter what one's analysis of the causes of environmental problems are, battle lines for a new kind of environmental management must be drawn at the community level. Clearly the world's environmental crisis requires political and economic analysis at the international level and global changes in the uneven, and selfish, use of natural resources, but that will not be a focus of this book. In my view, the ultimate solution to sustainable development will involve a radical change in lifestyles and patterns of production and consumption, along with a decentralization of power and a return to greater community self-sufficiency. The current trend towards greater global specialization in production offers everything to a few and so little to so many others. It remains to be seen whether or not those of us living in the privileged countries and social classes will ever be willing to forgo such wasteful treats as having raspberries flown to our homes all year round. I hope so, because the successful and responsible management of the environment requires the caring actions of individuals at the local level who are themselves gaining sustenance from it.[42] A just and caring use of the land cannot be entrusted to global market forces. No matter how it is achieved, we will need in all cultures a concerned and active citizenry to balance

their own needs sensitively with the needs of the earth to sustain itself.

Working against local knowledge and the local control of resources is the conviction of the average citizen, in the face of the enormous complexity of the world's environmental problems and the unassimilable quantity of information thrown at them every day through electronic information tools, that their knowledge is irrelevant. Yet it is this very complexity which makes the emphasis on local knowledge such a necessity. It is for this reason that there are many warnings about electronic technology in environmental projects with children in this book. It has utility, but only if it does not work against the fostering of local knowledge in children.

A further argument for emphasizing local environmental research by children is that genuine ecological understanding involves an understanding of environmental phenomena 'in place' – that is, in their complex spatial relatedness to one another. If one accepts the theories of developmental psychologists that young children (at least those under ten years of age) require direct interaction with phenomena to understand them, then it follows that children must first investigate small-scale, local ecosystems. An eight-year-old child who has once studied in detail the life of a pond and the many forces impacting this ecosystem will be better prepared to understand large-scale ecological issues than a child of the same age who has seen many films and read dozens of books on the Amazon region.

Much of children's learning all over the world is at the local level from their peers. We need to find ways to build upon this. The following description of such learning in Togo, Africa, is a clear illustration of how in many cultures children learn from one another without the intervention of any government, non-government agencies, or teachers.[43]

'Very early on, the young child becomes bound up with his peer group. From his earliest days he will have seen his big brothers setting off in the

[42] For a passionate series of arguments on the importance of finding the solution to global problems through local sustainability, the reader is referred to Wendell Berry (1987, 1990).

[43] UNESCO (1989).

44 For example, the Local Government Management Board of the UK produces useful publications for local government authorities. Address: Arndale House, The Arndale Centre, Luton, Beds, LU1 2TS.

morning for the pastures, seated astride bulls, cows or even horses, their nostrils steaming in the light of dawn. He will have seen them returning happily to the village in the evening. He will, above all, have seen them rounding up the scattered herd, with a shout here and an order there that brooks no disobedience. He will also have watched his sisters rising very early to help their mother sweep the compound and its surroundings, drawing water from the river, washing their little brothers and sisters and clearing up the dishes used the previous evening. He will have seen them prinking and primping and accompanying their mother to the local market to sell vegetables and other rural products. And as the years go by they will have seen their brothers, one after the other, leaving their cattle-tending tasks to go off with their parents to tend their land while their sisters progressively assumed the role of housewife.' (Nambou, in UNESCO 1989).

Finally, for logistical reasons, research and action with children must be at the local level if the environmental movement is to involve everyone. For the vast majority of children this is the only realistic level to which they can expect to have access; long-distance expeditions and national and international conferences must remain the kind of high-profile projects for the select few children beloved of journalists and politicians.

Local Agenda 21

While there is much talk about Agenda 21, the UN agreement for global sustainable development, it is the Local Agenda 21, that each community is asked to create, that is most relevant to children. Although Agenda 21 was an international agreement, two-thirds of its proposals can be achieved only through local action. Some countries are taking the mandate of the UN agreement seriously and are creating mechanisms of support for communities to create their own Local

Agenda 21s. In the United Kingdom, for example, over half of the local government authorities in the country claim to be working actively on the production of a Local Agenda for sustainable development even though they are not required to do so by law.[44] Many of these authorities are taking seriously the requirement within Agenda 21 that young people should be involved in project identification, design, implementation, and follow-up. Local Agenda 21 coordinators are being hired to establish forums for community involvement, and many of them are collaborating closely with the youth service and education departments within their local governments. Sustainable development must be a long-term process at the community level. It involves changes in work patterns and lifestyle and consumption patterns as well as fundamental improvement in the democratic nature of local decision making. Not surprisingly, local government authorities see children both as the easiest captive audience for education and as the most realistic one in which to begin to develop such deep changes in perspective. Unfortunately, the temptation with most local government authorities is to think of involving young people in a forum that may last only a single day. Although this elicits press coverage and exciting talk for a short time, such initiatives will have no lasting impact unless they are conceived as part of a larger plan.

Before they can educate others about sustainable development, community development and environmental professionals need to rethink their perspective on the environment and the role of citizens in development. The Local Agenda 21 officers in the United Kingdom are being hired to train others who are themselves educators, trainers, and public spokespersons: elected officials, teachers, union leaders, and so on.

An interesting scheme is currently being developed in the schools of Berkshire in the United Kingdom. The Groundwork Trust provides technical support to advise teachers, parents, children, and school caretakers to save energy in the school and, by reducing the fuel bill, to provide new financial resources for the improvement of the school grounds. By involving children in the monitoring of this process and letting them see where the savings can be applied, it avoids the hypocrisy of many conservation schemes funded by energy companies. Also, unlike many environmental projects, this strategy involves children in thinking about the economics of sustainable development.

Linking Local to Global Understanding

While I have argued that we have relatively few models of environmental education or action programmes that are truly based on residents' own definitions of local problems, it is even more rare to find programmes that simultaneously link these local problems to global issues. Sometimes, with particularly poor communities that are struggling to survive, the focus must at first be totally on local sustainable development. Residents of poor communities who have once been involved successfully in such a project are more likely to show interest in environmental issues that are shared with other communities and thereby to become concerned with global environmental problems. I will emphasize 'environmental exchange' or 'linking' in this book as an effective strategy for fostering a perspective on the environment that is grounded in the local definition of environmental problems but attempts to understand these problems in a larger context by having children from different communities share their research with one another.

The evolving field of development education is important for those who wish to help children connect their understanding of local development with development issues in other countries.[45] This began as a rather patronizing conception of education practised by development agencies and related to fund-raising for the 'developing countries', whereby children in the North were taught about the problems of the South. It now appears to be merging the goals of global education, cultural awareness, health education, environmental education, and children's participation, through the glue of the CRC, to become an important focus for a contemporary, progressive version of what was once called in some countries 'civic education'. Many of the most important resources recommended in this handbook are produced by development educators.[46]

Children and the Wisdom of Elders

It is popular among environmentalists to speak of the critical importance of rescuing the environmental wisdom of indigenous peoples. One must go further and extend this principle to senior citizens in general. Continuity between the generations in all cultures is necessary if those cultures are to maintain their distinctiveness and those aspects of their relationship to the land that have stood the test of time.[39] The 'Foxfire' programme, based in the Appalachian mountains of Georgia, has inspired thousands of high school teachers to work with their children to gather the enormous cultural knowledge of their communities, through interviews, and publish it.[47] Traditionally, children have reproduced cultures through their relationships with parents and grandparents. This process is breaking down in many parts of the world. Children in urban societies commonly know nothing of their parents' work and have little contact with their grandparents. Increasingly, they learn about how to be in the world through mass media, from people they never meet. The media carry important information about problems in the world, but they do not carry equally important local knowledge and local solutions to the particular place where children live. Here is an important opportunity for intervention in the management of the environment, for children are best placed to play the role of bridging the wisdom of the past with the necessary new understandings demanded by a rapidly changing world. Fostering the relationship between the knowledge and skills of the older generation and the developing knowledge of the young offers us the best opportunity for maintaining cultural continuity while working for economic development.[48]

[45] EDEV News; DEA Monthly Bulletin; Development Education Journal; Fountain (1994). Godwin (1993). For information on other organizations, contact the Development Education Association, 29–31 Cowper Street, London EC2A 4AP, UK. Council for Education in World Citizenship, Seymour Mews House, London W1H 9PE, UK. See also Steiner (1993).

[46] One example of the many valuable educational resources available from UNICEF is Clear Water – A Right for All (UNICEF-UK, 1989).

[47] Wiggington (1973); Wiggington et al (1991).

[48] Boulding (1987), Bowers (1993).

Figure 9:
A boy learning from an elder in Peru. The Bilingual Teacher Training Programme in Iquitos trains teachers to build curricula on this great source of local knowledge.
© AIDESEP.

carried by these artifacts; *colonistas* or colonizers who remember the Amazon frontier before it was transformed by agriculture and urbanization; and shamen, or wise men of the Indian groups, who share with children knowledge of the Amazon's forest resources.

Kaplan has developed an intergenerational model called Neighbourhoods 2000 that brings together senior citizens and pre-adolescent children to work on community research and planning.[49] Intergenerational programmes developed in the 1980s in the United States as a response to a growing pattern of intergenerational segregation in housing, health care, recreation, and transportation. Not only does this isolate elderly persons, but children and adolescents also lose the benefit of adult guidance and the wisdom of these senior adults. Since the 1980s many programmes have been developed to bring children and adults together in schools, youth centres, museums and libraries around such activities as music, drama, and hobbies. Kaplan's programme involves community research and planning, building upon the personal knowledge of all participants in a neighbourhood setting where both groups live their separate lives. By working together, children and seniors are not only able to generate useful neighbourhood planning proposals but also come to understand each other better through comparison of their perceptions and perspectives on the same neighbourhood. This programme includes joint land-use mapping, photographic neighbourhood surveys, reminiscence interviews in which seniors recount their community memories and experiences, autobiographical walking tours, and joint model building. All of this work is brought together in a final presentation to local community planners and human service professionals. The model has been carried out successfully in schools, neighbourhood youth centres, and senior citizen centres.

Some environmental educators bring seniors into the classroom and take children to learn from them in forests, fields, or urban neighbourhoods. But a few exceptional programmes, like those in the Peruvian Andes described in Chapter 7, are even more enriching to a community because they involve not a one-way process but an exchange, and sometimes even a three-way exchange, of knowledge between local sages, outside environmental experts, and children.

In the national programme of working children in Ecuador, described fully in Chapter 4, seniors play an important role in helping children understand how the environment has changed and is changing. In the earlier stages of the project, children are asked to interview grandparents or elderly neighbours about their memories of the environment in their childhood. From this they are able to make comparisons that establish an awareness in the children's minds of how their environment is changing. Furthermore, different elderly persons are able to offer different kinds of knowledge of the environment: women ceramicists, who share with children not only their knowledge of making pots but also the rich symbolism throughout the environment

The Political Nature of Environmental Education

When children begin to observe their environment and

[49] Kaplan (1990, 1991, 1994).

to ask questions about why things are the way they are, they may be quickly elevated to a higher level of social and indeed political consciousness. When social injustices are expressed through the environment, they can bring a child to a new level of consciousness in a particularly convincing, concrete way.

I think I was about ten years old when I first became aware of social-class differences and their implications. I had observed a team of painters daubing pastel colours on the council houses one street away from our house, and I ran home excitedly to discuss with my family what colour we should choose for our house. I thought we would be finally be able to change the grass green of our doors and windows to something distinctively our own. My mum laughed. I stood in shock as she explained that we could have no choice in the matter. I vehemently argued that we could. I had seen the men using different-coloured paint – all she needed to do was ask. I was wrong, and the next day I stood, hands in pockets and shoulders hunched, as I watched the men throw the assigned paint colour on our section of terrace housing. Perhaps it was that day that my class consciousness began. I remember my outrage in realizing that some people could choose to paint their house whatever colour they wished while others had no choice at all.

Engaging children in research and action on the environment in a grounded way is certain to lead them into asking questions about inequities in the use of environmental resources and about power and the abuse of the environment. Such activity can be clearly defended in any context, including schools, as a democratic process. But schools are rarely democratic institutions, and many other settings suffer from similar constraints in their functioning. Facilitators and teachers adopting the principles outlined in this book should defend themselves in democratic terms but should be aware that by adopting the principles of participatory democracy they are, in effect, engaging in 'radical democracy' and should be prepared for conflict with some over their orientation.[50] An example will serve to illustrate the

Figure 10:
A senior citizen working together with children in a neighbourhood of Honolulu on the 'Neighbourhoods 2000' intergenerational urban planning project.
© Tami Dawson.

point. One of the schools involved in the Environmental Exchange Project described in Chapter 10 was located in a community experiencing cultural conflict. The new school, built at the boundary of a Spanish-speaking and an African-American neighbourhood, saw itself as happy and culturally integrated. As the community-based environmental research proceeded, however, it became clear that the school had dealt with community conflicts by turning its back on them. Nothing in the school curriculum addressed the core issues of the surrounding neighbourhoods. The fifth-grade teacher (with 10- and 11-year-old children) who had chosen to work on the exchange programme was not prepared for the consequences of children interviewing residents about what they thought were the important environmental issues and finding out that racial discrimination was the number one issue. She decided, with the advice of the principal of the school, to end the children's research and withdraw from the exchange programme.

For some observers of education, the fact that community issues are always political and full of conflict leads them to conclude that community research by children will inevitably lead to the political indoctrina-

50 Aronowitz and Dhaliwal (1994).

tion of children. Anxiety over such criticism is undoubtedly another factor leading many teachers to retreat into their classrooms and to rely upon textbooks as the primary source of data for environmental and community study. The clear answer to this criticism, of course, is that civic education must involve exposing children to different perspectives and values in their own communities. This is at the very core of the meaning of democracy.

Anyone planning to involve children in a community participation project should be prepared to answer such questions as: 'What is the sense of educating children to participate when there is little or no genuine political participation of adults? Are we not misleading them by doing so?' The answer of course is that we are not preparing children for this society but for a better one. Nevertheless, this question has important implications for how one should proceed in working with children. It is not acceptable to foster in children a false belief in some kind of ideal democracy in which they will be able to play a central part. This is one major reason why it is so important that real projects be the focus of community study and environmental education with children, rather than classroom simulations of community and environmental decision making. It is also why it is more important that children understand the entire process of research, planning, and action, including, in most instances, recognizing the impossibility of their ideas being carried out to fruition. Such projects are of much greater value to the democratization of children than those that pretend, especially to the media, that it is a smooth, easy process for children to have their way. Children need to see the failures of the process and the limited influence of planners, as well as themselves, in determining what happens to their environment. The main goal of children's participation projects, then, is 'conscientization' – becoming aware through facing and articulating this difficulty.

Children's Developing Capacity to Participate

The Convention on the Rights of the Child recognizes that we should provide direction to a child's right to freedom of thought 'in a manner consistent with the evolving capacities of the child', and to the child's freedom of expression 'in accordance with the age and maturity of the child'. The drafters of the CRC were right to steer clear of trying to outline children's development in a manner that would make sense to all the member nations of the United Nations. There are, however, some principles that have relevance across cultures in guiding our efforts to allow children to be involved in their communities to the extent of their capacities and their desires.[1]

The most important principle to consider with regard to children's capacity to participate is that we each develop in different domains of intelligence at different rates. The developmental theory of Piaget was so well disseminated in educational circles that many who work with children still think in terms of his universal stages of development.[2] Piaget's theory emphasized logical-mathematical intelligence, and many believed that the same stages of development, with the same constraints on a child's competence, extended across all domains of intelligence. But children living in different cultures, environments, and social classes are exposed to different materials, experiences, and informal teaching by their families and neighbours, and this results in the appearance of different competencies at different times.

Rather than the development of a universal kind of intelligence, one should think of multiple intelligences in each individual, which develop at different rates according to both the innate capacities of each child and the particular opportunities he or she has to experiment with and exercise those capacities. For example, as a result of two years of research with all of the children in a small town in Vermont, in the United States, I observed that there were very real differences between families in the kinds of learning they valued and fostered in their children.[3] A number of the manual working parents expected their children to be competent with their hands, to be resourceful in the use of materials, to be observant in the landscape and competent in navigating their way through the environment. As a result, many of the children of these families were extremely competent in these practical domains of intelligence. The local elementary school, however, even though it had a relatively progressive approach to learning, did not recognize these qualities, and the children of these families did not score well in school tests. The children who did well were those whose parents had an educational ideology that was in accord with that of the school: language abilities and the knowledge of formal mathematics rather than the practical intelligences described above.

Parents all over the world know that certain children seem to develop more quickly or with greater competence in musical ability or in relationships with other persons, but the tendency in educational circles has been to say that the child with verbal abilities is the more intelligent one. Gardner offers a definition of intelligence that is more valuable in thinking about the

[1] This chapter has benefited greatly from the much larger review by Hart et al. (1996).

[2] Piaget (1963).

[3] Hart (1978).

[4] Gardner (1993), pp. 14–15.

[5] This section draws heavily from Daiute reported in Hart et al. (1995).

capacity of different children to participate at different times. He talks of it as 'an ability, skill or a set of abilities or skills, to solve problems or to fashion products, which are valued in at least one cultural setting'.[4]

The implication of this conception of intelligence for children's participation is that we should not have universal notions of what children can or cannot do at certain ages. We should rather provide a diversity of ways to be involved and media to use in order to maximize the capacities for all children to take part. It would be equally a mistake to have children segment themselves off into completely separate groups based on their particular strengths. So many of us remember the child in our class whom we all earmarked as the artist and left to lead the way in demonstrating how to draw the correct tree or flower for us to copy. Our goal should be to design opportunities in all domains of intelligence with a continuum or sequence of developing competency in mind. A good way to achieve this is to be honest with children about the issue of different competencies rather than pretending to them that they are all equally good. This should help lead to a spirit of cooperation between children both about sharing their knowledge and skills with one another and, at appropriate times, such as presentations to others, being comfortable about 'electing' one of their peers who is more competent in the relevant domain of intelligence to go forward on their behalf.

THE DEVELOPMENT OF IDENTITY [5]

While there is a diversity of theories of the development of identity in childhood and adolescence, the qualification must be offered that these theories are inevitably culturally biased, having been constructed in Europe and North America. It may even be that personal identity and self-concept are rather Western notions, and that a broader societal anchoring dominates individuals' orientations in other cultures. Nevertheless, to the extent that children develop identities, a feature common to all of the theories is that identity is a social process rather than something uniquely within individu-

als. An understanding of the social world and an understanding of oneself are constructed in a reciprocal manner, influencing and constraining each other.

The various theories are in agreement about differences in two periods of identity development that are particularly relevant to children's community participation: middle childhood and adolescence. They suggest that children and adolescents need somewhat different kinds of participation. Children from about eight to 11 years of age are seen as enthusiastic, outward-looking, and industrious as they forge what seem like independent identities, whereas adolescents are characterized as more inward-looking and philosophical, testing the identity constructions they have made for themselves. Thus, for children, groups serve as work places in which they demonstrate competence and the first flourishes of independence, whereas, for adolescents, groups serve more as a stage for trying out the identities they are creating.

The heightened sense of industry of the middle childhood period involves doing things alongside others. Children's awareness of the division of labour and potential to share opportunity develop at this time, and children need authentic recognition that their ways of mastering experience and self-image are reasonably consistent with how others view them. An organization for children of this age group should provide the impetus and resources for manageable and intellectually challenging projects, such as conducting community surveys. Children in this age group have enormous energy and enthusiasm for turning outwards to the world as a way of feeling their identity and gradually using the world as a mirror. But, while these pre-adolescents are propelled by a strong sense of industry, this can be frustrated by feelings of inferiority when their efforts are foiled or when they do not receive appropriate feedback. An organization needs to provide support if these children are to carry out their sometimes overly ambitious ideas. It cannot simply play a role in engaging children in meaningful, concrete projects; it must also make it a priority to ensure, as much as possible, against failure in these projects by supporting children's grand schemes with structure and practical resources. The organization must help the children learn to deal with failure when this becomes necessary. If both authentic projects and adequate supervision are provided, children at this age can become part of a community where their industry is valued and where they can engage in meaningful tasks with peers and adults.

As adolescents undergo major physiological changes, they experiment with different identities, seeking to consolidate their social roles. According to one of the most prominent theorists, Erik Erikson, the sense of identity is 'the accrued confidence that one's ability to maintain inner sameness and continuity is matched by the sameness and continuity of one's meaning in others' eyes' (Erikson, 1950, p. 74). Consequently, adolescents commonly test their emerging sense of self in various contexts, sometimes with strong symbols of dress, behaviour, or language. Since adolescents focus more internally, their projects need to allow for extensive comparison and contrast of self and others in emotionally intense contexts. Because symbols function as the observable glue of youth cultures, and these include aspects of language, dress, music, rituals, and activities, an important function for youth organizations is to provide a context in which youth can establish a culture in ways that positively impact their personal and social identities.[6] They must be flexible enough to allow members to form and reform their symbols and rituals. Organizations that have captured and maintained young people's interest have several important features (Heath and McLaughlin, 1993, p. 59). Youth organizations need to allow for complexity – in particular for young people's participation in multiple cultures, and multiple identities, defined in their own ways. In successful organizations, youth benefit from having the opportunity to play a range of roles and to be experts in these roles as well as apprentices. Adults in these organizations should not overdetermine the culture of the organization. Instead, they need to provide a trustworthy base, to maintain a sense of purpose, and to understand the issues,

purposes, and needs of youth as they define these things themselves. Adults can honestly convey their values and compare and contrast their values with those of youth, but this should not take on the form of an evaluation that can diminish the sense of responsibility and identity at work in the young people. Thus, supporting youth organizations is a difficult job indeed. Structure and support are crucial, as is positive role-modelling, but, if these organizations are going to attract and serve young people in a way that encourages them to participate in and serve their communities, adults need to allow the organization culture to be deeply informed by youth.

So much for some of the patterns of identity development which seem to unfold with age. These should not be taken as universals. Further complicating the story are the enormous cultural variations in identity and self-concept to which this book can only refer. For example, children in Asian cultures tend to describe themselves in more collective terms than children in North America. Clearly, whatever structures for participation are established, they must allow flexibility for children and adolescents to explore and develop their identities and actions in the world in ways consistent with their own cultures. It may even be that the 'participation articles' of the CRC reflect a Western bias. It is for this reason that these principles should be the subject of thorough reflection and debate before their widespread application in any culture.

The social structure of different settings in which children live plays an important role in their developing sense of competence. Environments like schools, emphasizing self-restraint and doing what one is told, can, if carried to the extreme, make children dependent and overly restrained, thereby spoiling their desire to learn and work.[7] At the other extreme, relying entirely on free play and doing what one likes to do can lead children to a feeling of confusion. Children need to be able to discover that they can accomplish pragmatic and realistic tasks. Such accomplishment makes them aware of previously unexplored potentials in themselves.

[6] Daiute and Griffin, 1993; Heath and McLaughlin (1993).

[7] Erikson (1980), p. 88.

8 Coles (1986).

9 See Erikson (1950) for a discussion of a child's psycho-social need to develop competency through ever larger scales of play environment.

10 Freire (1970, 1974, 1975).

11 Boulding (1987).

12 Summarized in Hart et al. (1995). See also Feffer and Gourevitch (1960); Flavell, Botkin and Fry (1968); Guardo and Bohan (1971); Broughton (1978); Chandler (1977); Selman (1980).

Self-Esteem, Social Class, Culture, and Participation

An overriding factor affecting children's desire and ability to be involved in community projects is how they feel about themselves. Very often this is tied to how they feel about their own social class or culture. Robert Coles has illustrated clearly through his research with poor children in the United States how damaging poverty and experiences with discrimination and powerlessness can be to children's sense of self and of their capacity to change anything.[8] Also, children with poor self-esteem develop coping mechanisms that tend to distort how they communicate their thoughts and feelings, and so group participation with these children is particularly difficult to achieve. In the poorest urban neighbourhoods of Brazil 'street educators' and teachers in non-formal or popular schools repeatedly explained to me that the priority in working with children living in poverty is first to build within them a strong sense of their identity within a culture.[9] Only from this sense of belonging, they explained, could children be expected to act effectively for themselves and for their community. For this reason, projects with children initially focus on the construction of expressions of their cultural identity, with a great emphasis on music, dance, and theatre. In creating these events, the children face the history of their culture and the roots of their poverty and discrimination, a process that results in 'conscientization', as it is called by Paulo Freire.[10] This is a useful point to pause and restate the overwhelming importance of culture in children's participation. Different cultures have different processes for involving children, at different ages and with different gender divisions of labour.[11] What may seem like a reticence to be involved on some children's part may sometimes be related to a different cultural expectation by these children of their role.

The most important principle to follow when wishing to involve children who seem less involved than might be expected is to identify situations and offer opportunities that are likely to maximize their ability to demonstrate competence. This points to providing a wide diversity of methods of participation and a diversity of different media of expression. One should also think of trying to foster children's sense of competency by allowing them to make decisions about things that are closest to them. Children who have never been able to choose or create their own clothes or to decorate their own sleeping space are less likely to feel that they can, or should, be involved in improving the environment of a community.

A word of warning is called for here. In some quarters in the USA self-esteem-oriented programmes are carried out in the belief that some group or category of children canot meet some particular standard of academic performance, and therefore special efforts are required to make these children feel good. Such efforts can easily be patronizing and offensive to the children, who discern that they are not being taken seriously. Ultimately, children need to be able to compete in the world, and one needs to be honest with them about their strengths and weaknesses and to offer them guidance from this honest base. All children have some special qualities, and it is certainly good to recognize these in supporting individual children, but not to the point of covering over their difficulties in other domains. This is often a delicate path to tread and is another reason that the qualities and training of facilitators of children's participation are so important.

SOCIAL DEVELOPMENT

The Development of Children's Understanding of the Perspectives of Others

The ability to participate depends on a basic competence in thinking about the thoughts and feelings of others.[12] The difficulty children have in decentring from their own perspective is important for anyone trying to achieve cooperative group work with them. Even during their early school years, children are at least intellectually capable of working with adults, but the adults need to be sensitive to children's limitations in taking the perspectives of others. Unfortunately, again, the theories are based largely on research with children in the industrialized countries of the North, and no doubt the development of social perspective-taking in children growing up in the Euro-Anglo tradition of individualism is different from that of children reared in the more collective traditions of other countries.

Nevertheless, while children in some societies might have a less marked egocentric phase than that discussed below, the underlying difficulty with simultaneous thinking about multiple aspects of a situation will appear in some form wherever one works with young children. In a very limited way, a child can take the perspective of others by the age of three.[13] But while they gradually become more aware that another person has feelings and thoughts, there is confusion until the ages of five or six between the subjective psychological and the objective or physical characteristics of the person's behaviour. For example, intentional and unintentional behaviours of the other person are not differentiated. Between the ages of seven and 12, children develop the ability to step outside themselves to take a self-reflective look at their interactions and to realize that other people can do the same thing. There is a gradually increasing capacity to coordinate one's own perspective with that of another person in a way that allows for anticipation of what the other might think, do, or feel. At first, children come to be able *sequentially* to take another's perspective, and recognize intent. Not until about ten years of age, or older, is there a recognition of the psychological relationship between self and other; that is, a *mutual* perspective taking. They can now recognize that a person may have multiple or mixed feelings, such as being interested but also a little frightened.

By adolescence, the individual is not only aware of the other person's thought, but also grows to be acutely aware that other people might be thinking of them.

Figure 11:
A critical phase in perspective-taking occurs between the ages of seven and twelve when a child becomes capable of putting herself 'in the other person's shoes'.

Such reflective capacities allow for strategic planning of interactions with others. Mutual perspective-taking is necessary for children to be able to organize themselves into enduring democratic groups. These same capacities also lead to the heightened sense of self-consciousness characteristic of early and middle adolescence, which often results in isolation or an extreme emphasis on relationships with peers and on how one is seen by one's peers.[14] These feelings have important consequences for whether or not an adolescent chooses to participate in programmes with others.

Beyond this mutual perspective-taking ability of adolescents, Selman hypothesizes a higher level of 'societal-symbolic perspective-taking'. A person can now imagine multiple mutual perspectives, forming a generalized societal, legal, or moral perspective in

[13] Selman (1980).

[14] Chandler (1977); Elkind (1967); Selman (1980).

Figure 12:
Developmental levels of social perspective-taking and how they are reflected in social relationships (after Selman 1980). (This scheme is based on research in the USA, and it may be more relevant to Euro-Anglo countries with their relatively individualistic traditions than to more collectivist cultures.)[15]

Developmental level in coordination of perspectives	Close friendships	Peer group	Leadership
Level 0 (approximately ages 3 to 7) Egocentric or undifferentiated perspective. Other's perspective not differentiated from one's own perspective.	**Stage 0** Momentary physical interaction.	Emphasis on physical connections and overt action (e.g. 'a big team', play games).	Recognition of a leader's physical actions (e.g. 'tells what to do') but not the rationale.
Level 1 (approximately ages 4 to 9) Subjective or differentiated perspectives. Recognition of differences in perspective.	**Stage 1** One-way assistance, e.g. someone who plays your favourite games with you.	A series of unilateral relations. Group activities thought of in terms of outcomes that benefit self or please others. Reciprocity based on physical acts only.	Obedience to authority 'until reaching a critical level of hurt feelings results in the leader's dismissal'.
Level 2 (approximately ages 6 to 12) Self-reflective or reciprocal perspective. Awareness of how others might view one's thoughts and feelings.	**Stage 2** Fair-weather cooperation. Cooperation around incidents or issues. Relationships tend to break up over arguments.	Bilateral (reciprocal) partnerships. Interlocking dyads. Reciprocal feelings of affection 'extend a chain from one dyad to another'.	Thoughts and actions tied to specific pragmatic effects are the basis of interdependence.
Level 3 (approximately ages 9 to 15) Third-person or mutual perspective. Ability to understand a neutral perspective.	**Stage 3** Intimate and mutual sharing. A system, not isolated. Possessiveness and jealousy often characterize this stage.	Concept of the group distinct from particular relationships. Cohesive because of common interests and beliefs. Expectation of unanimity suppresses differences of opinion.	Unanimity and team spirit are valued. Leadership is thought of in terms of personality differences. Obligation based on shared beliefs.
Level 4 (approximately 12 to adulthood) Societal or in-depth perspective. Ability to take the perspective of what is good for society; a legal or moral perspective.	**Stage 4** Autonomous, interdependent, i.e. relational systems which are flexible and change.	Interdependence of group process and individual differences are recognized. A pluralistic community united behind common goals but recognizing diversity.	An abstract concept of the leader's role.

[15] From Hart et al. (1996), after Selman (1980).

which all individuals can share. A person believes others use this shared point of view to facilitate accurate communication and understanding. This final phase, which can emerge at any time from the age of 12 on, is the one that allows for the most fruitful cooperative projects of children.

The sequence described here is limited to children's intellectual development and their logical ability to take the perspectives of others. It does not take into account such factors as children's understanding of the different roles people have and the power they possess. These factors must surely influence the degree to which children think it is appropriate to take the perspectives of others. For example, knowing that someone in a group is a policeman, and thinking that policemen punish misbehaving children, may override children's intellectual ability to understand the person as an individual and may thereby reduce their participation.

A useful way to understand how this scheme might inform work with children is to look at how 'levels' of perspective-taking, conceptions of friendships, peer relationships, and leadership might be related (Figure 12). Figure 12 can be used as a tool for designing organizational structures for the optimal involvement of children at different ages, as long as one remembers that one can only provide the opportunities and that participants will not always function in these optimal ways.

The development of self-awareness and the ability to understand others, as shown in Figure 12, have direct implications for how a child is likely to interact with peers and in groups which might include both peers and non-peers. Too often, such developmental schemes are used to express what younger children cannot do. Its purpose here is rather to help us think of what children can do if we design opportunities appropriately. Even though an organizing and coordinating stance cannot be expected until early adolescence or later, children at each age are capable of making contributions to group activity; preschool children, for example, can express their own preferences and enjoy participating in projects alongside others.

The Development of Social Cooperation

All over the world, children may be said to have a greater equality of status in their relationships with their peers than they do with adults, who hold authority over them. This greater equality of status between children is believed to be particularly important to the development of social cooperation.[16] Again, it must be noted that this theory was developed in the USA and may not apply equally to more collectivist cultures.[17] The theory holds that children are required to listen to one another and attempt to resolve disagreements in order to reach a common understanding. Six- to eight-year-old children are said to develop a strict direct reciprocity in their relationships to one another, that is, a child responds to another child's act 'in kind'. For children between nine and 11 years of age this strict reciprocity is transformed into a principle of cooperation, for, as described above, they are now able to attend to psychological considerations beyond the act. According to Youniss, this cooperation with peers is well in advance of cooperation with adults. The lack of true cooperation among children before nine years of age does not mean that they are incapable of participation in environmental projects, but it does mean that adults or teenagers need to take a greater responsibility in coordinating groups.

Following from this theory, it is tempting to conclude that, if children learn cooperation by having to face the need for reciprocity with their peers, then organizations that require children to work things out together, rather than walk away or use power, would develop better cooperative abilities. Unfortunately, there is little research on this subject. Some research has claimed to have demonstrated, however, that providing group-oriented rewards to a class was associated with a higher degree of cooperation than providing individual rewards to children.[18] A full discussion of this subject would of course need to consider the degree to which a culture is individualistic or collectivist in its orientation. Also, some have suggested that these

[16] Youniss (1980).

[17] Cox, Lobel, and McLeod (1991) review research on collectivist versus individualist cultures, finding that collectivist cultures stress communal needs, shared goals, and cooperation and are more likely to subjugate personal interests to the welfare of the group (Triandis, 1989). Unlike white Christian Americans, who remain connected to Anglo-European individualism, Asians, Hispanics, and Americans of colour with African roots remain connected to the collectivist cultures from which they descend. Cox et al. suggest that, in any organization, prompting may be necessary to encourage the cooperative norm among ethnic minorities, particularly if the organization is largely Anglo-European. More important, the organization must also create a climate where expression of diversity is encouraged (p. 842).

[18] Williamson, Williamson, Watkins and Hughes (1992).

Figure 13:
The promoters of 'adventure playgrounds' argue that the opportunities for creating settings for play with a rich variety of materials foster social cooperation in children: Hanegi Adventure Playground in Tokyo. © Roger Hart.

[19] Gilligan (1982).

[20] Riger (1993), p. 288.

[21] Kritt (1993).

[22] Smith, Boulton, and Cowie (1993).

[23] Dawes, van de Kragt, and Orbell (1990).

[24] DeVries and Zan (1993).

contrasting modes of being are revealed in gender orientations, with women and girls showing greater degrees of relatedness and interdependence.[19] Others have suggested that this contrast of autonomy with relatedness is more a function of one's position in the social hierarchy, with those who are not in positions of autonomy, including women, choosing to focus on greater degrees of connection and communal goals in order to survive.[20]

It is often thought that the best way to teach students how to do something difficult is to 'model' the behaviour, but modelling is antithetical to encouraging free and democratic inquiry – by showing the one way or preferred way to do something rather than encouraging children to construct their own solutions to tasks.[21] The most appropriate methods for promoting democratic participation in children are based on dialogue. Furthermore, it is now a generally recognized theory that people acquire patterns of action and interaction, not merely discrete behavioural sequences. Children and adolescents become more aware of their own and others' perspectives in disputes with peers and attempts to convince others, as well as through

differences of opinion which emerge in topical discussions. These reflective abilities can inform future social interactions. Although the guidance of an adult (in a moderator capacity) may be necessary at times, the participants should be encouraged to construct their own democracy as much as possible. A successful group will be encouraged to consider alternative suggestions from different members when discussing an idea or deciding how to go about tasks, and to be respectful of each other's contributions.[22] The successful group's activities will be designed expressly to reflect the values that the group members are interactively learning: reasonableness, orderliness, respect for others' feelings, equality, freedom to take risks, and the capacity to listen.

Finally, it should be noted that, in research with adults, the establishment of *group identity* has been found to be a factor of great importance in the development of social cooperation.[23] Having opportunities and support for children to build this sense of group identity would be of lasting benefit to their democratic development.

Communication and cooperation

Very young children are constrained in their ability to communicate because of their rudimentary language skills. From three to seven years of age children speak well, but use communication in a different way than older children and adults. Their fluid verbal facility to express their own thoughts, experiences, feelings, and desires might sometimes seem impressive, but they are unable to tailor their messages for an audience because of their inability to take in the perspective of other persons. This limitation reduces their abilities to be diplomatic and to engage in negotiation or compromise. These communicative skills develop gradually through childhood and adulthood. Such skills can, however, be fostered.

Even young children can be encouraged to work together in settings where a 'tradition' of talking about how they and others feel has been established.[24] Even though a child might want his or her way, such discussion can make the child aware of another child's point of view, even if only in that situation and for the time being. Such discussion cannot be expected to facilitate lasting development, but the processes established in the discussion can become an accepted way for dealing with disputes while overcoming communicative and perspective constraints among young children. Among older children, a milieu of open communication can also create expectations for the type of honest interchange conducive to establishing values and working with others.

Peer Relationships and Friendship Formation

In designing programmes for children it is useful to know how they spontaneously come together in groups to share interests, how friendships are formed and how they come to develop a mutual sense of belonging. Researchers have identified a number of 'roles' that children may occupy in their peer group, and have looked specifically at how peers are accepted and rejected. Dominance relations characterize peer groups from as early as preschool through middle childhood and adolescence, particularly among boys.[25] As they enter adolescence, group structures are less influenced by the exercise of physical strengths of their members than by characteristics that support the group's normative activities. No doubt experiences with democratically organized programmes would improve this transition away from physical dominance.

Friendship formation among preschoolers has been found to grow out of a mutual attraction through which partners reciprocate and complement each other's behaviours, leading to a 'climate of agreement' (Howes 1987). Youniss and his colleagues found that six- and seven-year-olds describe 'friends' as children with whom they share activities and things (Youniss 1980). By the time they are nine or ten years of age, children say that friends are people whom they know well and with whom they share interests or similar abilities or

who have compatible personalities. While participation in common activities remains an important basis for friendship formation in adolescence, other factors come into play at this time as well. Friendship becomes a much more reasoned relationship, with a great deal of shared values as well as similar interests, behaviours, and attitudes towards both school and patterns of educational activity (McCord 1990).

Age Mixing and the Values of Child-to-Child Learning

An important issue in the development of competency is the capacity of children with different abilities to learn from one another. Whereas it was once thought that children learned in groups of similar ability (commonly approximated by age), many people now argue, on the basis of theory and research, that it is good for children to work together in groups of varying ages and abilities, for in this way they learn more from one another as well as acquiring important skills of give and take. Interactions among peers provide greater developmental opportunities because adult–child interactions are usually characterized by adult instruction of children, whereas peer relationships allow for a greater degree of bidirectional give and take.[26] This greater flexibility in peer interaction allows children to test their understandings and adapt them to the requirements of ongoing interaction. Although same-age interactions might seem to provide optimal conditions for such experiences, there are other benefits of mixed-age and mixed ability groupings. Children of lower ability or younger age can benefit by being exposed to more sophisticated approaches to tasks. Furthermore, in research in schools, this has been found to have no averse effect on the most sophisticated children in the group, who may even benefit from an opportunity to demonstrate their abilities. Older children might try out assertive roles, such as helping to teach, while younger children might try to take advantage of a less threatening opportunity to seek assistance. In summary, mixed-age groupings are generally beneficial for all

[25] See for example Strayer (1989).

[26] Piaget (1965).

[27] Youniss (1980).

[28] Sarbin and Allen (1968).

[29] Alcoff and Potter (1993); Fivush (1994).

[30] Hart (1978).

participants, though too great a difference in age, such as adolescents and preschool children, can yield the same differential of power and knowledge that characterizes child–adult interactions.

Child–Adult Interactions

In contrast to their relationships with peers, the relationships of six- to eight-year-old children with adults is one of adherence to rules and the use of material rewards. Research in the USA, has shown, however, that by early adolescence children's relationships with adults is capable of being transformed from one of mere authority to reciprocity, as the individuality of both the adolescent and the adult is recognized.[27] Such developments, of course, vary greatly according to culture.

How adults are perceived by children is also related to the issue of social roles. Social roles should not be thought of as static ascriptions of function and power relations but more broadly in terms of behavioural possibilities sanctioned by society.[28] Children acquire expectations for people in particular roles, such as teacher or policeman, but, more broadly, we might say that individuals come to expect a particular range of behaviour depending on the social location of the other, that is membership in a group defined by race, class, culture or gender. For this reason a male teacher or policeman might find it more difficult than others to establish quickly a trusting relationship where a child feels comfortable sharing his feelings and working with, rather than for, him. On the other hand, there is the satisfaction for that male authority figure of knowing that, once he has demonstrated a different kind of relationship to the child through his behaviour, there is the possibility that the child will begin to see that social roles, and one's position in society, need not be fixed at all.

SUPPORTING THE PARTICIPATION OF GIRLS AS WELL AS BOYS

In pursuing the goal of enabling all children to have a voice in improving their communities and the environment we need to be aware of the special barriers to the participation of girls. Recently, feminist psychological theories have emphasized the role of political power in the formation of self-concept.[29] Playing the role of the 'other' by society, parents, teachers, and even peers is usually the foundation of girls' identity. This disempowers them, especially when they do not recognize the power imbalances. Special efforts need to be made in participation programmes with girls to counteract these socializing forces.

Throughout the world there appear to be many more organized opportunities in communities for boys to participate than for girls. In poorer families, this may reflect the much greater work demands placed on girls inside the home. In many cultures, girls are expected to apprentice themselves to their mothers from as young as three years of age and to engage in a gradually ascending series of challenging tasks, from collecting firewood to looking after siblings to preparing food. More often, boys remain free to play as they await apprenticeship to their tasks, which are commonly away from the home.[30] But other factors may explain the gender difference. Many programmes for children and youth were developed with a view to keeping them busy and out of trouble and, because boys are thought to get into more trouble, there are more such preventive programmes for them. Furthermore, many adults in all cultures think of boys as the children who need to be prepared to become decision makers as adults, and hence need programmes that offer opportunities to develop autonomy and decision-making skills. Girls, they feel, should be more protected and prepared for domestic roles.

Gender differences have also been found between the learning styles of males and females in classrooms in the USA. Girls prefer to use a conversational style that fosters group consensus by building ideas accumulatively. In contrast, boys learn more through argument and individual activity. It has been suggested that, in schools at least, most discourse is organized around male learning patterns to the detriment of the learning styles of girls.

The changing roles of women in families and the larger community in other cultures is too large a subject to be taken up fully in this book, but clearly a special emphasis on girls is another concomitant of the challenge of the CRC to involve all children to their fullest potential. Children of both genders should be given a say about their own life and their own futures. I further believe that it should be a human right for all people to have opportunities in their life to make contributions to shaping their communities.

The discussion I had with approximately fifty children in an Escuela Nueva in the province of Caldas, Colombia, suggests that for one culture, at least, the democratizing of children is having the effect of increasing equality of opportunity between the genders. In the Hojas Anchas school, described in Chapter 3, girls occupy positions of decision making and responsibility equally with boys, including the farming, carpentry, and nutrition programmes. During a long summing-up meeting with all the older children of the school, they made it quite clear that my observations were correct and seemed bemused by my persevering in questions on this topic. I therefore approached the issue from a different direction by asking them if they thought their mothers and fathers engaged in different activities and degrees of decision making in the home. After confirming that this was so, I asked them what would happen when they became adults. The girls and boys insisted on their feelings of equality in competency and in responsibilities. I asked them how this could continue if their parents were involved in very different occupations. The answer came quickly and surely from one of the girls: 'We're making a new kind of school in Colombia, and the kind of life we will have as adults will also be different.' Satisfied smiles around the room revealed a general solidarity with her position. This was all said with a remarkable degree of confidence and with no noticeable disturbing reaction from the head of the Junta Accion Communal (the local village government) or from the few parents who were sitting on the sidelines of the meeting.

Figure 14:
The much studied differences in the play of girls and boys is greatly influenced by the environmental opportunities they have. When allowed, girls also exercise 'environmental competence' in their play. Here, girls in Vermont have designed and built an intricate dam system in dirt, because they attended a school which did not discourage such 'dirty play' by them.
© Roger Hart.

At last year's National Congress of Street and Working Children held in the Brazilian capital, Brasilia, half of the 700 children participating were girls. It seems that this came about because of the democratic values of this new movement; I observed the same equality in the Philippines National Congress of working children in Manila in 1992. I hope these changes among children will lead to greater opportunities for the participation of all in the newly emerging democracies. Clearly there is a difference between community participation programmes with children and the kinds of opportunities society will offer girls and boys in work as they enter adulthood, but in keeping with the general argument of this book, even though cultures change slowly, the best way to transform one role in society is by practising that role.

[31] See the summary of the different theories of individual differences by Reiff (1992).

[32] Reiff (1992).

[33] Summarized in Reiff (1992).

[34] Gardner (1993).

RECOGNIZING INDIVIDUAL DIFFERENCES AND SPECIAL NEEDS

In order to design programmes that enable all children to participate, one needs to go beyond general patterns of children's development and their variation by culture, social class, and gender. One needs also to be aware of divergence in the ways of thinking and acting of individual children.[31] Furthermore, there are special considerations one must make in order to maximize the participation of children with 'disabilities'.

Most generally, it can be stated that different children interpret the 'same' situations, activities, tasks, information, etc. in different ways – a phenomenon that is called 'cognitive style' or 'learning style'. Teachers also have different cognitive styles, and becoming aware of one's style is an important aspect of preparing to work with children. Lack of awareness of one's own cognitive style and of the existence of diverse styles can lead to misunderstanding, and even intolerance, of children's styles that are different from one's own and the mislabelling of children as 'at risk,' or 'slow'. Research has also revealed that the two hemispheres of the brain process information differently; the right hemisphere functions in a global, holistic, visual-spatial maner while the left hemisphere is characterized by verbal, sequential, and analytical processing. While all individuals use both brain hemispheres, some may be more left- or right-hemisphere dominant, resulting in different ways of working within a group and with different media. Other psychologists have classified learning styles as reflective versus impulsive, what Reiff calls 'conceptual tempo'.[32] Recognizing this difference points to adopting a relaxed attitude to the pace in which different parts of a project are completed, being clear about the whole process, and, for some children, breaking tasks down into more manageable units. There are many other observed differences, for example, some researchers characterize thought as either abstract or concrete and organization of thought as either sequential or random.[33] In the face of this complexity, Gardner's theory of multiple intelligences has been useful in recent years to many teachers.[34] It redefines intelligence as the ability to create products or solve problems that are valued in one or more cultural settings. This concept can be used by the facilitators of any children's programme against the tendency of those who might wish to reinforce certain types of intelligences in order to label children as 'gifted', 'learning disabled', or 'at risk'. It can be used as part of a general strategy for inclusiveness. Recognizing multiple intelligences means using multiple approaches and media. Furthermore, one should take advantage of individual differences by using a committee structure, so that not everyone is working on the same thing. Children should be allowed to self-select activities with which they will be involved, and be allowed to switch if they feel things are not working out.

Children may have special needs because of orthopedic, visual, auditory, or mental challenges, and different accommodations must be made in order to include them. Children with orthopedic challenges have no overt impediment to participating fully in meetings or in office work. Their participation in research and action in the field may be affected but there are always aspects of the work in which they can comfortably engage. For example, in a community playground building project, a child in a wheelchair cannot climb steps to hand materials to someone. By simply having a wide diversity of roles in all projects, and by consistently describing tasks before asking for volunteers, there is no reason why all children should not find a valuable role to play and situations awkward to any child can be avoided.

Differences in intellectual capacity have already been discussed above. Visual and auditory challenges are of greatest concern in making full and natural communication possible. Without cues such as raised hands or body positions, something as elementary as turn-taking may pose a difficulty for visually impaired children. Even greater communicative challenges ensue when auditory impairment exists. Measures such as a signing interpreter or other accommodations must be used and a facilitator will need to consult with a specialist in order properly to invite children with these special characteristics to become participants.

A number of factors enter into how children with special needs are perceived by other children. Most obviously, young children may not be able to anticipate how others feel, or may not be able to modify their behaviour to take into account their understandings of other persons' feelings. As reported above, although some evidence of empathy has been found among children as young as three years of age, small children are not able to coordinate their thinking with someone else's; when there is an incongruence between the thoughts of self and other, one's own thoughts and feelings inevitably take precedence. Only later are children able to reflect upon their thoughts and actions so that they can use their knowledge strategically in interactions. But there are also irrational fears, such as the

mythology of contagion. Also, to the extent that the social cognitive processes that contribute to prosocial behaviours rely on comparison of self to others, these same processes may be the source of fears and antipathies. If it is explained that a child is 'just like you', except for some observable difference such as a wheelchair, leg braces, the loss of a limb, or blindness, it is understandable that another child might want to assert how he is indeed different from that child. In fact, it has been found that rejection of children with more minor disfigurements, such as the lack of a few fingers, is more intense and widespread among children than rejection of those in wheelchairs, because the desire to accentuate the difference may be especially strong. All of these issues which might arise in trying to make any programme truly inclusive offer extremely valuable opportunities for children to learn, through discussion, the true meaning of participation and citizenship.

[1] Hart (1992).

CHAPTER 3

Organizational Principles

The previous chapter, on children's developing capacities, was designed to serve as a guide to their participation, but questions of how adults can work with these growing capacities are equally important. Unfortunately, while there is a sizeable literature on organizing with youth, very little has been written concerning participation with children. The following principles are drawn from a combination of personal experience, child development theory, and a small, but growing, literature on democratic schooling.

AVOIDING MANIPULATION AND TOKENISM

In a previous publication on children's participation I used a ladder as a metaphor to illustrate the different degrees of initiation and collaboration children can have when working on projects with adults.[1] Though somewhat simplistic for explaining a complex subject, this metaphor has been useful as a basis for discussion on how adults can support the involvement of children to the maximum of their desire and capacity. More important, it was meant to show what is not participation. As can be seen from Figure 15, the first three rungs of the ladder are unacceptable. All children may operate at one of the upper rungs of the ladder depending upon their ability and interest in a particular project. But this does not imply that any project where children are operating at level 4 is necessarily inferior to one where they are operating at level 8. To clarify, I will illustrate each rung of the ladder with examples of children's participation in environmental projects.

Manipulation or Deception

Manipulation, the lowest level of the ladder, refers to those instances in which adults consciously use children's voices to carry their own messages. For example, adults might produce a publication that includes drawings by children, but with no participation by children in selecting the drawings or editing the publication. The drawings, taken out of the context in which they were made and the instructions that were given, can be used by adults to argue a perspective of children that may be totally inaccurate. If, however, the book makes the criteria and the selection process clear and offers no pretence that children were involved, then this is not manipulation. Another example is seen when a placard against toxic waste is hung around a young child's neck for the child to march in a demonstration, with no attempt made to have the child understand the issue according to his or her ability. This is not a good way to introduce children to democratic political action.

Deception is more common. It refers to those instances where adults, with good intentions, deny their own involvement in a project with children because they want others to think that it was done entirely by children and believe that it would diminish its effectiveness to refer to the participation of adults. A common example is seen when an adult designs a garden, has children carry out simple planting, and then tells journalists and photographers that the children designed and built the garden. This kind of project is all too common. Another example is found when adults promote books of children's work as though they were strictly child-produced when they were not. This can result in such gross exaggerations of children's ability that other adults may respond in disbelief or, worse, in a patronizing way. There may have been no conscious attempt to manipulate children's views, but the effect is similar. And so I have relegated it to the lowest level of the ladder.

Beware also of referenda and opinion polls with children. We can expect more of these as the idea grows that children should have a voice, and they do have some potential, but statistics from such research instruments are easily manipulated even with surveys of adults. The risk is greater with pre-adolescent children, given their varying capacities for understanding the purpose of such research instruments.

Decoration

Decoration is seen when children wear costumes or T-shirts promoting a cause, but have little notion of what the cause is all about and no involvement in organizing the occasion. This is one rung higher than manipulation because adults do not pretend that the cause is inspired by children; they simply use children to bolster the cause as though they were understanding participants. I do not wish to imply that children's dance, song, or theatre performances are undesirable. The problems arise when children's involvement is ambiguous. If, for example, they appear in the middle of a demonstration on some environmental issue and sing a song about the issue written by someone else, but have had no opportunity to understand the issue themselves, then this is a decorative and even possibly manipulative use of children. If, on the other hand, the children are simply giving a performance and it is quite clear that the music is written by someone else, then we can enjoy the performance without being concerned about where it falls on a ladder of participation.

Tokenism

Tokenism is a particularly difficult issue to deal with, because it is often carried out by adults who are

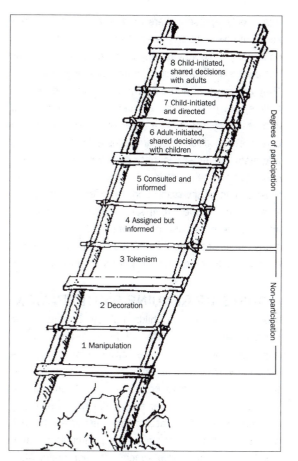

Figure 15:
The ladder of children's participation: while the upper levels of the ladder express increasing degrees of initiation by children, they are not meant to imply that a child should always be attempting to operate at the highest level of their competence. The figure is rather meant for adult facilitators to establish the conditions that enable groups of children to work at whatever levels they choose. A child may elect to work at different levels on different projects or during different phases of the same project. Also, some children may not be initiators but are excellent collaborators. The important principle is to avoid working at the three lowest levels, the rungs of non-participation.

strongly concerned with giving children a voice but have not begun to think carefully and self-critically about doing so. The result is that they design projects in which children seem to have a voice but in fact have little or no choice about the subject or the style of communicating it, or no time to formulate their own opinions. Tokenism is an extremely common form of involving children; I hope that by thinking more about it we can begin to transform these instances through the application of certain principles which will enable us to nudge the projects a little further up the ladder. We need to look carefully at children's conferences, for example. It is common for articulate, charming children to be selected by adults to sit on panels, with little opportunity to consult with their peers whom they purportedly represent. Rarely is the audience given any sense of how children are selected and hence of which children's perspectives they represent, but this does not even seem to concern many audience members. They are more affected by the symbolic impact of a child's presence, just as certain audiences are impressed by the appearance of a person from a certain ethnic group or other oppressed minority. This is tokenism. Tokenism is not, however, an inevitable consequence of involving children in conferences. Children can be involved in conferences at the highest levels of the ladder. To involve them as tokens will impress the press and politicians and may entertain many audiences, but children learn from such experiences only that democratic participation is a sham.

MODELS OF GENUINE PARTICIPATION

It is not necessary that children always operate at the highest possible rungs of the ladder of participation. An important principle to remember is *choice.* A programme should be designed to maximize the opportunity for any child to choose to participate at the highest level of his or her ability. We have previously discussed some of the factors affecting this ability, such as cultural attitudes to children's participation, age, and the particular competencies of each child. Also, children may not wish to participate to the maximum degree of their ability in all projects. A child who is capable of leadership may be quite happy building a wall for a project initiated and guided by children who are less able in this role but are more interested in designing or managing that particular project. In the Escuelas Nuevas, or 'new schools' of Colombia, I was most impressed to discover that children are commonly comfortable working under the coordination of elected younger children and can clearly articulate, using democratic principles, why they are comfortable with the situation.

Assigned but Informed ('Social Mobilization')

The fourth rung of the ladder, 'social mobilization', is the most commonly used approach to children's participation by international development agencies working in the developing countries. Unfortunately, it is common for social mobilization to be carried out in a manner that does not meet the requirements of genuine participation and hence does not further the goals of the democratic socialization of children. Only by looking closely at each example and at the particular culture in which it is found can we discover whether it is participatory or not. It is often difficult to judge where a social mobilization project lies along the continuum of regime-instigated to truly voluntary activity. Only a person from within the culture who also understands the political system can make this judgement. The size of a project alone is not enough to make it unacceptable. In many large-scale mobilization projects, although the children may not have initiated the project themselves, they may well be fully informed about it and feel real ownership of the issue, and may even have been involved in a critical reflection on the issue. Even large-scale environmental clean-up campaigns, with children gathering garbage created by adults, may be acceptable under the right circumstances. In this example, one would need to ask whether the project was designed simply to use the children as free labour or as part of an exercise to begin their critical reflection on the causes of such littering, and on how children might influence the responsible adults to change.

Social mobilization can be used effectively as a first stage in more substantial participation projects with children. The Programme of Working Children (PMT) in Ecuador, which will be discussed in the next chapter, uses festivals, parades, and other mass demonstrations as a first step in enabling children to see that they can have an impact on the world and in attracting other children to be involved (see Figure 25, p. 67).

Another common example of children's social mobilization in environmental issues is the assignment of children to catalyze the actions of adults by educating them on an issue. For example, some schoolchildren in New York City were named deputy mayors by the mayor of New York during a water crisis. After receiving lessons on the problem and on what they could do to help conserve water, the children were deputized with badges and sent home to carry this message to their parents. Yes, this was a low-cost solution, but everyone seemed to benefit from this creative response to a real crisis in the city. The sarvodaya development movement in Sri Lanka carries out effective social mobilization events, in the form of village dance performances through which children communicate fundamental health principles to the village.

Social mobilization alone achieves very little in the democratization of children. These efforts carry simple messages from the top down – that is, from adults to children – and have only a short-term impact. They must be quickly followed with more genuinely participatory experiences, or what will remain in children's minds is the notion that children are to be used when needed, rather than the idea that the children's perspectives are themselves important.

Consulted and Informed

Projects can be designed and run by adults yet still have virtue as participatory projects if children understand the process, are consulted, and have their opinions treated seriously. City-wide surveys of young people's opinions like those carried out by the cities of Seattle, Sacramento, and Berkeley in the USA and by Toronto in Canada can also be excellent examples of children's participation, especially if they involve those who were surveyed in the analysis and discussion of the results. At a minimum, children should be informed fully of the purposes of the survey, should be asked to volunteer for the survey, and should each be fully informed of its results.

Figure 16:
The solar box cooker project, sponsored by Children's Earth Fund, was a good example of social mobilization with children that can both inform them and enable them to play an awareness-raising role with others. In Nigeria, a teacher explains how and why isolators are used and how to make solar box cookers, while at the Rio 'Earth Summit' more teachers are invited to become involved. © Etinan Institute, Nigeria.

ADULT-INITIATED, SHARED DECISIONS WITH CHILDREN

Most projects carried out by communities are not meant for use by any particular age group but are to be shared by all. Usually the most politically powerful age groups (those over 25 years of age) dominate the decision making. The goal should be to involve all persons, but, given the natural tendency to exclude certain groups, adult-initiated projects should pay particular attention to involving the young, the elderly, and those who might be excluded because of a particular personal characteristic or disability. This is an important level of involvement on the ladder, for, if adults cannot foster a sense of competence and the confidence to participate at this level, then the upper rungs of the ladder are unlikely to be reached.

It is easier to convince children and adults that young people should take part in the planning and design of environments for their own use, so this may be a good first project. In these kinds of projects, it is important to assume nothing about what children want, even if there are severe constraints on what you can help them achieve. The constraints should be made part of the open discussion with children at the earliest possible stage in the participatory process. The Children's Environments Research Group, for example, has assisted schools and community groups in working with children to design play spaces in Harlem and the Bronx, New York. Although children usually rush to request swimming pools and baseball fields, it does not take them long to discover that the available spaces and resources are inadequate for these kinds of activities.

To achieve real shared-decision projects, children need to be involved in some degree in the entire process. The temptation is to involve them only in the conceptual design and to assume that the technical details, which commonly compromise the project and erode its original scope, are not part of children's concern but should be left to the adult initiators and such professionals as engineers or architects. This is a mistake. Even if children cannot have a voice in these discussions they should be able to understand how and why compromises are made. In this way, they will be less likely to assume that their participation was merely token and more likely to gain a realistic idea of how environments are created.

Child-Initiated and Child-Directed

Projects in this category are particularly difficult to find except in the world of children's play. But play is an important training ground for many of the fundamental qualities we wish to foster and should not be ignored. Regrettably, adults in North America and Europe are tending more and more to programme and manage children's activities, including their play. There are, however, ways in which adults can help without directing. For very young children, the secret is to set the stage for play. Good preschool and kindergarten teachers know the kinds of environments and objects that three- to six-year-old children like to use in their activities. They know, for example, that sand allows for cooperation between children. In a similar manner, many communities in Northern Europe have developed adventure playgrounds for older children (usually between eight and 14 years of age). These are settings with plenty of loose materials, particularly wood, and tools for children to use, and a small crew of 'play leaders' to support but not to initiate or direct children's play and building activities. Children who have learned to cooperate in such settings are better prepared to make useful contributions to their communities.

It takes particularly observant adults to notice children's initiatives, allow them to happen, and recognize but not control them. I was impressed by the teachers at an elementary school in Vermont who allowed children to develop their own environmental clean-up project. The children had observed that the stream behind the school, which was full of tiny fish and which they valued highly, had been polluted by oil during a clumsy oil tanker fill-up operation. The fifth-grade children (ten- and 11-year-olds) organized a rescue operation for the fish, requested to telephone the Environmental Protection Agency (EPA) themselves, and waited to hear from the officials what they should do next.

Regrettably, more often children will either carry out such projects secretly or will be intimidated from even beginning them because of fear that adults will not understand their desire or capacity to carry them out. Sometimes the children will conclude that they must operate secretly. My favourite story in this regard is that of the secret vegetable garden built by eight-year-old Peter, also in Vermont. Peter longed to grow food for his family, but his father would not allow him to work in his garden. So Peter 'stole' seeds and developed his own garden a few hundred yards away from his father's. Peter's two tiny gardens were less than four square metres in size, but he managed to produce a variety of vegetables. As they matured he would sneak them into the baskets after his father had harvested his own garden. In this way he enjoyed the feeling of competence in his own abilities as a gardener as he observed how his large family unwittingly consumed his corn and squash at dinnertime.

Child-Initiated, Shared Decisions with Adults

After I published my first version of the ladder of participation, some people complained that surely the eighth rung of the ladder could not be the highest level of children's participation because adults are still involved. But my goal is not to encourage the development of 'children's power' or to see children operate as an entirely independent sector of their community. If children initiate their own project, they should be allowed to continue to direct and manage that project. If, however, they choose to collaborate with adults on a project that they themselves initiated, I can only applaud this as a demonstration of children who feel sufficiently competent and confident in their role as members of the community that they do not find it necessary to deny their needs for collaboration with others. Well-organized groups of teenagers understand that, although they may be able to carry out projects themselves, they may need to work at some stage with adults in positions of power. A sensitive observing adult can also offer help on a project to children, although the line between an adult offering assistance and children feeling that they have no choice but to accept it is often an ambiguous one.

It takes some time to establish a climate of trust wherein children feel that to involve adults does not necessarily mean subjecting themselves to adult control. An example comes again from Vermont. Ten-year-old boys had designed a 'blind' (hidden observation post) in their classroom in the Wilmington Elementary School and were observing other children's behaviour. Earlier, they had enviously observed me taking groups of children from a neighbouring class into the woods each morning to observe animals from behind the blind we had built. These boys were using the forms I had designed for studying animal behaviour with their own classmates! Fortunately, their teacher was good at picking up on such initiatives and supported the children by suggesting ways they might improve their observations. This activity became a valuable means for the class to learn about themselves. Children took turns observing classroom behaviour from the blind throughout the day. Then, during the daily classroom discussion period, their observations were used to help interpret conflicts in the classroom and to suggest new strategies for organization and management of the room. We use words such as *animators*, *promoters*, and *facilitators* to describe the kinds of professionals who give life to the potential of young people, but all of these words suggest that the critical skill in adults is to initiate. What we equally need are adults who are good at listening to and observing children in order to know better how to respond.

ALTERNATIVE STRUCTURES FOR CHILDREN'S PARTICIPATION

The best opportunities for democratic experiences for children come from sustained involvement in a group. With regular attendance in the same group, adult facilitators can establish with children clearly understood processes, roles, and rules. This offers the best opportunity for all children to develop their own orientations to participation in ways that build upon their particular proclivities and desires. There are a wide variety of structures for children's participation, but it is remarkable how rare it is for these to be made explicit, even in children's and youth organizations.

In any organization where adults are formally

[2] Earthnauts, 5108 Woodgreen Cove, Austin, Tx 78745.

responsible for children there will be some issues on which adults must maintain the final word. For example, a book contract negotiated and signed by adults on behalf of children may obligate a group to produce a book of a certain length. The children need to understand from the beginning the constraints of that contract and that although they might be able to design the book and its contents, they cannot decide to produce a newspaper or video instead. Again, the principle to follow is honesty and clarity from the beginning about the extent of children's power.

Although it is common for groups to be vague about the democratic structure for children's participation and children's relation to adults, there are important exceptions. Earthnauts, based in Austin, Texas, in the USA, is an independent corporation of adults, children, and teenagers.[2] It has a board of directors with an equal number of young people and adults and has adopted a team/task model of management with no hierarchical power structure. Committees are formed around specific projects for as long as the projects last, and the leadership is shared between adults and children. Each adult board member is paired with a student member and each member of the team has one-half of one vote in all policy decisions. In this way children are involved in all phases of negotiation and consensus building with the group.

Many schools in many countries have some kind of student government structure with a limited range of responsibilities. The details of student government structure and election process vary from school to school. Many high schools in the USA have a student government with a president, secretary, and treasurer, and a representative from each classroom. The election is often a sophisticated affair modelled roughly on the national elections. Children use their creativity to present their ideas, give speeches, and hold press conferences during a brief period. Press conferences are held as open panels in which children from the entire school are encouraged to ask questions about

what they would do if elected. Adults from the community are invited to serve as a jury for the election, but children also sit at the jury table so they can learn to be jurors at a later time.

The student government of the 'New Schools' of Colombia determine the types of committees there will be each year and then the student body elects officials for each of these committees – the fish farm committee, the worm farm committee, the recycling committee, and so on. There are also elected offices for each class of children. The representative system works well to enable all children to feel they are involved in school decisions. The classroom representatives make 15-minute summaries of the regular central committee meetings to their classmates. There are also general assemblies in which all students are allowed to speak on the predetermined agenda. Parents and town councillors may also participate in these general assemblies. The students are allowed to call extraordinary meetings when special needs arise, such as dissatisfaction with the elected officers.

One of the issues the New Schools are struggling with is how frequently to hold elections. In one school, elections are held every two months, thereby guaranteeing a high degree of participation of students but also perhaps consuming a little more time than might be desirable given the quite elaborate election process. Other schools work with a six-month or even a year-long election cycle. At the beginning of each year the school government produces a Manual de Convivencia (Manual for Coexistence). This document, prepared by the student government together with parents and teachers, replaces the taken-for-granted nature of rules in traditional schools, which are handed down by the school administration. The manual includes sanctions for children who fail to meet the norms. Clearly, these democratic practices are likely to lead children to a deeper belief in democracy than any number of songs or recitations of democratic principles.

The Issue of Representation

Whatever form of democracy one adopts, there will be times when a group needs someone to represent them. Yet it is surprising how many adult organizers all over the world still insist on selecting children themselves, even when their programmes are in other respects participatory. There seems to be a fear that children will not do a good job of electing representatives. The electoral processes of the New Schools in Colombia illustrate that children in the early elementary school grades can, with practice, understand the principles and the values of electing competent, interested, and responsible peers for different committees in the school, regardless of differences in age or gender (see Chapter 7). As the introductory section of this chapter explained, children's capacity to coordinate the perspectives of others develops gradually, but this does not mean that they are incapable of democratic representation; in fact, there is strong reason to believe that children will greatly improve their abilities to take the perspectives of others and to progress in their moral reasoning as a result of rotating experiences with democratic representation.[3]

There should always be some process, fair and transparent to all, for forming committees. Volunteering is sometimes acceptable but is so commonly based on unstated criteria, such as a child's knowledge that he or she is one of the favourites of the facilitator or, conversely, a bully whom the other children dare not challenge. There are many different schemes that the group can use, and the children can be involved in selecting the system. Sometimes it may be appropriate simply to have a rotating representation, but this seems to remove the opportunity for children to think seriously about the nature of the particular task and who would best be able to represent the group and would most benefit from the experience. The Escuelas Nuevas use a system of elections that are so frequent and involve so much discussion of the importance of involvement that every child gets elected to serve on committees.

Although the youngest children in these schools are only six and do not fully understand what representative democracy means, the teachers in this system find that through frequent practice children gradually become more reflective in their choice of candidates and more responsible voters.[4]

I have been struck by the reticence of some facilitators to face the issue of democratic representativeness clearly, even when they are otherwise highly committed to giving children a voice. I have found this to be particularly true when it involves 'their' children representing the group elsewhere, such as at a conference. Street workers in the Philippines have spoken to me with discomfort over their selection of the president, secretary, and treasurer of the various working children's associations themselves, but emphasize the importance of children's competence and responsibilities in these tasks and their need to be in control of assessing this. There is generally a lack of guidance on the subject, and this is an important area for discussion among all of us who are concerned with children's participation. I discussed with the Filipino street workers how one solution to the dilemma of wanting competence but desiring a more democratic system would be for all of the children to have experiences as apprentices or shadows alongside older, more experienced children. This would offer opportunities for learning and demonstrating competence, and would also provide continuity when the adolescents move out of the group into adulthood. Furthermore, as long as they can see the consequences of their decisions, they would gradually improve their voting behaviour.

Establishing Rules and Decision-Making Structures with Children

Many facilitators working with children in participatory projects shy away from establishing any explicit rules for decision-making processes. Fearful of imposing their own structure, they provide no structure. But this is impossible, and the frequent result is that ad hoc rules

[3] Doise and Mugny (1984).

[4] Schiefelbein (1991).

5 Much of the thinking of this section is drawn from Educators for Social Responsibility (1991; see also Charney (1992); Power, Higgins and Kohlberg (1989); Steiner (1993).

are established in the process, often by the adult, and confusion reigns. The alternative to authoritarian structures is for a group to establish its own rules and its own decision-making processes. This is necessarily an ongoing process in any highly participatory group. It is most important in any such group that all the participants feel they can pull the group together at any time to address problems and establish new rules to deal with them.

A facilitator who is desirous of establishing democratic process with a group of children needs to introduce them to alternative decision-making structures and to have them look closely and critically at the way they make decisions in their own lives. Educators for Social Responsibility, a group of educators based in Cambridge, Massachusetts, who produce material to support teachers engaged in socially relevant work with children, have produced some useful guidelines for educating for democratic participation in elementary schools.[5] They suggest that children be introduced to six different models for decision making through a discussion of examples. This is just a theoretical introduction to decision making, because in fact many decisions are made by an informal combination of a number of these models.

Authoritarianism

Children also know this style well, for it is typical of most schools. The final responsibility for the decision rests with one person or with a small group. Giving children the chance to talk about the ways they have experienced this and ways it could be avoided is a good start to the discussion of alternative decision-making structures.

Delegation of responsibility

This is a category that is much more common than representative democracy in work with children. It is a blend of authoritarianism with representative democracy in which the people in control turn over decisions to someone else whom they select. It can be an appro-

priate strategy for adults to use with children as a training approach, as a way of systematically assigning children to activities offering greater and greater degrees of responsibility through experience. Unfortunately, this is commonly used with children as if it were representative democracy: children are delegated by an authority to carry out tasks for a collective as though they were representing the interests of the collective.

Random Choice

Children are familiar with this method, which is often used in their own games. It is used to avoid bias, as when a teacher randomly selects the first person to present to a class. Children know it well as a method used in sports to decide who will kick off and from what side of the football field.

Direct Democracy

In direct democracy everyone has the opportunity to participate in the decision-making process and to vote. The decisions are made through a majority vote, although the rule may vary as to whether a simple majority or a three-quarters majority is required. Many children will be familiar with this system.

Representative Democracy

This is a common system in schools that try to be 'democratic'. It is necessary when large numbers of children are involved but it is often used unnecessarily instead of direct democracy. Representatives are usually elected by a majority vote, although unfortunately they are often selected from a limited number of choices. It is important for children to be critical of how this initial set of options is selected.

Consensus

With direct democracy, the goal should be to achieve the maximum degree of consensus. Some groups may aim to make all of their decisions in this way, although this can be unhealthy if it results in individuals' consistently repressing their perspectives. Consensus does not mean that everyone agrees completely with a proposal, but only that it is acceptable to them after engaging in a discussion of everyone's ideas and taking the different perspectives into account.

By discussing each of these different approaches one at a time with children, it is possible to provide them with a language that will enable them to develop their own democratic processes and rules. One could create a wall display to show the six models graphically, with examples of each provided by the children themselves. Educators for Social Responsibility also suggest having children create skits in which they role-play each of the different decision-making models around a common problem, such as how a family might decide to celebrate a special event. If children are keeping logs about a project, they might systematically try to record how these different models are variously used by the group from day to day.

SOME SIMPLE PRINCIPLES OF DEMOCRATIC PROCESS

There are a few principles that I find helpful in keeping a project at an acceptably democratic level of participation:

- The children should understand the intentions of the project and should have volunteered for the project after these were explained to them.
- The organizational structure and power relations should be made clear to all participants at the beginning. It is all too common for children to discover late in a project that they do not have the degree of decision-making power they thought they had. This can lead to resentment and a sense that democratic participation in general is a sham. A useful way of doing this so that children of all ages will understand to a degree is to make a pictorial diagram.[6]
- Rules should be established through dialogue at the start of the project and amended by dialogue

throughout. This does not mean that adults may not impose some rules upon a group; this is an inevitable reflection of the power relationships and different responsibilities of adults in any society. It does mean, however, that the rules should be clear to all and that any member should feel free to request discussion of any rule at any time.

- All children should have equal opportunity to participate if they wish in all phases of a project, even if this may mean that, because of age or experience, a child is initially simply observing the work of others.
- Bringing children into a project at the last minute is a classic error, guaranteed to lead to only token involvement. A simple rule for avoiding this pitfall is always to try to make the entire process of any project transparent to the participants. Then, if children are not involved from the very beginning, they will at least understand the history of the project and be able to assess their role in it.
- Similarly, while not all children need to be equally involved in all phases, it is essential that, to the extent of their intellectual capacity, they are fully informed of the history and complete scope of the project and where they currently are in the process. This is very important if one is sincere about sharing control of the decision-making process. Because of different ages, degrees of experience, and interests, some children may wish to be involved in the action phases of a project rather than in research and reflection. The facilitator should explain the importance of all phases and make sure that no children are excluding themselves because of a sense of incompetence. It is all too easy for the more literate children to take over the research phases of a project just as the artistically competent children dominate the artistic products. On the other hand, the children themselves may feel that they want the most talented children to carry out certain phases in order to guarantee a high-

[6] For a participatory approach to creating such a diagram, see Pretty, Guijt, Thompson and Scoones, (1995), pp. 241–3.

quality product. Again, transparency and the establishment of democratic principles within the group are the best strategies for a facilitator struggling to balance these different considerations.

Following these simple principles, it should be possible for children always to be operating at one of the upper rungs of the ladder of participation.

ORGANIZING MEETINGS

It is generally recognized that groups of more than ten or 12 individuals do not work well for achieving high degrees of participation with people of any age. The ideal group size for children to work together and achieve a sense of cohesion, while also allowing a diversity of viewpoints, seems to be four to eight. With a group of this size, it should be possible for each child to feel involved. Depending on the age of the children, these groups may or may not remain stable over time. Children in the early school years frequently change their friendships and may prefer to have a completely flexible arrangement for group structure. While they should be free to change, it is also valuable for the facilitator to discuss clearly with the group the value of maintaining continuity and learning to work with people who may not be their closest friends; this is one of the main values of being part of such a project. It is often valuable for children to work on problem solving in pairs before coming together as a group. This maximizes their ability to identify their own ideas and have them expressed. It is also an excellent means for enabling children who are new to a group to establish personal relationships with others.

Large meetings are periodically necessary for the support of group identity. They are also valuable for introductory and closing sessions in which everyone is kept informed of each other's work. There may even be times where a whole group should come together for brainstorming, but in all instances these large-group meetings should be as brief as possible in order for everyone to feel involved and to reduce domination by a small vocal minority.

It is often necessary to find ways for subgroups to merge their ideas with one another. An excellent solution for both the smaller groups and the larger group is to use large sheets of newsprint on the wall with felt pens, which enable a facilitator to document all that is being said in a combination of written and graphic form. The more artistically talented the facilitators, the better they will be likely to capture the ideas of the group in a concise way and in ways that children with limited reading skills will be able to understand. The important principle to remember is that the facilitator is simply supposed to be the 'pen' of the group. Facilitators can stress that they are simply working as the group's tool by periodically reminding group members that they can add pieces to the wall graphic either by drawing directly on it or by sticking on it pieces of their own work. Ideally, the recorder is different from the person verbally facilitating the group's participation. If they know how to work well together, it is often best to use two recorders to keep up with the momentum of the group. This is a task that is difficult for pre-adolescent children to carry out, for it truly requires the ability to hear what all individuals are saying while at the same time maintaining a sense of the direction of the group and also focusing on the highly creative act of transforming what is being said into written and graphic form. As discussed above, such high levels of coordinated thinking develop slowly in children.

Simulation and Role Playing: Practising Participation

This book is about direct participation in projects rather than simulation. There are, however, ways for those who have not been involved in projects before, including teachers, to play with the idea of participation before engaging in it directly.[7] The Living Space action packs produced by the Neighbourhood Initiatives Foundation in the United Kingdom are a good example.[8] These kits are based on the idea of changing

[7] Ward and Fyson (1973); Nelson (1984) van Matre (1979, 1990).

[8] Iltus and Hart (1995) and Gibson (1993).

> ## Box 3: The Houses Game
>
> *The Houses Game, developed by Bishop, Jones, Russel, and Mills, was, like so many other useful ideas, published in the* Bulletin of Environmental Education *(now* Streetworks*) (Jones, 1979).*
> *How to go about it:*
>
> 1. *Houses: Use the pattern to draw up 12 houses on an A4-size stencil for duplication. Each player needs one sheet, or 12 houses. Cut out, fold, and insert slots. See diagrams. No gluing is necessary. You now have 12 houses with back gardens.*
> 2. *Site: A piece of land is represented by a piece of A4-sized paper. You will also need glue.*
> 3. *The task: Each person has to get all 12 houses, one of which is a shop, on the site in as interesting, convenient, and inexpensive a layout as possible. This has to be done in consideration of the following:*
>   *a) Sun: Sun must get to each garden. A decision about orientation must be made here, and the sun on the wall helps. Gardens do not have to face directly onto the sun but should be within roughly 45 degrees.*
>   *b) Footpath: There must be a footpath to every house; no one must be cut off.*
>   *c) Parking: Cars can be parked right by the houses (in which case roads must be shown) or in a group or groups around the edge. Roads can enter the site anywhere.*
>   *d) Open space: There must be as large a possible an area (or areas) of open space, marked as such (using green pen). It does not all have to be in one piece. A play area should be identified.*
> 4. *Finishing: When a final solution has been achieved, the houses are glued down, and footpaths, roads, parking, and open spaces are drawn in on the site.*
> 5. *Evaluation: Each individual is given an evaluation form for his or her design, or, if time permits, one for everybody's. If each person has one form, the whole group looks at each in turn and a count is made of the votes in each box on the form. The leader simply asks, 'How many people think it is very attractive?' or 'How many people think it is fairly expensive?' which is quick and enjoyable, but it is like any public ballot – votes are 'influenced'. If you choose to get all students to fill in their own forms on each design, there is then a need for someone to count ticks in boxes and produce a summary. But this is fairer (it is also a mathematics exercise).*
>
> *These are the basic rules for the game, which can be played by people of all ages. Only the number of issues, the connections between them, the verbal skills, and perhaps the sophistication of the results will change.*

one's own surroundings, beginning with that which is closest to oneself, and expanding outwards in concentric circles: room, home, street, housing estate, neighbourhood, town, landscape. The base materials are simple 3D layouts: an inner-city waste site, a patch of suburban land for a proposed housing estate, a landscape model on which a whole town could be planned. The kit also includes cardboard cutout houses, pipelines (coloured threads), bus routes (string), roads (narrow-gauge masking tape), and so on.

In participatory planning and design with children it is often necessary to liberate the children from the

Figures 17 and 18: A reduced version of the cutout sheet to be used by the children in playing the Houses Game, and a finished sample display.

constraints of the traditional designs with which they are familiar. Especially when one has a limited amount of time with a project, showing children a series of slides of an extremely wide range of ideas from around the world, some of them bordering on the outrageous, can liberate them to think openly.[9]

Brainstorming Workshops

At many times during a project, a group may need to liberate itself to think broadly and richly about a subject without constraint upon their creativity. There are different strategies one can use, but all of them should stress inclusiveness – that is, that everybody's ideas count. The goal is to propose as many ideas as possible, so that the chance of coming up with a good one is increased. There is, however, a danger that the group will go off on a particular tangent without exploring a diversity of possibilities. One way to avoid this is to begin by having children draw some of their ideas on paper or discuss them with partners before coming together in a group. Ideally, two people should record the group's ideas on large sheets of newsprint on a wall with felt markers so that everyone can see. Two children can record ideas in turn so that the group does

not have to lose its momentum by waiting for the recorders. It is the facilitator's job to make sure that everyone feels that all ideas are acceptable, and they should remind the group periodically that there should be no judgements, no matter how outrageous an idea may seem. The group should also be reassured that it is fine to build upon the ideas of others.

A brainstorming approach for very young children can begin with a collage. In the design of a play environment, for example, the children might be asked to draw all the features they would love to see, cut these out, and pin them onto a wall collage as a first step. It is then a very simple matter to group the different elements and spin off ideas from them in the more traditional verbal maner of brainstorming. In another version, for older children, members of the group write

9 Lee-Smith and Chandry (1990).

their ideas down on separate pieces of paper and stick them onto the wall. This is particularly useful when brainstorming is required on a number of separate topics. The value of keeping the combinations on separate pieces of paper is that the ideas can subsequently be moved around as the group moves into the phases of classifying, clarifying, and evaluating them.

COMPETITIONS

Adult organizers of children's involvement in environmental events frequently turn to competitions as a quick and easy way to get children's perspectives expressed and in a manner that guarantees adult control. The organizers of children's conferences, for example, sometimes turn to drawing competitions to decide who should attend, but although this may seem to be an improvement upon the usual tendency of adults to pick the articulate or socially confident child, it is still most inferior to such alternatives as asking children who are involved in environmental projects to elect their own representative.

Competitions may be thought of as antithetical to the concept of children's participation as espoused here, with its emphasis on inclusiveness, but this need not be so. It depends in part upon the degree to which the rationale for the judging and the results are shared with the children themselves. The Mazingira Institute in Nairobi, Kenya, conducts a highly interactive competition, with the children's ideas being shared with thousands of children and adults (Box 4).[10]

Another good use of competitions is for children to work in groups to prepare proposals for environmental improvement. Urban planners in the city of Nottingham, England, designed a competition for local improvement linked to an anti-vandalism campaign. Nearly 400 children entered the competition. They were asked to select a derelict site or building and make proposals for its improvement that would enhance the area's environmental quality. Five of the 'local improvement scheme' proposals designed by the children were implemented.[11]

A straightforward way of avoiding the individualistic nature of most competitions is to arrange for a prize that goes to the school or organization to which a child belongs. An example is the annual art competition for local schools in the Peak National Park Planning Authority in the Peak District area of England, which offers a special prize of an engraved oak plaque (carved by a local craftsperson) and a selection of half a dozen trees for the best overall school entry.[12]

In 1990, the WWF in Italy initiated a nationwide school competition on the theme 'Let's Design the Future'. Through its Panda clubs, several thousand copies of a manual were distributed to school classes to help them produce proposals for 'alternative futures' in their local environments. The 'competition' was more complex than the typical 'school contest' in that more than a poster was required. The projects were presented in an array of media – site plans, videotapes, models, theatrical pieces, photo exhibitions, and so on. The winning team – a junior high school class from one of Palermo's poorest quarters that had 'imagined' the transformation of an abandoned eighteenth-century botanical garden into an 'ecological park' and 'community museum-workshop' – was awarded a one-week stay at one of the WWF's nature reserves. The group was also invited to produce working drawings and cost estimates with the town's architect.

ENGAGING WITH THE NEWS MEDIA

Children's environmental projects are popular with news media all over the world, and the temptation for many groups is to invite the media in at the earliest opportunity. To do so is to risk trivializing the important work of which young people are capable. Rarely do the media describe the process of children's involvement; the tone is more normally one of a patronizing superficiality. Children's work is applauded without specifying why it is important or what it may influence. The implication is usually that for children, they have done a good job, but that their work is not a serious contribution of relevance to decision-making. Because children are

[10] Lee-Smith and Chaudry (1990).

[11] Oakley and Russel (1979).

[12] Oakley and Russel (1979).

Box 4: Competitions Where Everybody Learns, from the Mazingira Institute in Nairobi

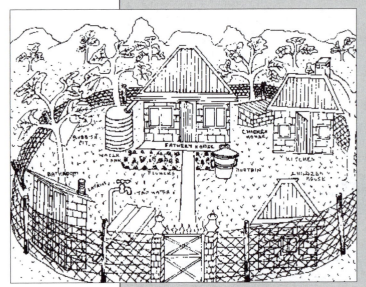

Figure 19:
'A dwelling place for my family', drawn by a child in the competition on shelter (note the water tap and latrine are placed too close together).

Mazingira means 'environment' in Kiswahili. Since 1979, the International Year of the Child, the Mazingira Institute in Nairobi has been exchanging information with primary school children about their environment. As part of its programme of research, networking, and documentation for environmental improvement in East Africa, the Institute has established a children's project using mass communication techniques for two-way communication and learning. A regular series of illustrated learning packages, including comic books containing stories, articles, posters, games, and puzzles, are mailed out to all the primary schools in Kenya and to some schools in other parts of East Africa. An important part of the programme is an annual competition in which children answer questions and send in essays and drawings on an environmental or developmental theme. Not only do the children receive prizes for themselves and their schools, but the information they provide is also considered as valuable data to be shared with others. The winning entries are printed in another full-colour package distributed to all participants. Each school receives ten copies of the package, necessitating print runs between 50,000 and 250,000. Topics covered have included tree planting, water management, wood fuel, tree seedlings, health and nutrition, water and sanitation, and occupational environmental hazards. The first competition, held in 1979, revealed so much information about the use of Kenyan trees and shrubs for fuel, fibre, food, and building and medicines that it was published in a book.

One competition question revealed that 80 per cent of Kenyan children clean their teeth with chew sticks made from different species of plants or shrubs. This led the Mazingira Institute to engage in research with the Kenyan Medical Research Institute on the subject. They discovered that chew sticks are effective as toothbrushes, and after that extension packages on chew sticks were sent out to schools, health centres, and teacher training colleges.

In 1989 a competition was held on the subject of shelter. Children were asked to find out from their elders about the health and safety of traditional houses and the rationale behind their designs. Second, they were asked to draw their own house and evaluate it and to include a discussion of how waste was dealt with and whether the methods were safe and healthful. These questions were followed up with a request for a description of how they would design a good house and what they would do to make it safe and healthy. An example of one of the contributor's submissions is shown in Figure 19. These competitions clearly lead to discussion in the classroom and a great deal of learning for both teachers and children. In a country with limited published resources for children to use, this low-cost approach of distributing learning packages that are highly interactive has proved extremely effective as a way of combining mass media with the educational system to mobilize children and their communities, particularly the elders of those communities. It is a model that is being used in other parts of Africa and is even stimulating the development of local clubs.

Excerpted, with permission, from Lee-Smith and Chandry (1990). For further information on the Majingira Institute and the Majugira journal contact them at Box 14550, Nairobi, Kenya.

capable of engaging on a level that is of relevance to real improvements in their environments, the media should be educated by the young people and the facilitators they are working with about the authentic nature of the projects, and this is best done when a project is already established. The media can often give a great boost to the initial phase of a project, but one needs to judge whether one really wants the applause of an uncritical observer or the serious commentary of an educated one.

A particularly effective way to have the children or teenagers in one's project become educated in their dealings with the media is for them to become journalists (see Chapter 11). Whenever possible in each project, some members should elect to become journalists or press officers for the organization. They can even produce their own press releases and prepare press conferences, thereby influencing the quality of information that is broadcast. Without too much effort, children can be helped to see when they are being treated in a patronizing or tokenistic way by adults through such experiences.

MONITORING PROJECTS

A project sponsor may require an evaluation of a project, and this may necessitate the hiring of an outside, independent evaluator. The reader can refer to the large literature on evaluation but it is important to remember that too often evaluators look for product outcomes in quantifiable terms when the emphasis in children's participation projects should be the process.[13] This means that you may need to educate your sponsor a little by suggesting that, rather than an evaluation in the sense of a simple 'before' and 'after' comparison, what is needed is an ongoing monitoring of the process. If an outside evaluator is to be hired, you should stress the importance of including qualitative data, including children's critical self-commentaries, for only in this way can process be evaluated.

Whether or not evaluation is required, it is necessary for any participatory group to look critically at the processes of working together in order to be able to improve upon its performance, and this demands self-monitoring involving all participants. At a minimum this should entail regular discussions but, ideally, it might also include log keeping by children and facilitators. To help children learn to be self-critical, it is important for facilitators to build critical commentary into their own practice. One way is to ask some specific questions at the close of each discussion group or work session, such as, 'What were the things you most liked and disliked about this session?' or 'Was there anything we could have done today to make our work easier?' From such systematic examples children will begin to see the importance of monitoring.

The 'New School' described in Chapter 5 has an excellent monitoring system for group work. Each classroom of children maintains a large logbook which carries a record of every day's activities. Children take their turn, in pairs, to fill out this record. In this way, children share the review of their progress as a class, a role normally limited to teachers.

[13] For an excellent review of the evaluation of the social aspects of development, see Oakley and Marsden (1990). See Sabo et al (1996) for participatory approaches to evaluation with children.

CHAPTER 4

New Models for Involving Children and New Institutional Alliances

Figure 20:
A boy collecting firewood in Nicaragua. Such work for the family presents an opportunity to introduce local actions with children (such as the planting of woodlots close to homes) which can improve livelihoods, reduce a family's workload and better maintain local natural resources.
© Maria Morrison/ UNICEF.

The conception of children's democratic socialization promoted in this book requires new kinds of institutional structures. This chapter includes reviews of some useful models. Innovation can also come from a revision of existing organizations for children. Indeed, a number of case studies in this chapter are of institutions, normally thought of as quite conservative, where innovation has enabled them to become models of how to foster democratic development. There remains a great divide, however, between children's organizations and the adult organizations that make decisions about the communities in which children live, including those decisions that most closely affect children. For this reason, examples are also included of new kinds of links between children's organizations and adult institutions such as local community organizations, local governments, and local environmental planning agencies.

HOUSEHOLD ENVIRONMENTAL MANAGEMENT

For thousands of years, children all over the world have been involved in environmental work for their families. This commonly involves work that has a direct impact on the natural resources that surround them, particularly in rural areas: collecting firewood, foraging for food, and shepherding animals. Sometimes this work is excessive and exploitative, but often it is a natural apprenticeship to the responsibilities of adulthood. In these cases, it is an appropriate place to try to foster more ecologically responsible actions where these do not traditionally exist. For those cultures in the Northern Hemisphere in which household work is a rare phenomenon, household environmental management represents an entirely new opportunity for children who are commonly denied all opportunity for meaningful work.

In recent years, children all over the world have begun to serve as catalysts for responsible environmental awareness and action within their own families. Commonly this has involved the mass media communicating issues of conservation to the family via the children, rather than encouraging dialogue between vehement children and the families over environmental issues. Children are commonly effective, but sometimes self-righteous carriers of environmental messages. There is a danger of abuse of this uncritical channel of communication. For example, teachers who commonly feel starved of environmental education teaching materials may be happy to use materials provided by electrical power companies, which in some countries are required by law to supply a certain amount of public information on conservation. Not surprisingly, the materials provided by these companies are biased, suggesting, for example, that energy wastage is a problem caused entirely by household consumers and that children should learn (and teach others) to switch off lights, turn down thermostats and use less hot shower water. These are certainly valuable lessons for saving electricity at home but are only ethically acceptable as lessons if prescribed within the larger context of alternative sources of energy production and the commercial waste of energy. Teachers should beware of programmes that require actions of their children without reflection. We need more than personal action from children. We also need them to develop an orientation towards critical analysis and reflection on environmental issues if we are to develop a citizenry capable of independent environmentally responsible behaviour.

It is important to remember also that not all parents in all cultures will be receptive to their children educating them about the environment. Authoritarian family structures may leave little room for such a catalytic role for children. This consideration points to the value of the interactive models proposed in this book, whereby a dialogue is established between children, parents, and some development or environmental agency. The chapters that follow contain excellent examples of children as the dynamic force in establishing domestic programmes of gardening in Peru, water management in Sri Lanka, and fish farming in Colombia.

COMMUNITY SCHOOLS

Many would argue that the kind of radical approach to environmental education described in the previous chapter will be impossible to achieve in most public schools because they are by definition conservative guarantors of the status quo rather than institutions of social change. But it is because I have seen such a great range in degrees of democratic structure, even within schools in the same country, that I know significant change is possible, especially if a variety of other institutions and professionals become involved. Furthermore, public schools are the single most important institution for children in most parts of the world. We need to convince governments that making them centres for promoting local democracy and community responsibility is not only in the interest of achieving sustainable development but also, in the long run, the best guarantee of the kind of national political stability that schools are supposed to offer a nation-state.

There are a number of important ways a school can influence the development of children as democratically competent and responsible members of society:

- the nature of teachers' relationships with the children, including the way rules are set and discipline is administered
- the extent to which the curriculum allows for decisions to be made by children and encourages collaboration with others
- the extent to which children are involved in the government of the school
- the extent to which the curriculum is related to the daily lives of the children and their community
- the relationship of the school's democratic structures to the democratic structures of the surrounding community
- the content of the curriculum.

While community participation has long been recognized as an effective strategy for development, there have been remarkably few attempts by nations to foster community participation of children or youth through their public school systems.[1] Most public schools in most nations remain completely isolated from their

[1] For some notable exceptions, see Ward and Fyson (1976); Ball and Ball (1973).

[2] Dewey (1900).

[3] It is surprising that the global movement for elementary basic education, entitled 'Education for All', does not recognize the environment as 'basic'. Government education agencies all over the world claim they are trying to convince poor parents of the importance of schooling for their children, but there are remarkably few programmes which stress the relationship of schools to the child's or the parent's work or to the everyday struggle of families for survival. Niger, for example, has extraordinarily low rates of literacy which the World Bank claims it wishes to help the country raise, but the schooling continues to be entirely in French even though nobody speaks French in the villages! Even if the Education for All programme is able to increase school attendance it is not going to help children lift their country out of poverty if teachers and children continue to be trapped inside their classrooms using a foreign language and alien texts, unable to make connections to the local environments, the local culture's use of that environment, and the children's daily work in that environment.

surrounding communities and their environmental problems. It is difficult to imagine how a citizenry can become interested in democratic participation except by experiencing its benefits, yet civic responsibility is still taught as a classroom subject, through texts, like the remainder of the school curriculum. Even in the progressive educational philosophy of John Dewey, and the many that have followed it, democracy has been taught in a simulated manner by using the school as a microcosm of society.[2] Now, with the growing global recognition of the environmental crisis and the rush by many nations to develop environmental education programmes, it is critical that we stress the need for a genuine involvement of children in the environmental issues of their own surrounding communities.

Primary schools are particularly important because they are the institutions most children in the world attend. Unfortunately, many teachers have no interest in conducting field-based activities with their children or are fearful of doing so. We need to convince developmental and environmental NGOs that schools can be the focus for long-term strategies of local sustainable development.[3] While our ultimate goal should be to make the linkage of schools and their curricula to community development a universal of basic education, an initial solution is for nongovernment environmental organizations to play the role of a 'go-between.' They can help by linking community development and environmental goals with state-mandated curriculum goals for schools. This requires collaboration in designing programmes with teachers and continued in-service support so that teachers learn to satisfy their curriculum goals through research and action on the local environment.

One of the great barriers to the assimilation in schools of the kind of community- and problem-oriented approach to environmental education described in this book is the extent to which public school curricula are fixed, often by the state. For persons approaching a school with a proposal to collaborate on community environmental research, it is important to assure teachers that environmental education is not a new, separate subject but a focus that can be integrated into all subjects. This is possible because environmental education does not involve a new content area of the curriculum (see Figure 21). What is academically 'new' about environmental education is the ecological perspective. This perspective should not be taught as a separate subject: it is too important and is best understood as it is applied to the science, social studies, and arts section of the curriculum. In this sense it is like the language arts (reading and writing). Like the language arts, ecological thinking can be learned in the study of each subject area. As is true with the language arts, however, some schools may find it desirable to have a time slot in the curriculum to highlight environmental issues. The most obvious reason for doing this is to offer special opportunities to integrate the learning from the separate social studies, science, arts and language arts, classes through local community research and action – a field-oriented class. It is possible to do this through each of the separate subjects but, in schools with many different teachers teaching each subject, this may involve too much out-of-classroom time organization. This special environmental education class would then focus upon coordinating all of the children's community research and action projects with all other subjects and teachers.

A more serious barrier to the approach to environmental research and action proposed in this book is the degree to which children and their teachers can be involved in the pursuit of problems that they identify in their community when the mandated curriculum is laid out in too detailed a manner. A straightforward way for teachers to surmount this barrier is to annotate the required curriculum outline regularly with the activities the children are carrying out on their environmental projects. This can become an effective weekly classroom planning activity, ideally done together with environmental advisers. In this way, a predetermined curriculum can become a valuable check upon the different skills and kinds of knowledge being fostered by the children's environmental research, rather than a barrier to that research. It means a little extra planning time, but that is true of all good teaching.

For many families around the world, a formal school system requiring regular daily attendance may be impractical because of the work demands on children or the irrelevance of the national curriculum to their daily lives and those of their families. Various types of non-formal schooling have been developed, often by local communities themselves, with little support from either public or private agencies. Focusing directly on the basic learning needs in a manner that is sensitive to the particular problems of a community results in a more flexible solution than the standard government primary school system can offer, with its standard duration sequence, age structures, and pedagogical techniques. These schools not only have been able to offer such innovations as school calendars that vary according to community work demands and a combination of productive work and learning, but have also often been able to develop curricula which are more relevant to the community.

The most exciting aspect of the non-formal schools I have observed is their potential as a model for integrating the goals of educating children with the larger goals of community development. During my visits to the following school it was often difficult for me to understand where the work of children in school ended and their participation in the larger community organization began, for they took place in the same building and were in many respects the same thing. The Centro de Formaçâo do Educador Popular Maria da Conceiçâo in Recife, Brazil, is many things at once: a preschool, a day-care centre, a literacy school for six-year-olds, and an elementary school (until 11 or 12 years of age, but for some children until age 14). It is also a professional training centre for teenagers who have completed their elementary school

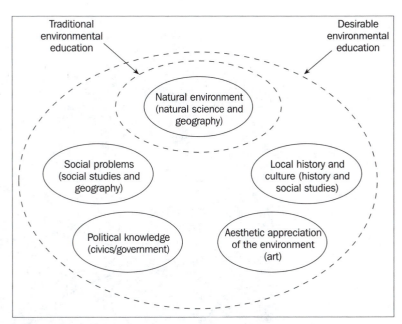

Figure 21:
A comparison of traditional and desirable environmental education.

training, and now work part-time on schooling and part-time for the centre. It is the location for meetings of the residents' council and for a variety of special community groups, many of which emerge out of the concerns of teenagers such as a group that was formed to stop avalanches in the area. The centre is very proud of being part of the popular movement for the poor, and serves as a training centre for 'popular educators' from Recife and elsewhere with courses in organizational management and educational methodology.

The centre began with a preschool and gradually expanded, developing its methodology from experience and improving upon itself. The group found that the best way to animate community participation in the running of the school and of extending the school into the community was through the traditional culture of this region, primarily music and dance. The school now continues through fourth grade. It is not public but has some funds from the federal government. Its emphasis is on social and cultural identity for the residents of the community. Like the centre in general, the school is concerned with improving the life of the community

Figure 22:
The bilingual programme of teacher training in Iquitos is now enabling teachers to build upon local environmental knowledge: here a teacher works in the field around the theme of hunting with bow and arrow.

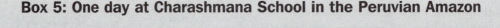

Box 5: One day at Charashmana School in the Peruvian Amazon

Teachers trained in the Bilingual Teacher Training Programme of the Peruvian Amazon at the Instituto Superior Pedagogico in Iquitos, are bringing a new kind of education to the children of the region. In place of learning only about remote places and ways of life in a foreign language, they are now building upon their knowledge of their own community and daily lives using both their native language and Spanish. The result is a schooling that is better integrated, more highly motivated, and better suited to building cultural resistance and sustainable development for their community.

Ini Niwe: *Do you remember the story of how the Shipibo learned to fish? Did you ask your parents and grandparents about the story?*

Rono: *A long time ago the Shipibo Indians used to fish exclusively with barbasco (a natural poison). One day the Incas appeared. They knew how to fish with arrows.*

Soi: *But the Shipibo Indians were envious of the*

Incas because they could fish bigger and wider fish with arrows. So the Shipibo Indians decided to bury the Inca alive.

Sina: *That's why the flood came as a punishment, and that's why all the Shipibo indians died. The only one that survived was the one that saved the buried Inca. He and his wife were the only Shipibo Indians that stayed alive.*

Ray: *Ah! But when the Inca Indian wanted to save the Shipibo Indians, he asked them to go up the hill and be safe from the flood. But the wife of the Shipibo Indian was very tired and couldn't go up the hill. 'I cannot keep going anymore. I have to stop', she said. Then she became a termite.*

Ini Niwe: *And then what happened to the Shipibo man?*

Ray: *He survived. The Inca gave him two wives and they started to increase in number, teacher. But by then the Shipibo Indian already knew how to fish with arrows. After that everybody learned to fish with arrows.*

Ini Niwe: *How about you? Have you already learned how to fish?*

Nita: *Oh yes, I can even catch zunjaro [a big fish], teacher!*

Rono: *Teacher, from the edge of the water I can fish sardina, paco and bagre [different kinds of fish].*

Ini Niwe: *So let's go and fish in the little stream.*

Once at the stream, the older children start to fish with arrows using their own canoes. The younger children use hooks and start to fish from the edge. The children scream with happiness every time they catch a fish. After fishing for at least forty minutes, they have caught 17 fish of different kinds: boquichicos, sardinis, tanas, bagres, bugurquis, movias, and two very pretty zungaros. Right there at the edge of the stream, the children observe the different characteristics of the fish species they catch.

Ini Niwe: *Rono, you separate the different fish and form groups.*

Rono: *How should I group them?*

Ini Niwe: *However you want.*
Rono organizes different groups of fish according to size, big and small, and the other children make different groups according to their spikes or scales and teeth or no teeth. With the oldest children, the teacher makes an analysis of a physical phenomenon when a fish is caught with an arrow, what is called light refraction. The teacher asks the pupils how they manage to catch the fish when they throw the arrow directly where the fish is placed.

The children talk about how they learn to calculate where the fish really is, and who taught them. The children mention their parents, their grandparents, and their older brothers. After that the teacher demonstrates an easy experiment, putting a spoon inside a glass of water.

When they come back to the classroom, the teacher summarizes everything they have observed and experienced in the stream. The younger pupils draw the different fish and group them in the same way they did at the stream. The older children also draw the refraction of the light with the teacher's

help and then make a summary of the subject. After the children finish their drawings and summaries, the teacher shows the children the two trays with the different fish.

He writes down the way they are represented mathematically and then asks the children to do the same for the fish without scales. Some children fail at first but Ini Niwe explains again. The children continue doing exercises with other groups using other environmental resources such as flowers and seeds. When they finish, the older children invent riddles, and the youngest play and sing with Ini Niwe in their own language. The teacher then gives them reading books with a short story also in their own language. It is a story of a black lizard that hunts a duck in the stream. After the two groups have read the text in silence, they do comprehension exercises. Ini Niwe then starts working with the younger children, beginning by asking: 'What kind of fish did you catch this morning?'

The children quickly describe the pana fish and talk about its behaviour and qualities. They also use a drawing of the fish and title it with its name.

Figure 23:
Drawing by Sharup Kantash Semu (six years old) from C N San Juan de Manchan, Pueblo Achuar.

[4] Schiefelbein (1991); Torres (1991).

Starting with the name of the fish, the children learn how to read and write a new consonant with respect to its syllables and they start to create words and sentences combining the syllables with the new ones they have just learned. After the younger children finish reading and writing the syllables, the older children start reading the short story aloud. Everybody listens to them. After they have all read or listened to the story they organize a play about the story. The children volunteer to be the character they want to represent. Finally, Ini Niwe bids good-bye, telling them that tomorrow they are going to Mrs. Bawan Rama's house to observe and learn how to make a ceramic bowl, even though most of them already know how to do it.

Adapted from a translation by Maria Fernanda Espinosa of Kanatari: Seminario de Actualidades, No. 550 (2 April 2, 1995). Published by CETA, Putumayo 355, Apartado 145, Iquitos, Peru.

through cultural development and political struggle. The curriculum is organized around different themes, and the final event each month is a party with a play, dances, and speeches integrating all that the children have learned on a theme in that particular month.

The entire centre is concerned with community development, so children and teenagers spontaneously become involved in and even initiate community projects. Children and teenagers belong to a variety of special community groups. At the time of my visit, the government was proposing to make the community into a tourist area because of the attractiveness of its traditional culture. Many residents fear that much of their traditional culture will be lost if tourism develops. The children involved in this project interviewed old people to document the history of the community and thereby help the resistance to tourist development. 'Cultural resistance' is generally an important theme for the school, but it received special attention during this effort to confront tourism.

While organizations like these could benefit from the availability of technical assistance from environmentalists and environmental educators, in terms of organization and the relationship of school to community, as well as the approach to identifying and acting upon community issues, they are more advanced than the vast majority of public schools, in either hemisphere. Unfortunately, because these schools are not connected to the state system, it is much more difficult for children to move on to higher levels of education.

Many different models of progressive schools around the world respond to a number of democratizing principles of community schools described at the beginning of this section, but the 'New schools' of Colombia, described in Chapters 4 and 7, are particularly important because they have so successfully developed an eclectic model that incorporates all of these principles in various degrees. In such a model there is no need to call for a special environmental programme; it is integral to the whole concept of the school, for, if school is organized for the children to identify and work on community problems, it cannot help but work on the community's physical environment.

The New Schools programme in Colombia is a highly successful, well-evaluated, new approach to schooling.[4] Furthermore, it is a low-cost innovation. With only 10 per cent in extra expenses, it can serve as a model for many poorer countries. It is now found to some degree in 18,000 of the 24,000 Colombian public rural schools, including all of the smaller schools with one or two classroom teachers. It is difficult to summarize the many ways in which the New Schools model is innovative, for this is a sophisticated model that has evolved over 20 years. This book concentrates on the environmental and democratic community activities of these schools, but a general review of the model is first necessary to reveal the multiple ways in which children are imparted with the knowledge, skills, and concerns for democratic citizenship.

As in other Latin American countries where rural

children spend considerable amounts of their time working and where schools are very small with only one or two teachers, the quality of rural education in Colombia was poor. Children's attendance was necessarily erratic as they responded to the pressures of the agricultural seasons, so they found themselves continually repeating grade levels and making little progress. This led to experimentation with mixed-age classrooms, and with a flexible curriculum. Such experimentation was easier because most of the schools have fewer than 50 children enrolled. Further innovations were borrowed from countries that had experimented with alternatives to traditional classrooms.

A programme was created that allowed children to learn more successfully, both individually and in small groups with other children, thereby liberating the teacher to function as a facilitator who could respond to the demands of the children as they moved through the curriculum themselves. This kind of model, generally called 'active learning', includes learning corners, which allow for simultaneous class activities; school and classroom libraries for groups of students to pursue advanced questions; and new types of organizations to enable children to function as a coordinated democratic community. One of the greatest problems in transforming a traditional model to such an active learning model on a national scale is the great cost and time required for teacher training and retraining. Primary strategy in Colombia was to disseminate the programme through weekly teacher-to-teacher meetings between the schools of each district, thereby enabling teachers to help one another with the radical redefinition of their role on a regular basis rather than in an isolated workshop.

COMMUNITY DEVELOPMENT ORGANIZATIONS

An ideal way for children to participate in community development is through community-based organizations. In many villages and urban neighbourhoods, these orga-nizations already provide a means for adults to participate in community improvement or community events. It is extremely difficult, however, to find examples of children's participation in research, planning, or decision making in community organizations. Commonly, children enthusiastically try to join in the physical phase of projects, such as carrying pipes in a water project, but this seems to go almost unrecognized by the adults of the community, even when children carry out a substantial portion of the work. Community-based organizations need help in recognizing the capacities of children and how to involve them. It is difficult for children's organizations or schools to approach a community-based organization with an offer of collaboration. They have no history of doing this and no prior examples of such collaborations. In many instances they do not even know of community-based organizations. This is an important area for environmental and development NGOs to initiate. Our own work in the Children's Environments Research Group with children's groups, schools and community-based organizations in New York tells us that there is a need for an ongoing NGO to serve as an intermediary between these types of organizations, and that it takes years to establish lasting collaborations because there are no pre-existing channels of communication.

CHILDREN'S AND YOUTHS' ORGANIZATIONS

It might be thought that the best place to find careful consideration of democratic principles with children would be in organizations established specifically to cater to children's out-of-school play, recreation, and learning. Regrettably, however, explicit principles of democratization of children are the exception rather than the rule.[5] Certainly there is great emphasis on the learning of responsibility, but not too many organizations in their statements of aims and principles recognize that this is best learned by democratically involving children in the management of the organization. Interestingly, the greatest exceptions seem to be

[5] See Smith (1981) for an account of organizing in youth clubs.

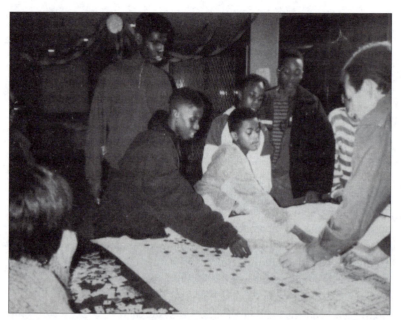

Figure 24:
Teenagers producing a map of their current recreational use of the neighbourhood and what they consider dangerous locations as part of the Safe Play project, at the Phipps Houses Community Development Centre in the West Farms neighbourhood of the Bronx, New York.

[6] Benjamin (1976). See also *Play Rights Newsletter* and the *International Children's Play Journal*.

[7] The text is extracted from the aims and principles of the Children's House Society. For further information, write to the Children's House Society, Victoria Chambers, 16–20 Strutton Ground, London SW1 P2HP, United Kingdom.

dren's spontaneous learning through play and exploration in a consistent environment over time, with good role models nearby, could well be the basis for establishing the kind of deep, affectionate caring that is needed as the basis for a lifetime caring approach to the environment.

Another interesting example which is even more explicit about the democratic structure required of members is the Children's House Society in the United Kingdom. The society exists to establish children's houses primarily for ages five to 11, that provide for the leisure activities of these children. By establishing such houses, the society seeks to provide the place with an atmosphere in which responsibility and mutual care may be nurtured among children.[7]

What happens in a children's house depends on the children. Sometimes it is just a place to be. But also, as far as possible, opportunities exist to encourage children to exercise and develop any interests and talents that seem important to them. A children's house should, ideally, be a building on its own, for example a house, a custom-built hut, or a converted shop but it may be part of a community building – for example, rooms in a church, community centre, or block of flats, in which case it is essential to its character that it be clearly designated so. Children are encouraged to regard the space they are using as their own and to be responsible for its management and activities.

The formation of a children's committee, consisting entirely of children who, with the assistance of the guardian, decide the activities of the house and formulate any rules, is basic to the concept of the children's house. The members of the first, temporary committee should be agreed between the guardian and the initial group of children, who are the first members of the house and consist of about six individuals. When the membership has reached about 20, and when the guardian considers the children to be ready, a proper children's committee of about seven children should be elected by a secret ballot of all house members. This committee should be re-elected anually, and election

institutions that have been established in industrialized countries for children who have been in trouble with the law. Similarly, in countries of the South, many of the organizations working with children living or working on the streets have more explicitly democratic structures and practices, to be discussed below. But first let us consider younger children and the success 'playworkers' have had in involving children in the management of their play settings.

In Europe, many of the organizations that provide opportunities for children's play have democratic structures to a degree that is unknown in organizations established for children's learning. Of particular note are the adventure playgrounds of Northern Europe. The professional playleaders who work in these institutions are models of the kinds of facilitators needed in children's democratic organizations. While the environment is not a stated specific focus of these centres, inevitably, and in a very natural way, the environment becomes a focus of much of the children's work. There is a sizable literature on adventure playgrounds and their management.[6] In Chapter 1 it was argued that there is a strong theoretical basis for believing that chilto the committee is open to all members of the house. The children's committee elect their own officers – chairman, secretary, treasurer, and others. Short committee meetings are presided over by the chairman, with the guardian in attendance to give guidance on procedure. The children's committee may call a general meeting at any time with the permission of the guardian. Before the house may be used for any purpose other than as a children's house, the permission of the children's committee must always be obtained.

ORGANIZATIONS FOR STREET AND WORKING CHILDREN AND OTHER CHILDREN LIVING IN POVERTY

It might be thought that children living in marginal conditions of survival should not be involved in community projects, but I believe that, as long as these projects are genuinely based in the children's own priorities and those of their peers or family members, there is much for them to learn and to give by their involvement. The degree to which children living in extremely difficult circumstances, such as street and working children in some programmes in certain countries, are beginning to understand their rights and become more involved in determining their own futures was introduced in Chapter 1. Some people might wonder whether, for children struggling to make a living, the priority should instead be with schooling, which offers them the development of literacy as a way out of poverty. This is an understandable reaction to a type of activity that has long been relegated to the voluntary and alternative margins of public school programmes. But programmes that offer disadvantaged children the opportunity to learn about their rights while practising them are much more valuable than programmes which accept these children's economic circumstances and offer them only poor, ameliorative versions of traditional educational programmes. When literacy is a central part of children's community participation programmes it is

likely to be highly effective, because language is being used in ways that are fundamentally relevant to the children's lives rather than in the abstract way it is used in most school language curricula. Another argument is that many street workers are very aware of what Paulo Freire calls the danger of the oppressed becoming the oppressors.[8] While 'empowering' children or building a sense of identity and self-worth through the promotion of individual rights, one needs simultaneously to foster a sense of responsibility towards others. This is one reason that even extremely disadvantaged children should also be involved in community development.

'Communities' for street children do not fit the usual geographic concept of community, for many of these children are homeless. For those who are not, their first community of concern should probably be their peers – that is, other children in similar conditions. A superb example that recognizes this is the restaurant programme of the Butterflies street children's organization in New Delhi, India. The restaurant, in a bus terminal, is run by children who have found their way out of street life through working with the

Figure 25:
In Macquinoise, a small village of 500 inhabitants in Belgium, children wanted a house for themselves. The Service de l'Animation worked with the children, found an old house that was to be demolished, and together restored it as an asset to the community. An adventure playground was developed on land behind the 'children's house'.
© Service de L'Animation, Brussels, Belgium.

[8] Freire (1970).

[9] Dallape and Gilbert (1994).

street workers of Butterflies. The children earn money by serving meals to bus passengers, but a special section of the restaurant also offers very low-cost meals to other working children.

For homeless children with no family, the focus of their research and action must necessarily be their own struggle for survival, but in well-designed programmes even these children are asked continually to remember their peers as they pull themselves out of their difficult conditions. A good example of how children in difficult circumstances can be helped to analyse alternative options for their future, and, through this process, come to serve their community better, comes from ENDA, a well-known non-government organization in Zimbabwe.[9] A participant in a recent ENDA training workshop for urban educators describes how a boy from Nkayi, a rural area in northern Zimbabwe, came to the city of Bulawayo looking for work. The aid organization Freedom from Hunger not only gave him information on job opportunities in Bulawayo but also worked more comprehensively with him to analyse his options. He concluded that he should return home and start a gardening project there. Freedom from Hunger provided fencing materials, and he recruited six other boys and began selling vegetables. This led to the construction of a live-in shop on the site for all of the boys and the expansion of employment to other children.

More commonly, children are living in difficult circumstances with their families in communities with many environmental problems. The following account of a national programme for working children in Ecuador illustrates how valuable participation programmes can be for children whom society has pushed to its margins.

El Programa del Muchacho Trabajador (PMT), the Programme of Working Children, is a national organization in Ecuador that uses children's rights as an organizing focus and the CRC as a basic referent in all its activities. It has demonstrated that a large environmental programme, involving the genuine participation of children, can be achieved at a national level in only one year. There are, however, two special factors in

Ecuador. First, the country is smaller than most. Second, and more importantly, PMT already had a national system of centres for working children and children otherwise at risk because of poverty. Each of these centres, called Espacios Alternativas, has a dedicated, trained coordinator committed to empowering children to become active agents in defence of their rights and improvement of their lives according to the United Nations CRC.

From its headquarters in Quito, the staff of PMT reach working children in Espacios Alternativas (Alternative Spaces) in all provinces of the country. These spaces, located primarily in poor urban areas, offer opportunities for children to learn informally to defend their rights, through play, learning, discussion, and action founded on the principles of the CRC. They learn about their histories, both individually and collectively, and, through play and artistic activities, develop an identity in their multicultural society. The goal is to convince these children from the age of six to 16 that they are citizens with the rights and capacity to create their own future. As many as 80 children in each Espacio are free to attend three to five voluntary meetings per week. The locations vary depending on the available spaces in their community: public schools, Catholic schools, community organizations, and colleges and health centres.

The environment was collectively chosen as the theme for 1993 at the annual conference of children and youth of PMT. The environment is, of course, a fundamental part of the CRC and hence a worthy theme. Its choice by the PMT children, however, came out of their own enthusiasm for the subject, no doubt inspired in part by the general growth of the environmental movement in Latin America. PMT intends to continue its plan of developing a theme each year taken from the CRC. From the start of the environmental programme however, it was believed that this would have some special value for consolidating the children's rights movement in Ecuador because of the visibility of local environmental actions to community residents.

Building upon this national structure of Espacios Alternativas, PMT was able to establish environmental projects in 21 provinces and 23 cities, with a total of 70,000 children. Most of the centres were in public schools that had space available after school. Many of these schools had not previously included any study of the local environment but were subsequently persuaded to incorporate the programme into their regular curriculum; and some middle-class schools reprinted the PMT materials for their own use.

Supporting the Espacios Alternativas and their environmental programme is a large developing network in defence of children's rights at the community level, with families, neighbourhood organizations, schools, churches, and youthful volunteers, and at the city level with government institutions and influential individuals. This is achieved through a large parallel programme of social mobilization of the public in defence of children's rights through TV, radio, and the press.

The earliest phase in each of the three major environmental regions of the country involves establishing a system of technical consultants to provide information and ongoing support to the programme. It was hoped that, by working first with ecologists from throughout the country, children could be guided to choose ecological actions that would not fail because of infeasibility. This network of ecological experts was also useful for collaboration in the design of numerous booklets used by the children and the programme promoters.

The central concept of the programme is the training of youth units in each city to work as the promoters (animators or facilitators) of environmental groups. With such a dual age-level approach to the participation of young people PMT was able to have a remarkable multiplier effect, with each small group of four or five teenagers working with as many as 80 pre-adolescent children. Each city established a local support group to serve as the training programme for these youth units. With this remarkable national structure in place, PMT began phase I of its project in March 1993. A detailed

account of the action research strategy used by PMT is offered in Chapter 5.

The project was initially conceived as a one-year undertaking because each year the children of PMT vote to work on a new theme of the CRC. It was their intention from the beginning to make this movement so strong that its momentum would be maintained through a variety of other institutions. Many schools have certainly been affected by children's enthusiasm for this project, but the traditional resistance of public schools in all countries to innovative extracurricular activities and their failure to incorporate activities that involve children's participation in their surrounding communities have been well documented in this book. However, even though PMT has continued to work on different themes of the CRC each year, the environmental theme was so interesting to the children and had such community support that it has remained central to the work of most Espacios Alternativas. In many of these spaces, there are now three-dimensional maps serving as bases for continued developmental diagnosis and action.

Figure 26:
While the PMT process begins with a fairly typical 'social mobilization' phase, with banners and festivals, it quickly moves on to the significant involvement of children in the identification and diagnosis of community environmental problems.
© Roger Hart.

[10] IUCN (1991). For further information, contact Walia B.P. 215, Mopti, Mali, or IUCN, Sahel Program, Avenue du Mont-Blanc, CH-1196 Gland, Switzerland.

CHILDREN'S ENVIRONMENTAL CLUBS

Thousands of children's organizations all over the world are devoted in one way or another to the care of the environment: conservation clubs, natural history groups, environmental action groups, subchapters of national environmental organizations like Friends of the Earth, and ecology clubs. Many of these are based in schools, though some are based in communities. They rarely have a democratic kind of structure. To my knowledge, however, there are no children's organizations devoted to the other side of sustainable development – that is, to community development with a focus on economic issues and livelihood. While it may at first seem appropriate that children should be concerned primarily with defending and improving the environment, and that economic activities should be more the concern of the adult world, the contemporary view of environmental care, as expressed in this book and in much of today's environmental movement, is that the perspective of sustainable development should be promoted. There are many community service groups in which children and teenagers play various social support roles in their communities. Perhaps in the near future we will begin to see children and adolescents forming sustainable development clubs, community development clubs, or groups for environmental justice.

Tens of thousands of children around the world receive newsletters and magazines, often with an environmental focus, which give them suggestions for activities to carry out themselves, usually in their own home. The best of these are interactive, with children sending materials to the newsletters that are reprinted and sometimes even analysed and used as data, as was described with the Mazingira Institute under 'Competitions' in Chapter 3. Sometimes these newsletter or magazine subscribers are encouraged to form clubs, which then become more effective in the development of local action and in the provision of useful information to be sent back to the newsletter for others to benefit from.

An excellent example is *Wallia*, produced by the International Union for the Conservation of Nature in Mali, West Africa.[10] By some estimates, Mali is considered the third poorest state in the world. Desert covers much of the land; only 12 per cent of the country is arable, and much of that is overexploited and deteriorating. For this reason, environmental care is a major priority for the nation. As part of their demonstration programme on the integrated use of natural resources for arid and semi-arid areas, IUCN established public environmental awareness and environmental education as major priorities. *Wallia*, the name for the stork or messenger bird, the bringer of hope which marks the return of the rainy season, is designed to awaken curiosity and stimulate action in the children of the nation. Though similar in many respects to the Mazingira Institute's magazine described in Chapter 3, it is designed for secondary school pupils aged 13 and over. The magazine is a twenty-page low-cost black and white bulletin produced three times a year, once for each of the school's trimesters. Before this age, the children of the West African countries speak many different languages and their command of French is inadequate. This is a major problem in this part of the world, where materials are still produced in the former colonial language, making environmental education of the type proposed in this book extremely difficult. Perhaps in the not too distant future, bilingual and bicultural education will develop here as they have in other parts of the world, and village presses will begin to produce publications like *Wallia* in local languages so that primary school children can use them and achieve greater communication with their parents on environmental topics.

A further sign of the formal nature of the curriculum in this part of the world and its removal from the community is that the *Wallia* activities are not carried out in the regular school curriculum but are extracurricular and voluntary. The modest print run of 5,000 copies reaches an enormous number of children, with one copy for approximately ten to 20 pupils. Most schoolchildren have no books of their own, so *Wallia* is often the only written document they can read and sometimes even keep. When the magazine began in 1985, children generally sent in their solutions to the riddles and games presented in the magazine. The interactive nature of the magazine has led to large amounts of information being volunteered by the children. They take the initiative to send in drawings, legends, guessing games, and suggestions for articles.

An important feature of this publication that enables it to become interactive is that twice a year the production team visits the 25 schools that receive *Wallia* to run presentations. Not only does this stimulate debate at the time, but it establishes a direct relationship between the children and the producers of the magazine, which encourages them to think of it as an interactive publication. School representatives also attend an annual national young people's camp which further fosters the idea that *Wallia* is an organization for children, not just a distant publication produced by strangers.

Because the publication is produced and used in combination with schoolteachers and is received consistently over time, it has been able to serve as a catalyst for children working with their community. For example, in the Ningari region of Mali, where guinea-worm is very widespread, the children have organized themselves and, with the approval of the traditional village chiefs, have developed an information campaign. Teams of five pupils each from 11 different villages in the region now travel around their communities explaining how one can get guinea-worm and how to create a process for filtering water that can prevent it.

CHILD-INITIATED CLUBS, NETWORKS, AND PROJECTS

All over the world, children form unions with one another without adult initiation. It has been rare for these child-initiated groups to look outside themselves or engage in any noticeable projects of social or environmental improvement. Children's spontaneous organizations are usually focused on play, recreation, sports activities, or a shared hobby. There are many signs in the northern industrialized nations that the environment is a domain around which children will sometimes organize themselves without adult initiation, partly because of the overwhelming amount of information available on the subject. Another reason may be the ability of children to network with one another and with organizations that provide information. The rapid expansion of electronic networking through personal computers in children's homes and in schools seems to be spurring these developments. Responsive, available adults are always important to these initiatives, but there is still a qualitative difference with groups that begin this way. At the time of writing many groups are simultaneously establishing electronic networks on the global system of communication called the World Wide Web, and it is impossible to present any clear view. With luck, schemes will emerge that successfully connect the initiatives of groups that are on the web with those that are not, for the danger is that electronic networking, rather than being a panacea for the world's environmental ills as many believe, will become yet another way of separating the privileged elite from those who have little.

It was largely in response to the unprecedented growth of child-initiated projects in the USA that a large national organization, called Earth Force, was established to help create alliances that would enable the efforts of individual children and small groups to become part of a national effort.[11] Earth Force has formed partnerships with many of the existing environmental NGOs, the mass media, most notably television, and major corporations to run massive national campaigns such as 'Pennies for the Planet' where children raise money for the World Wildlife Fund to use in the protection of the habitats of migrating wildlife. The organization is working hard to find ways of making these campaigns relevant to the interests and concerns of the thousands of members. For example, in 1994, 145,000 children voted in a national ballot which resulted in 'preserving wildlife as the issue they would

11 Earth Force, 1501 Wilson Boulevard, 12th floor, Arlington, VA, 22209, USA.

[12] An extremely valuable resource full of ideas for working with children are the Outbreak Information Packs produced by the United Nations Environment Programme, P.O. Box 30552, Nairobi, Kenya.

[13] Lorenzo (1988).

[14] Lorenzo (1990, 1991).

first like to work on. But no matter how successful such campaigns might be in attracting large numbers of children, they are inevitably destined to be rather top-down affairs and hence are best thought of as stimuli for more lasting local initiatives.

At the time of writing, Earth Force is experimenting with 'town meetings', the US equivalent of 'children's hearings' (Chapter 9) as a way of promoting local initiatives. The long-term success of Earth Force will probably depend on the degree to which it can foster and support community-level initiatives by providing information and resources to help children contact one another and forge coalitions with NGOs, environmental professionals, and government officials at the local level throughout the country. The important issue of how to establish programmes which are fundamentally local but also connected to regional or global efforts is discussed in Chapter 10.

ENVIRONMENTAL NON-GOVERNMENT ORGANIZATIONS

Most large environmental organizations have not found ways of bringing their expertise down to the community level in their work with children. They have relied instead upon films, magazines, and correspondence clubs, which, though highly informative, do not generally offer children the kinds of direct experiences called for in this book. The media they prepare exhort children to be active and provide clear accounts of small actions they can do themselves, but this cannot substitute for shared projects designed and executed with one's peers and with adults.[12]

The World Wildlife Fund in Italy is a model of how a very large organization can take its work down to the local level and thereby make it interactive. The WWF in Italy has over 300,000 members, of whom about 170,000 are under the age of 14. Approximately 100,000 of these young members are involved in over 5,000 school-based Panda clubs and approximately 70,000 are individual junior members. The environmental clubs work with local partners to animate community projects with children. The association's Education Department has produced numerous publications and a quarterly journal, *Teaching Green*, that is distributed to over 150,000 teachers. Workshops and seminars on various topics are offered regularly for teachers and activists at the local, regional, and national level. As can be imagined from the WWF's international and national statutes, the association emphasizes nature and wildlife appreciation and conservation, but recently it has begun to focus on urban environmental education.[13] In 1990, 'Let's Design the Future' was launched as one of the organization's three major programmes.[14] It involves children's participation in envisioning, analysing, designing, and communicating alternative desirable futures for their local environments, whether urban or rural. An example is the Aspromonte case study described in Chapter 6.

One of the great benefits of national environmental NGOs is that they can mount large-scale research efforts with children as participants. A remarkable series of national scientific surveys has been conducted by Wildlife Watch, the young people's wing of the Wildlife Trusts, one of the largest environmental clubs for children in the United Kingdom. The programme began in 1971 with the help of the *Sunday Times* newspaper as a national study of stream pollution to be undertaken by families. The overwhelming response prompted a second survey, using lichens as air-pollution indicators. As a result of public enthusiasm the project grew into an organization, and a partnership was formed with the Society for the Promotion of Nature Conservation (now the Wildlife Trusts). This partnership now operates independently of the newspaper, and currently Wildlife Watch has over 20,000 members, with many more children joining in the club's activities. Similarly, the Young Ornithologists Club, the junior wing of the Royal Society for the Protection of Birds, has for 16 years involved children in a survey of birds in backyards. With the help of *Blue Peter*, a children's television programme, and a national newspaper, the number of scientific observations has gradually increased; in 1995, almost 30,000 children recorded bird life in their gardens during a special one-hour period. Scientists have begun to take note of the research conducted by these young surveyors as a useful resource on the changing bird populations of the United Kingdom.

DEVELOPMENT NON-GOVERNMENT ORGANIZATIONS

While community participation has been central to the agendas of international and national NGOs concerned with development, this has seldom involved children. An important exception is the so-called child-to-child approach adopted by many organizations as a useful strategy for expanding health care knowledge (see Chapter 5). At the time of writing, there is considerable enthusiasm among a number of development NGOs to begin to involve children and youth in their community development initiatives, not only in strictly child-to-child activities but also in child-with-adult projects. From discussions with staff at such organizations as Actionaid, Plan Aid, Save the Children, and UNICEF, which funded this publication, it is clear that the CRC has been the catalyst for this. A sign of the newness of this interest is the current paucity of publications on the subject.[15] There are exceptions, though, and an important pioneer in involving children in development efforts has long been the Sarvodaya movement in Sri Lanka.

The Sarvodaya movement is a successful self-help initiative involving a large percentage of the rural population of Sri Lanka. Sarvodaya, meaning 'upliftment of all', relies greatly upon Shramadana, the sharing of labour, or self-help.[16] A few thousand villages have children's groups with children aged six to 16 years, as well as youth groups for people under 30 years of age and groups for women, men, and senior citizens. The primary strategy for introducing Sarvodaya to a village is through children. Preschool teachers trained in Colombo, the capital, start preschool groups in a village. Using traditional Buddhist principles and media

Figure 27: The Sarvodaya Children's Groups of Sri Lanka: ten-year-old boy standing proudly by the water tap area he manages in the village of Nellikolowalta, near Kandy, in the mountainous centre of the island. © Roger Hart.

of communication – dance, song, and puppetry – the children carry development messages to their families. This is done both through performances, which most of the village attend, and by the children copying messages home in the form of changed behaviour, such as personal hygiene activities like brushing teeth. From this modest beginning, children's groups and mothers' groups are formed. In the children's groups, the children carry out projects with a high degree of participation. The goal of the activities is to develop the capacity of children and youth to play a sustained role in their communities, rather than simply to provide cheap labour. The leader of the movement, A. T. Ariyaratne, puts it this way: 'Shramadana – voluntary sharing of labour – is primarily a psychological technique for personality awakening and only secondarily it is an essential process in building up an economic infrastructure in the community where there is less capital and plenty of idle labor'.[17] He goes on to specify what he means by the personality awakening of youth: 'Real maturity or development as a person is achieved when the youth no longer is the object of external influence, be it from environmental or "karmic"

[15] Hart (1992), Johnson, Hill, and Ivan-Smith (1995) is a recent excellent exception.

[16] Ariyarante (1978, 1980).

[17] Ariyarante (1978) p. 3.

[18] During the final stages of writing this book, Maria Rosario Mascellani, a deeply committed person, who has worked vigorously with Arciragazzi for years to improve children's participation in Italian communities, died suddenly. It was a great loss to many throughout Italy. Ray Lorenzo, who also works as a consultant with Arciragazzi, translated the writing of Maria on this subject to serve as the core of this summary.

[19] An evaluation and two volumes of edited monographs of children's councils in France are available in French from L'Anacej (the National Association of Children and Youth Boards) at 15 Rue Martel, 75010, Paris, France. A published summary report is also elsewhere in English (L'Anacej 1995).

[20] Since the founding of the first council in Schiltigheim in France, some communities, such as Aulla in Italy, allow the children's council to go beyond the role of having a voice to make some autonomous decisions and manage a limited budget (about 10 million lira or approximately $7,000 US a year, in Aulla).

sources, but is a subject who can change at his own will both his environment and his "karma" because he has recognized the power of the "self-mastering mind" he is endowed with and which he now knows how to use for the progress of himself and society.'

In the village of Nellikolowalta, near Kandy, in the mountainous centre of the island, 36 boys and girls between six and 16 years of age manage the community's 15 taps. Two to four children who live near a well gather to clean the tap area and to tend the garden surrounding it. The elected water-tap leader, aged 14 years, checks the working of the 15 taps and, if he has a problem he cannot handle, reports it to the preschool teacher, who also serves as the organizer of the children's groups. The children also proudly shared with me their garden plots created in a variety of styles and degrees of success near their homes. The children's group meets on Sundays and has an elected leader, also aged 14 years. The fact that the project involved almost all the children of the village made me wonder if this met my criterion for genuine participation. For an outsider from a Western democracy, with its stress on the freedom of the individual, I could not help but wonder, with so many children involved and such a well-organized system of environmental care, if there was any coercion for individuals to join. My conclusion, upon talking with the children, was that they were genuinely involved in their projects and enjoyed tending the water tap areas and gardens. I took this as a warning of the danger of applying universal standards of participation. The great success of this project should be evaluated within the context of a culture that has a greater degree of collective effort and a more consensual form of democracy than my own.

LOCAL GOVERNMENT CHILDREN'S COUNCILS

In the town of Narni in the Umbria region of Italy, I observed a three-hour children's meeting during which all of the town's elementary schoolchildren met to

present their ideas for the redesigning of recreational space in the centre of the town to the mayor and all interested citizens. The hall was packed beyond its capacity and no one seemed to leave early. The children's moving and articulate presentations led the mayor to declare to the crowd around midnight that his ideas had been changed about the competencies of young people, and that now he intended to include children as well as teenagers in his city council meetings.

Cities and towns in several countries are now experimenting with the involvement of children, usually teenagers, in their decision-making bodies.[18] The system for their involvement varies, but at the time of writing there had been little comparative research on this important experiment.[19] In 1979, the International Year of the Child, the mayor, the town council members, and several teachers in the city of Schiltigheim in France decided to create a permanent structure for the town's youth in which they could share their perceptions of the city and offer suggestions to the administrators – a setting in which adults could work with children. In this first experience the adults were perfectly explicit in saying that the denomination 'council' was not to be taken literally. 'The Youth "Council" had the right to make *suggestions* while the [adult] Town Council had the right to make *decisions*.'[20] In this manner, the first youth council in Europe was born.

Sixteen years later, there are approximately 740 councils with various titles following the two main ones of 'children's councils' and 'youth councils' operating in France. In addition, there are many such councils in other European nations – Belgium, Switzerland, Austria, Germany, Portugal, Poland, Hungary, and, most recently, Italy. In some countries, national associations (like Anacej in France) were instituted to improve the exchange of information and the coordination between local experiences. The councils represent settings for dialogue between children, youth, adults, and the local authorities and have helped in many cases to improve the quality of life in towns and cities for adults as well as children.

The municipality and its 'educational partners' (teachers, principals, headmasters, etc.) organize the council. There are no national rules regarding a standard organization for children's and youth councils. Taking into account the political, social, and cultural diversity of the locality, each city has developed its own rules. The ages of the young councillors vary from town to town – in some cases from ten to 13 years, in others ten to 15 years. In some French communities, local administrators have decided that 'dialogue is more profitable with older youth' and have raised the eligible age limit to 15 to 18 years (it is interesting to note that, in Brazil, children of this age can vote in national presidential elections!). A specific number of 'young citizens' are elected by their peers from their schools or neighbourhoods for a period of one to three years. Anacej suggests 30 young representatives for a city of 25,000 inhabitants for two-year terms. The elections are normally held at the beginning of the school year on school premises or in youth association centres. Sometimes the elections are held in the official town hall, especially in the case of very small municipalities.

Immediately following the elections, the young councillors usually meet with the (adult) mayor to present their proposals and criticisms. In general, these discussions treat such issues as city planning, traffic safety, quality of everyday life, and problems concerning living together in some neighbourhoods and school-related issues. Often the children express their worries about the future and concerns over employment, crime, and lack of cultural opportunity. There are no limits to the themes discussed and often the debates are cutting. Usually, the mayor leads the discussion, responds immediately to the simpler problems, and suggests that the young councillors work on the more difficult issues throughout the year by participating in various commissions. In some exceptional cases, the children elect a 'junior mayor'.

Usually, the children's councils meet once a month to improve and refine their proposals. The themes treated by the various commissions are similar from town to town: playgrounds, school life, solidarity and social issues, information and communication, culture, and recreation. Generally the commissions have an adult reference person who coordinates their activities. This figure usually comes from the organization that promoted the council, from the adult town council or from the municipal staff. In some cases, the children have preferred to organize themselves and call upon adults only when they need them. During their meetings, the children often summon adult resource persons who aid them in specific themes, such as architects, planners, or environmentalists.

At the end of the school year, a plenary session is held with the mayor and the adult town council to review the work carried out and the decisions taken. In some cases, an additional session is held at mid-year to report on work in progress and to decide urgent matters. These sessions are open to the general public.

Examples of results attained by the numerous children's councils include:

- bicycle paths and skateboard tracks
- playspaces and intergenerational open spaces
- radio and TV programmes managed directly by youth
- library of European youth journals and publications
- surveys concerning the needs and perceptions of children
- a permanent urban environmental observatory
- various initiatives of international solidarity with children in developing countries
- numerous programmes of environmental education and action.

L'Anacej has made a start with a self-critical evaluation. Their report confirms what one might expect, that there is an over-representation of middle-class children, but also points out that the representation of children from

[21] Coggin (1968, 1974).

[22] The greatest source of information from the experiments of this period is the *Bulletin for Environmental Education*, published ten times a year by the Town and Country Planning Association in London. Its successor, *Streetwise*, is now published by the National Council for Urban Studies. See also Ward and Fyson (1976); Ward (1978); Armstrong (1979). Bishop, Kean and Adams (1992) is a recently published history of this period of innovation.

'blue-collar' families is six times greater than with the adult councils. L'Anacej reports that some commentators feel the relationship to the promotion of local democracy is not all positive and that there is a danger of manipulation, such as in the way adults intervene to structure propositions. There has been an equal representation of girls. The analysis also reveals that it is not always the best academic students that are elected. There is a need for further analysis of the functioning of these important experiments in children's civic participation. There has been great variation in how they have been set up, and this should allow for a fascinating evaluation and comparison both within France and with other countries.

LOCAL GOVERNMENT ENVIRONMENTAL AGENCIES

For many countries it is not possible at this time to envisage children's participation in local government council meetings, but there are many ways in which government planning agencies can support the work of schools and other organizations operating with children on environmental research. This section draws entirely from experiences in the United Kingdom, which in the 1970s and early 1980s was so progressive in involving its environmental planning departments in work with children. Although most of the examples were in urban planning, much of what is described here is relevant to other kinds of agencies: public heath, water, waste management, agriculture, horticulture, forestry, conservation, and the management of natural resources. In some countries there are even some agencies with one or two officers working specifically on sustainable development issues who could greatly increase their effectiveness if they collaborated with children.

In 1967 the Education Department of the County of Wiltshire made an innovative decision to involve hundreds of children in research on the impact of a major motorway through that part of rural England.[21] Children from 36 schools, both primary (under 11 years) and secondary (over 11 years), became involved

in a diversity of projects: traffic counts and surveys, effects on industry and commerce, farm boundaries and land use, ecological studies of flora and fauna, land and house prices, and historical and archaeological investigations. The project took five years to complete, and many of the children were able to follow its progress as they moved through primary school and passed on to secondary school. The aim of the research project was to form a basis of comparison between conditions before the highway was completed and those that would prevail after its completion and use. The children's involvement was seen not merely as an educational experience but also as a project for helping the surrounding communities understand the planning process and for the children to provide useful scientific data. The Nature Conservancy became enthusiastic about the children's research on flora and fauna and what happens to the plants and hedges along a country road when it is misused because of the arrival of a new highway, or what happens to animals in a wood when their habitat is cut in two by a motorway.

This was one of the earliest projects in what became a national educational experiment in the United Kingdom in the 1970s and 1980s. Children of all ages became investigators of their local communities. Unlike the field trips of the past, this new kind of environmental research was not limited to rural areas; the city was embraced as equally important for environmental study. Because of these two characteristics, the two decades of experience in the United Kingdom are full of valuable lessons.[22] Regrettably, since the late 1980s the social, economic, and political climate has been much less conducive to this kind of activity. There are signs, however, that the call for children's participation in local Agenda 21s may rejuvenate these important institutions.

The Value to Planners of Working with Children

Involving children in environmental planning benefits planners as well as the children. It provides information to planners about children's use and perception of the environment so that children's own needs are better planned for. Planning is all too often a response to the perspectives of a select group of local adults and public participation is limited largely to voting. Children cannot even vote, yet they often know a great deal about the local environment. Indeed in many countries those who are most knowledgeable about the local environment are the children and the elderly, two groups who are usually denied access to meaningful public participation.

A less obvious value of having children work with planners is that they can conduct useful research to supplement the planners' own survey work. There are many examples in the United Kingdom of children conducting large-scale research projects that would have been impossible with the manpower available in most planning departments. There is a danger of using the children as 'cheap labour' but it is sometimes acceptable for children to carry out survey work that would be difficult for the planning department to achieve with its own small staff. For example, even though the categories of a land use survey may have been designed by a planning department, they can often be of great educational value to children as they work in teams to make detailed maps of their community, especially if they can engage with the planners in a critical evaluation of the categories used. The issue of how children can be involved in the design of community surveys, including the identification of indicators, is discussed in Chapters 9 and 11.

Involving children in planning is an effective way of fulfilling the long-term goal of improved public participation in planning.[23] Many countries are establishing laws for the participation of citizens in planning, yet the ability of individuals to carry out this right is unevenly distributed. The reasons for this are sometimes economic, which cannot be corrected simply by education alone, but the more children learn about the environment and how it can be affected by the actions of individuals, the more they will be interested in making greater demands for more genuine participation in the future. The strategies many planners used for children's participation in projects in the UK in the 1970s and 1980s was more radically democratic than what existed for adults in the same communities. By investigating real issues in their community, using democratic principles for talking with public officials, and reporting their research and planning results both to decision makers and to the general public, children were having more of a voice than their parents had ever had.

The Value to Children's Groups of Involving Planners

Anne Armstrong, a planner who worked for many years to involve schoolchildren with planning issues in London, explains how schoolteachers and others involved in the environmental educational and participation of children might benefit from the contribution of planners:[24]

1) Planners have access to materials that are not usually available in schools. Maps, models, survey data, histories, and monographs are all available in planning departments and are of great value to children's projects. To avoid a constant trail of requests, planners may decide to prepare 'resource packs' – information in envelopes including maps, slide sets, and perhaps printed trails suggesting initial routes children can take through their community, with information noted alongside the trail on the map.

2) Planners can help design the research and planning process by children. Teachers of children are seldom trained in how to take children through an entire research process leading to recommendations and actions.

3) Planners can be lively adjuncts to the teaching process, especially in the early stages of a project, and can convince children that they are engaging in something serious. Furthermore, planners often know more about their local area than do the teachers or facilitators of the project.

[23] The Skeffington Report by the government of the United Kingdom in 1969 required the participation of residents in local planning and recommended the collaboration of departments of education and planning at the local level to achieve this.

[24] Armstrong (1979).

[25] Armstrong (1979), p. 69.

[26] Armstrong (1979).

[27] Armstrong (1979).

How Can Planners Become Involved?

In the United Kingdom there was the great advantage of a central, independent organization to introduce planners into the territory of children's participation. The Town and Country Planning Association, an independent body unafraid of taking on challenging causes, in 1971 established an education unit to serve as a resource to the profession. The Royal Institute of British Architects and the Royal Town Planning Institute followed suit. While it may be difficult at first for planners to leave their agency to volunteer to work directly with schools or other groups of children, it may well be possible to make the resources of planning departments more available to those who work with children – large-scale maps, data, photographs, slides and reports – although the reports are often written in a language that would require some translation to become accessible to children. The question next arises as to how best to make these resources available to the schools. The London Borough of Hammersmith found it effective to produce a catalogue for teachers of what was available in their planning agency.[25] Other agencies found it more effective to establish Urban Study Centres independently from the planning department and to stock these with the relevant resources so that they would be available to large numbers of groups working with children.

A planning department can also serve as a link to other agents of government. Armstrong describes how a local geography teacher worked through the offices of a planning department to take his children to visit the town council's nurseries to examine how their greenhouses functioned, in order to help the pupils in their own design work for the school greenhouse.[26]

As a result of the government legislation requiring public participation in planning, the United Kingdom's many county planning departments had their own schools liaison officer. Some planners took advantage of this situation and involved children in planning projects. In the absence of such enlightened initiatives by planners, it should be possible to invite a planner to come and talk about their work with a group or class of children. The children can prepare questions about their community in advance and the exchange might lead the children to think of projects that they would like to initiate. The planners' cooperation might then be maintained for future collaboration as the project develops. Another good time to invite a planner is when children have completed an evaluation or plan of their own and they want to get an official reaction.

How Can Planners Work With Groups of Children?

The typical response of a government agency in working with a school is to send a staff member to give a talk to children. This is rarely a good way to begin. Unless planners have had a great deal of experience in working with children, they are likely to offer presentations that are not sufficiently relevant. It is preferable to put them in the position of being a resource. One way to do this is to have the children begin an investigation and then to visit the planner in his or her office to ask questions. Alternatively, it can be very effective for children to accompany planners on surveys in the community, walking side by side and exchanging their different perspectives. Armstrong describes how this learning can be mutual and how, even after she had spent several years as a planner in Kensington, children were continually bringing her new knowledge of the community.

Armstrong also describes a successful open house at the Town Hall of the Borough of Hammersmith, also in London. Two hundred children attended the 'Plan Away a Day'.[27]

The purpose was 'to offer a variety of urban studies activities, with a strong emphasis on fun, in the hope of interesting children in the local area and planning, making the town hall seem more approachable and showing that the people who work there are, after all, human beings.' Events included the planning of a local cycle path, a photography workshop, model

Box 6: Case Study on the 'GreenIt' Programme of the United Kingdom

The Black Country Groundwork Trust in the industrial midlands of the United Kingdom developed the GreenIt programme, a business partnership with schools, as part of a national effort to rescue blighted areas. Children work to improve the landscape of damaged or neglected land owned by the business and, through a process of critical evaluation, plan the design and execution of the improvement. The project works primarily with schoolchildren aged ten to 13. By upgrading the land, Groundwork helps the business behave more responsibly towards the environment and make the lands more attractive to the public while simultaneously improving its commercial prospects. The movement was initially established by the Countryside Commission of the national government, but 32 local, self-sustaining Groundwork trusts – coalitions of local business people and local government leaders – have now been formed with high degrees of autonomy throughout the United Kingdom.[28]

The children are invited to make proposals to corporations for improvement of their sites. Through a process of consultation and negotiation between the children and the companies, these proposals are then funded by the company. Children are involved in all aspects, from site survey, through analysis, the use of computer-aided design, plant and material selection, liaison with the client, costing, and finally the implementation on the site. Considerable effort has been spent by the programme organizers to convince teachers of its relationship to the National Curriculum of the United Kingdom in a wide range of subjects. In addition to developing the kinds of research skills described with other projects, this programme emphasizes the need for children to become competent in preparing proposals that will

be convincing to businesses and that include an understanding of the costs involved. To this end, the children are expected to develop the skills of collation, presentation, speaking, and listening.

The initial emphasis was upon the improvement of the landscape of industrial sites. For example, the Kendray Primary school in Wakefield, Yorkshire, developed landscape designs for the Dunlop Slazenger International Corporation, which has a plant located in their area. One of the school's classes divided themselves into four (companies) for the purpose of providing alternative landscape designs and layouts for the company. Their designs included ideas that they obtained from the workforce of the company. The programme has gone on to work with other kinds of settings. For example, the children of Laurence Haines Elementary School in Hertfordshire designed seating areas for the Watford

[28] While the local Groundwork Trust is designed to be self-sustaining, the GreenIt programme receives funds at the National Coordination Office at Groundwork Black Country from the RTZ Corporation and the Department of the Environment of the United Kingdom. For further information, contact GreenIt, Black Country Groundwork Trust, Red House, Hill Lane, Great Barr, West Midlands, B43 6ND, UK.

Figure 28: Children working to improve the landscape at Bronx Engineering in Dudley in the West Midlands industrial area of England.
© Groundwork Trust.

*General Hospital grounds. Research involved inter-
viewing the site owners, observing how seats are
currently used, and interviewing patients who used
the site. This research resulted in a presentation to
the district health authority estates manager. In
Rochdale, Lancashire, children from five schools in
the Kirkhold Estate have conducted research in*

*collaboration with the police as part of the Rochdale
Safer Cities Programme. Their research on problems
with the homes of elderly residents, for example,
resulted in recommendations for low-cost measures
to prevent crimes against these particularly vulnerable residents.*

Figure 29:
A flyer produced by
the Borough of
Hammersmith,
London, describes
'Plan Away a Day', an
opportunity for
children to under-
stand and become
involved in city
planning. This is one
of many activities
organized by street
workers to involve
children in local
urban issues.

making, housing design, a competition to design a riverside trail, park improvements, designing a river
sculpture, a newspaper documenting the events of the
day, learning to solve spatial layout problems with paper
models, observing wildlife along the riverside, and a
poetry competition.

'SHADOWING' ADULT ENVIRONMENTAL PROFESSIONALS

An under-used opportunity for children to participate is
for them to work alongside or 'shadow' a skilled adult
environmental professional. This is not a new idea; it is
simply an informal version of apprenticeship. With time,
as in an apprenticeship, the children can become
useful participants in the work. Pre-adolescents can
work with wildlife conservation staff on the ringing of
birds, for example, or assist urban forest managers with
tree surveys, and teenagers can work with a wide range
of professionals, from agricultural advisers to the staff
of environmental protection agencies.

The city of Curitiba in Brazil is well known for
creative approaches to community development and to
environmental management. When the new botanic
gardens were inaugurated, boys from a nearby low-
income community vandalized the flower beds. The
solution adopted was a lasting one: hire the children as
garden assistants.[29]

BUSINESS PARTNERSHIPS WITH SCHOOLS AND COMMUNITIES

With the current enthusiastic climate for private–public
partnerships, it is surprising that there are not more
examples of corporations collaborating at least with
schools surrounding their plants. Box 6 offers an introduction to the potential that exists if you have a
public-minded company as a neighbour. The danger, of
course, is that the company may be more interested in
using children as an inexpensive public relations media

[29] McKibben (1995),
p. 87.

tool than fostering in them a critical attitude to their local environment.

COMMUNITY ENVIRONMENTAL CENTRES

To achieve the goals of Agenda 21 at the local level, every community should have an independent centre as a base for public participation in development and for ongoing community-based evaluation and management of the environment. Rather than being part of a school or any other institution, it would stress its independence as a centre for all ages and all social groups. As described above, non-formal schools sometimes approach this ideal, for they are located within integrated community development centres with a wide range of services and learning opportunities for all ages. But there is a great advantage in creating centres with an environmental focus. There are few models of such local centres in the world, and most of these do not seem to incorporate children systematically as working partners in the research effort. The 'urban study centres' and 'environmental resource centres' of the United Kingdom are valuable examples even though they emerged out of a concern with problems of the built environment in low-income areas, and hence emphasize housing, local employment, recreation, and the distribution of services over natural resource issues. It is not difficult to imagine how the example described in Box 7 might be expanded into an even broader mission.

The urban studies centres of the United Kingdom not only began to correct the nature-orientation bias of environmental education but also added a new political dimension. Children did not just study the environment but investigated it with a view to change. But in wishing to correct the general failure of schools to address the everyday urban environment, these centres, and the *Bulletin of Environmental Education* which inspired so many teachers at that time, had their own bias – towards the built environment. The need remains for centres to bring together these two professional worlds of environmental concern under one roof.

ENVIRONMENTAL SUPPORT CENTRES FOR COMMUNITY ORGANIZERS, FACILITATORS, AND TEACHERS

Not all communities have the capacity to initiate their own environmental centre. They need a system to recognize and build upon the capacities existing within communities. In Boxes 8 and 9, two superb examples are offered, one from Scotland and the other from Colombia.

THE DEVELOPMENT OF NEW ROLES FOR ADULTS: ANIMATORS, FACILITATORS AND PROMOTERS

Clearly the qualities of a good facilitator of children's participation are not the same as those traditionally possessed by teachers or most others trained to work with children. Facilitators set the stage for children to work with one another and support them in this rather than serving primarily as the transmitters of knowledge. This does not mean that they should hide their own knowledge and skills, but they should use these in the context of children themselves actively identifying issues and finding solutions. The facilitator is a resource to help guide children to a multitude of resources, not the least of which is one another. These persons are sometimes called animators or animateurs in Europe, and often go by the powerful name of promoters or streetworkers in Latin America, but in all cases the goal is to distinguish their role from that of a traditional teacher.

Facilitation is an important part of the work of the best teachers, of course, but I have found the clearest proponents of children's participation to be 'street workers' who help working children on the streets and 'playleaders' working in adventure playgrounds.[30] We need more adults who understand the importance of fostering children's sense of their lifetime right and responsibility to develop to their fullest and use their capacities in socially and environmentally responsible ways. These effective facilitators seem to be largely self-trained. The difficulty for most adults is in knowing how to fade into a different role once children are

[30] See Dallape (1987); and UNICEF (1987) on street-workers and Benjamin (1976) on playleaders.

Box 7: Case Study on the Notting Dale Urban Studies Centre, England

A number of innovations in environmental education in the 1970s in the United Kingdom came out of or were shaped by the highly dynamic education unit of the Town and Country Planning Association. Wishing to stress a new urban orientation to environmental education, the editors of the Bulletin for Environmental Education, Colin Ward and Tony Fyson, used a clever piece of wordplay to present their new vision. Environmental educators had long used the expression fieldwork, to which they now added the term streetwork. Similarly, there had been for some time a series of rural 'field studies centres' throughout the United Kingdom for use by visiting classes of schoolchildren. The name urban studies centres immediately captured people's attention to the need for places from which children could

engage in serious research on the urban environment. In their original conception, these were to be centres for environmental education, participation, and action for people of all ages, not just children. While their primary function would be to serve the community in which they were situated, they would also serve as a residential base for visitors from suburban rural areas wishing to understand the city or for visitors from other cities. By the end of the 1970s there were 23 urban study centres in the United Kingdom. The one that comes closest to the original conception of Ward and Fyson was the Notting Dale Urban Studies Centre described in some length here.

The Notting Dale Urban Studies Centre, located in a multicultural area of West London, serves as a base for local children and youth, as well as adults, to investigate and discuss the changes taking place in communities surrounding the centre. For a few years it also functioned as an urban field study centre for classes of children from outside the city who visit it for a day or a week to explore the urban community. Over time, the children gradually add to the archival and survey resources of the centre, helping it become more and more a community resource. In this way it established a political potential as a centre for community participation that would be difficult to achieve within even the most open-minded of community schools.

Groups of children from surrounding schools use the Notting Dale Centre as a base to conduct investigations about the local environment. The children go out with tape recorders, cameras, and pencil and paper to document existing conditions. They might interview residents, local officials, or people who work in the neighbourhood. On their return to the

Figure 30:
At the Notting Dale Urban Studies Centre, children put together an issue of the *Silchester Sun*, a community newspaper. For an introduction to urban study centres and environmental resource centres, see Ward and Fyson (1976); Kean and Adams (1991); and the journal *Streetwise*.
© Roger Hart.

centre, they transcribe recordings, print photographs, and type reports. Materials assembled by previous groups of children are retrieved from files for reference and comparison. Teachers and centre staff assist children with their tasks, engage them in discussion, and offer guidance in making decisions when requested. Working together in small groups, the children sift through, discuss, and interpret their material, and put it in the form of a newspaper to take back for printing and circulation around their school. Over the course of time, much material has been collected by groups working at the centre. It has become a repository of perceptions about the local environment through the work of young residents. In effect, the centre houses a vast array of archives – statistics, minutes, briefs, case studies, correspondence, newspapers, and the students' own documentations – that describe life on the public housing estates in the area, and ideas about environmental changes, why they were happening, and how they could be improved.

involved – listening, supporting, and being a resource when needed. For teachers as well as facilitators, one of the keys to professional development seems to be to discuss one's difficulties on a regular basis with others who share a similar desire to develop.

The professionals with the greatest potential for helping children develop into competent, caring, and active citizens are teachers. Unfortunately, there are commonly great forces bearing down on them, reducing their capacity to lead children to become independent, responsible, and hence critical thinkers. In addition to the inherently political nature of environmental education when practised in a participatory manner, there are some practical reasons why environmental education, when practised in a field research-oriented manner, makes radical demands on teachers:

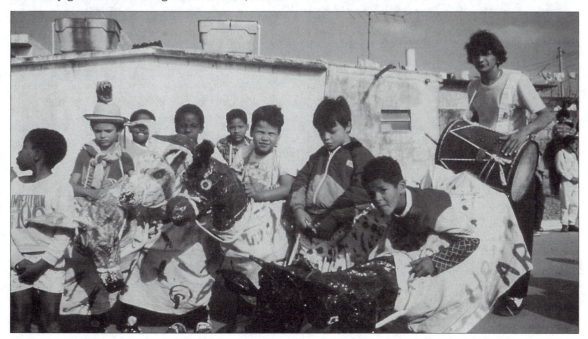

Figure 31:
Children in a low-income neighbourhood of Sao Paulo with a street animator employed by the Secretaria di Minor (Department of Childhood).

Box 8: Case Study on The Environmental Centre, Edinburgh, Scotland

The Environmental Centre was founded in the mid-1970s in Edinburgh, Scotland. From its inception, its goals were to foster a practically based environmental education in the schools that would lead both children and community groups to take direct responsibility for improving or conserving their local environment. Unlike the urban studies centres, which are used directly by children, the idea was for this centre to serve as a project and information resource base for teachers, youth workers, and local community education workers to obtain information packets, audiovisual aids, and environmental field-

work kits, as well as training, transport, and assistance with project supervision. The orientation of the centre was more towards nature conservation projects than the urban studies centres, but what distinguished it from traditional nature study was its commitment to action projects for children in both urban and rural areas. Serving a large region of Scotland, the centre was to support and disseminate model schemes which could serve as examples for other agencies to follow up rather than to provide ongoing support. For each successful model 'how to do it' reports were prepared, supplemented with exhibitions, slide tape productions, and in-service training courses for teachers and youth and community workers.

One of the innovative aspects of this environmental resource centre was the recognition early on that it was not enough to reach children only through the schools, but that this should also be done through youth schemes, adventure playgrounds, community associations, and 'out-of-school' clubs. By identifying key adults in local communities who were willing to act as coordinators, they were able to set up young environmental groups in these organizations, which became autonomous settings for initiating projects within their own local area. In fostering these groups, two kinds of support were offered to them by the Environmental Centre: assistance in designing locally based environmental surveys and self-help improvement schemes such as tree planting, stream and canal clean-ups, and gardening projects, as well as rural outreach projects whereby both children and adults could visit a natural area surrounding the cities.

Many of the projects initiated by the Environmental Centre, and the local environmental groups it spawned, did not involve a research phase

Figure 32:
The square metre cornfield has enabled thousands of children to plant and manage their own mini-farms, regardless of whether they live in rural or urban areas. This is one of the programmes introduced to schoolteachers, children's and youth organizations, and community groups by the Environmental Centre in Edinburgh, Scotland.
© Environment Centre.

by the children. Instead, projects that were already identified by adult residents were given extra support in the form of tools, transport, contacts, and technical support from the centre staff in order to 'take off'. By encouraging these adult groups to be open to the involvement of young people, all that was required to achieve their participation was to begin the action projects. A good example was the improvement of Coalie Park, including the River Leith. The sight of a few adults using grappling hooks, rakes, and ropes down by the river's edge quickly attracted a band of children, who then worked for eight hours a day to clean the river. This set the stage for more reflective work with the children on local environmental projects by inviting them to become a member of 'Coalie Park Community Project'.

Recently, the Environment Centre has embraced the sustainable development goals of Agenda 21 with a number of new projects. The 'Grounds for Learning' project, with its emphasis on making the immediate school environment a microcosm for responsible environmental management, is described in Chapter 7. A truly innovative idea that has taken hold in dozens of schools across the country is the 'One Metre Square Cornfield'. Children as young as three years of age have planted corn or oats or barley in a simple square metre plot, followed its growth, harvested it, and then thrashed, winnowed, and milled it in order to create flour for them to bake bread. In this amazingly simple project, any child can begin to discover directly the roots of their daily sustenance (see Figure 32). All that is required are a few seeds, fertilizer, and yeast for the bread. From this basis, children are able to compare traditional farming with modern farming methods around their community and thereby begin to understand different kinds of impacts we have on the environment in order to provide food.

- the physical separation of schools from their communities
- the lack of vehicles for transportation to the field, based on the belief that the school is a complete, self-contained laboratory
- fixed timetables, preventing sustained focus on a particular topic
- a disciplinary structure that is antithetical to the idea of an integrated or ecological approach to the environment
- the authoritarian structure of schools, which is contrary to the democratic notion of children as inquiring citizens, who should be able to ask questions of any other citizens, and particularly of those in positions of public responsibility
- the fear of losing control, or a sense of competence, when a classroom transforms from a teacher-centred to an inquiry-based mode, with children now asking questions to which the teacher may not know all the answers
- standardized evaluation procedures, which often measure children's performance in terms of knowledge of distant and generalized phenomena, rather than their local knowledge and understanding of how to do research themselves.

Teacher training has been too much concerned with knowledge divorced from a sense of its relevance to the communities in which children live. In addition to the training of facilitators, we need more teachers who can take on a facilitating role in their schools. The schools are the most universal centre for children and offer the most possibility for global change. When children pursue independent lines of inquiry, the teacher becomes, ideally, a resource guiding his or her young investigators to a wide variety of sources in pursuit of solutions to their problems. This problem should be addressed head on by any school wishing to foster this

Box 9: Case Study on The 'Green College', Colombia

The Colegio Verde, or 'Green College', located in Villa de Lleva in Colombia, is a radically new conception of a college. It is founded on the principle that everyone has something to learn from everyone else and shatters the elitism of college systems in many ways, such as inviting college students from Bogotá to lectures by local farmers. It is experimenting with a variety of ways to serve as a learning resource for the sustainable development of communities.

An interesting example for this handbook are the herbaria being created by primary schools in the region. With the help of their parents and through interviews with neighbours, the children of each school are constructing for their community a herbarium reflecting the collective plant knowledge of that community. Regular visits by a botanist from the Green College enable children to show the scientist what they have learned, to complete and confirm their plant identifications with him, to consult on plants they have not been able to identify, to provide him with specimens that he does not

have in the regional herbarium based at the Green College, and sometimes to offer him plants that he himself does not know. In these instances, the plants are sent to Bogotá for identification and, if necessary, to the Botanic Gardens in Kew, London, which is an international centre for plant identification. In this project, children are excited by the idea of playing a useful role as scientists for their own community with the possibility of extending the frontiers of knowledge. Creating a herbarium can be as fascinating to a child as collecting stamps or baseball cards, with the added fulfilment of knowing that the finished product is of interest to a larger community.

This is just one example of the many ways that colleges could serve as regional environmental resource centres for communities that are too small to have their own permanent environmental centre but, with assistance, could create an archive and a place for periodic meetings in their primary school.

ideology among its teachers. We need approaches to professional development that enable teachers to support one another as they move together to transform their practice.

Unfortunately, the retraining of existing teachers for the kind of environmental learning proposed in this book is much more difficult than that commonly required for introducing new curricula. For most teachers, it involves some radically new notions of the relationship of the school to the community, to the outdoors, and to other persons who can become collaborators in teaching. In the ERA Project in the Peruvian Andes, this retraining is being achieved by two or three workshops per year lasting two or three days

each. But often more time is required because of the need not only to learn new skills but also to rethink school–community–family relationships. Furthermore, these radically new curricula require some new teaching materials that are relevant to the local environment and culture. Commonly these must be created by teachers themselves, ideally with the assistance of environmental advisers. Consequently, for the first year, a new programme can be very demanding of a teacher's time. In addition, there is a need to develop in-service programmes to support teachers in developing their curricula in situ.

A four-year-old teacher training programme in Iquitos, in the Amazon region of Peru, is an excellent example of what is required. The Instituto Superior Pedagogico has collaborated with the inter-ethnic Association for the Development of the Amazon to develop a six-year bilingual teacher training programme.[31] Its purpose is to break from the inappropriate tradition in schools of teaching Indian children in the Spanish language about information that is completely divorced from their everyday lives in their Indian language communities. Rather than relying upon texts prepared in distant urban locations, the college is working with student teachers to produce new, locally relevant materials based upon the Amazon environment and the particular culture's knowledge and uses of the environment. Student teachers are trained to bring persons from the community who possess considerable knowledge about the environment into the classroom and, with these persons, to take the children into the fields and forest surrounding their school. Such a radical transformation of a school curriculum has a great impact not only on what children learn but also upon the larger community, for it revalorizes their own knowledge.

The staff of the teacher training college have found it necessary to support the student teachers directly in their introduction of this new concept of schooling to their communities. Initially, there is often considerable resistance from adult members of the community, who have long believed that the school should be teaching only abstract knowledge of the world in Spanish, for this represents the future for their children. Coming to understand that local knowledge is valuable and must serve as the basis for children's understanding of the Amazon can dramatically transform a community image of itself and the central role its residents must have in controlling decisions about the use of their environment and in training future generations to care for it.

One student teacher described how he behaved in returning to his village with his college professor. Walking back from a field to the village the student dropped a basket of manioc and begged his teacher to do the same. He hurriedly explained that he had seen his relatives arriving in the village through the trees and

that they would never understand why he should be carrying manioc after being in college for four years. It took a great deal of effort for the adviser to persuade the student of the value of turning this event into a dialogue with his family so that they could learn to see the relevance of local knowledge to children's schooling and to understand why primary environmental care is important to all communities.

At least as important as the training of new teachers is the professional development of those who are already teachers but wish to improve their practice. Many teachers might think of attending a workshop, but the challenges to teachers of improving their approaches to children's community and environmental learning in the ways proposed here cannot be satisfied simply by attending workshops alone; it requires ongoing critical reflection of one's teaching practices. In recent years, teachers in a number of countries have begun to re-evaluate and transform their own practice dramatically using action research: a repeating cycle of problem identification, planning, action, and reflection. Chapter 5 involves a detailed discussion of how to involve children in action research on the environment. The same processes can enable teachers or facilitators to identify and act upon aspects of their work with children that are in need of improvement.[32] Just as important, we also need educational administrators and evaluators radically to redirect their practice to the support of education for local sustainable development.

Finally, it must be noted that children exposed to democratic participation are more likely themselves to be able to serve as democratic facilitators. Some of the best streetworkers are those who were themselves street children who experienced excellent programmes. For this reason, in long-term programmes and schools, it is important to encourage older children to work with younger children as soon as they are able.[32] As the theoretical literature of Chapter Two revealed, there are great benefits to both the learner and the young facilitator.

[31] Programa de Formacion de Maestros bilingues de la Amazonia Peruana, Apartado 591, Iquitos, Peru.

[32] Robottom (1985); Elliott (1991); Stuart (1991).

2

CHILDREN'S PARTICIPATION IN PRACTICE

Introduction

This section begins with an introduction to action research because it should be the basis of all initiatives: whether they be the planning, design, construction, management, or monitoring of environments or public awareness and political action projects. This book does not concentrate on all of the specific environmental actions children can do, for there are dozens of useful guides available.[1] Beginning in this way will guarantee that children's actions grow out of their concerns and those of their communities rather than from some external agenda. Also fundamental to the action-research process are the means for children to look critically at themselves in any project through the incorporation of methods for monitoring the achievement of the project's goals, including the process of achieving them.[2] For these reasons, Chapter 5 should be seen as introductory to the other chapters of this section of the book.

A society that offers a full range of democratic, participative opportunities for all children does not exist. In some societies and cultures, participation in certain aspects of life may be well advanced and encouraged. In other cultures, those same advances may not be possible, but there may be opportunities in other areas of social life. There is unlikely to be a single great leap forward in any culture in the degree of children's participation or in the types of settings where children can participate. On the other hand, children may be able to change people's notions of what is possible. It is therefore important to help them strategically choose an arena that, although it may lead to challenges to the

community, will not put a child in conflict with or be an embarrassment to the child's parents.

Opportunities are likely to be greatest in those areas of life that are most commonly understood as the child's domain and where there is the least need to come up against other conflicting views. For example, in industrially advanced countries where children spend most of their non-school hours in play or recreation, they may have a high degree of control over their bedroom, the garden or yard of their home, the street, the sidewalk, and the local playground. In some countries, opportunities for children's participation can also arise beyond the immediate home environment in those settings designed predominantly for children. These might include the management of school grounds, children's hospitals, children's and youth's services, or even the advisory boards of national organizations serving children or youth, such as children's television stations or environmental organizations. In some European nations there are growing opportunities for children to participate alongside adult citizens in community open space and recreation planning, and some towns are even experimenting with children's participation in local government.

Figure 33 ignores the issue of cultural constraints. It is designed simply to illustrate the development of children's interests and competencies in relation to the wide range of potential opportunities that exist for children of all ages to engage in serious participation projects with their community. The ages should be seen as very approximate.

[1] Particularly useful examples of environmental action guides are produced by the Council for Environmental Education (1990) and United Nations Environment Programme (1994).

[2] For a review of methods involving children in the evaluation and on-going monitoring of projects see Sabo, Hart and Iltus (1996).

Figure 33:
Children's developing capacity to participate in environmental research, planning, and management.

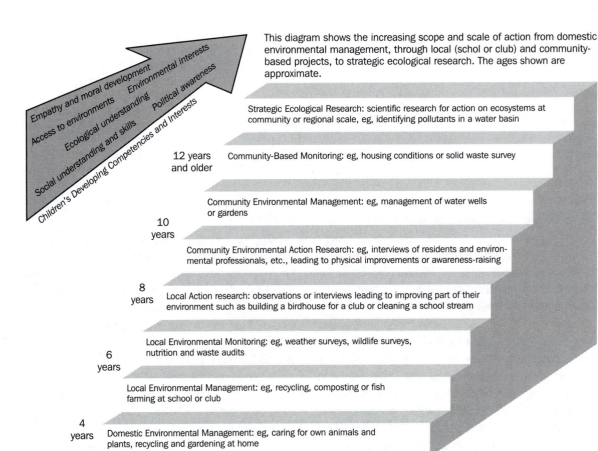

This diagram shows the increasing scope and scale of action from domestic environmental management, through local (schol or club) and community-based projects, to strategic ecological research. The ages shown are approximate.

Empathy and moral development
Environmental interests
Access to environments
Ecological understanding
Political awareness
Social understanding and skills
Children's Developing Competencies and Interests

Strategic Ecological Research: scientific research for action on ecosystems at community or regional scale, eg, identifying pollutants in a water basin

12 years and older   Community-Based Monitoring: eg, housing conditions or solid waste survey

Community Environmental Management: eg, management of water wells or gardens

10 years

Community Environmental Action Research: eg, interviews of residents and environmental professionals, etc., leading to physical improvements or awareness-raising

8 years   Local Action research: observations or interviews leading to improving part of their environment such as building a birdhouse for a club or cleaning a school stream

Local Environmental Monitoring: eg, weather surveys, wildlife surveys, nutrition and waste audits

6 years

Local Environmental Management: eg, recycling, composting or fish farming at school or club

4 years   Domestic Environmental Management: eg, caring for own animals and plants, recycling and gardening at home

Action Research with Children

The ability to evaluate environmental issues critically as a guide to action is basic to the development of competent, responsible environmental behaviour. This means, at some level, that each child should know the fundamental processes of research. They will not always need to engage in a thorough investigation before acting on the environment, but they should learn to operate on the basis of a critical analysis and with an awareness that there are different values surrounding human use of the environment. Community projects conducted by children should be guided by research if children are to act in ways that fulfil the important and difficult task of balancing community priorities for the improvement of living conditions with the imperative of ecological sustainability. A test of the degree to which children in any environmental programme are involved in a critical evaluation of community issues is the extent to which their projects look the same. If they cover all the same kinds of problems, then the children could not possibly have been centrally involved in identifying environmental issues themselves.

Regrettably, of the many hundreds of projects in my files involving environmental actions by children, very few describe a process for involving children in research.[1] When they do, it is usually research on problems that have previously been identified by adults rather than the children themselves. I have reports of dozens of litter clean-ups – reflections of many adults' limited conceptions of how children can identify and act upon environmental priorities.

The emphasis of this section will be upon action research.[2] Action research is distinguished from conventional scientific research by its goal of improving a social situation through an understanding of it. It is also distinct from the impartiality of orthodox research in that the investigators are, at least to some degree, investigating themselves. Research should not be the activity of a select few but, rather, the fundamental starting point for all people to look critically at their social and environmental condition as a basis of acting to change it. In adopting an action-research perspective, in comparison with the scientific tradition in which many of the readers of this book will have been trained, it is important to recognize that the investigator's perspective will probably change through the process of carrying out the research, and that this change is desirable. It is important that a research team document change among themselves in the process of their investigation; evaluation is not a separate, objective process but a fundamental part of the action-research cycle. Action research, then, is in accord with the theory of conscientization as articulated by Paolo Freire and as described in Chapter 2.

More traditional research, including experimental research, is also important to environmental investigations by children. It may be interesting for children to conduct research on the different crops they can grow in their school garden or farm by making experimental plots and comparing growth in each of these. Such experimental research was conducted by children of the fish farming committee of the New School in Colombia, described in Chapter 7, who needed to find out at what altitudes to build their fish ponds and which fish would flourish the best at different altitudes. Many

[1] An excellent exception is a guidebook for involving high school students (over 12 years of age) in research by Hungerford, Litherland, Peyton, Ramsey and Volk (1990).

[2] Participatory Research Network (1982); Society for Participatory Research in Asia (1982); Kassam and Mustafa (1982); Dallape and Gilbert (1994).

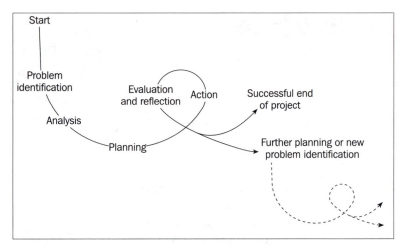

Figure 34:
The action-research
process.

not been centrally involved in this phase, they need to be told the history of the project, including who defined it and why. Ideally, children will be involved in some projects where they engage in a critical analysis of local community development and environmental issues from the perspective of different members of the community, including themselves. Even for children who have already been introduced to ecological concepts, there are important benefits to having them suspend temporarily their externally derived definition of environmental problems. The goal should be initially to liberate them from any preconceptions of what is or is not an environmental problem by stressing the need for community involvement in problem identification.

Helping Children Evaluate their Own Environment

For all children there is great value in beginning an environmental research or action project by evaluating their own everyday environment. To do so stresses that their own experiences are a relevant starting point for reflection on environmental issues. They are also experts on the subject, so the approach offers special support for those children who may not feel that they know much about anything. From this, they can go on to a larger community-wide analysis of environmental issues. In the Environmental Exchange Project, described below, the project begins with children preparing individual drawings and written statements summarizing their evaluation of their own environment and an image of their 'twin' environment. These were simultaneously exchanged, by mail, with their corresponding environmental pen pals. This enabled the children to engage in multiple comparisons of perspectives upon their own community and their 'twin' community. The Ecuadorian Working Children's Programme (PMT), described below, also begins by having children compare perspectives. They have found that it is particularly effective to have the children interview grandparents about their childhood as a way of discovering changes in the environment.

references exist on how to conduct such research in environmental and science education textbooks. But it is necessary to describe here the fundamental phases of action research, for the goal of this book is to support the participation of children in investigating and acting on environmental issues that are important in their own lives and the lives of their communities – a kind of research that has not been emphasized in environmental and science education textbooks.[3]

The research process described below is relevant to all age groups, with only the degree of sophistication varying. It is difficult to specify a lower age limit for children to engage in research. Following a general account of the process is a case study of research by children aged six to ten years at a public school in Vermont in the USA. Admittedly, the school is very small, with only two classes and a mixture of ages in each class, so that the children benefit from the kind of age-mixing described in Chapter 2, but the more important point is that it has a fundamentally progressive approach to education, which stresses from the earliest ages the importance of children working on their own projects with their teacher acting as a support.[4]

PROBLEM IDENTIFICATION

Problem identification is basic to the creation of a truly participatory project. If some participating children have

[3] An excellent exception is Hungerford et al. (1990). It is for use by children in their teens, but is similar to the research approach described here.

[4] For another example of research with very young children see Schwabl (1989).

[5] Good examples in the English language are Van Matre (1979, 1990).

For the many children in the world who live in poverty and struggle daily for survival, this process of documentation and critical reflection on their own environment and the resources it does and does not offer will be more than a starting point; it will be the focus of their environmental actions. Children who work and even sleep on city streets can benefit greatly from the kind of critical personal environmental inventory offered by many of the methods described below. Such analyses can be a valuable means of communication with the supportive adults who work with them. They can also be of great value for use in groups with their peers, enabling them to achieve a more complete understanding of one another's lives. In such instances, the products should clearly belong to the children themselves; one solution is to encourage them to construct personal books on their environment, even if, for non-literate children, this book is made up largely of pictures and maps. By building upon an analysis of their own daily lives, street and working children may be able to develop joint plans for the improvement of their living conditions. From such experiences, it becomes more realistic to expect these children to collaborate in projects for a larger community beyond themselves.

Research on their everyday environment can also be of importance to children of wealthy families. Sweden has long placed a strong emphasis on research and policy to reduce children's traffic accidents. Recently, schools have begun a new strategy for further reducing the number of injuries and deaths. Children as young as seven are involved in research on the areas where they walk and play in order to identify danger. The data are then used to inform parents, other children, and public officials, including traffic planners, school grounds officials, and the police.[6] This kind of research could be further developed by having children do research with the elderly on the safety of elderly citizens.

Addressing Different Perspectives and Values in the Community

If the goal is for children to work on a project that specifically addresses the quality of their own living environment, such as the absence of play facilities or, for teenagers, the need for a place to meet, then the problem identification phase is over and the project can proceed directly to a diagnosis, beginning with research on the perspectives of others. If, however, the children are also to work on problems that concern a broader age range of community residents or on environmental problems that extend beyond the awareness of any residents, the problem identification phase continues.

By considering all perspectives from the beginning of a project, children learn to work in a fundamentally democratic manner. This is valuable because planning rarely proceeds with such egalitarian research. The children's research can sometimes stop here with a broad statement of what the community collectively thinks its problems are. With broad dissemination to the community, through one of the many methods described in Chapters 8 and 11, this research effort can serve as a valuable catalyst to community action.

Surveying Community Residents

Children need to learn how to decide whose perspectives should be considered in diagnosing a problem. In particular, they need to include those groups of residents whose perspectives are often not considered in community development efforts, such as the elderly, the poor, and the disabled. Interviews of these different groups can be conducted in a number of different ways, depending upon the age and competencies of the children and upon a particular culture's orientation towards children and how they should relate to adults. These issues are discussed under 'Interviews' in Chapter 11. Whichever interview method is used, the children should use a community base map for recording the locations of problems identified during the interview.

Environmental Professionals as a Source of Information

An important perspective for children to consider is that of environmental science. A community is unlikely to

[6] Bjorklid (1995).

be aware of all the environmental problems facing it, now and in the future. In agricultural and other rural communities in particular, the utilitarian goals of human communities need to be balanced against the lives of other living things, whose 'perspectives' are unlikely to be fully revealed in a community survey. Here is a valuable role for environmental professionals, and again the children can be the interviewers, identifying environmental issues and locations of these in the community to add to their summary map of issues and problems to be considered. Most environmental professionals are not yet familiar with this kind of work with children and will need help in realizing the potentials and pleasures of their role. A discussion of such an expansion of professional roles was offered in Chapter 2 with the example of British environmental planners.

Elected Officials, Government Agencies, and other Decision Makers

Children also need to know as much as possible about the plans and ideas of those professionals and others who have decision-making power in their area. Children should not be 'protected' from information which adult facilitators might think is beyond their realm to influence or which they fear would deter children by showing them their relative powerlessness. It is basic to the process of conscientization that children confront such knowledge at all stages in the process to the maximum of their intellectual capacity. Whether or not children will be able to interview these actors directly or not will depend upon the culture. If not, there is always an analysis of newspapers and, for older children, accessing local government records.

Mapping the Issues and Including Ecological Concepts

Community surveys are likely to result in the identification of many problems, but a number of these will be the same and many more will fall into the same category. If the data are collected on maps it will be possible quickly to create a collective map showing all the problem locations identified in the community. But not all environmental problems are specific to a particular location – air pollution, for example. Therefore it is necessary to produce a table or chart as well to enable the children to integrate all the different problems or issues. This is an important stage, and it need not exclude the non-literate children. Classification can be readily carried out in a large wall-chart format using graphic symbols. Very young children can create a classification table as a collage using graphic elements either drawn by themselves or cut out from magazines. In the process of discussing this classification the children will be well on their way to prioritizing the issues mentally. The most likely graphic structure for organizing the classification will be columns with headings, such as housing problems, water pollution, and agricultural problems.

Now is the time to introduce or remind children of ecological concepts, for they will be able to see their relevance. The use of introductory books and films by the children can be interspersed with discussions of their relevance to their developing diagnosis of the problem.

Whether or not children mapped the data when they collected it, they will now need to map it. By mapping the phenomena, children may see ways in which issues in their village or urban neighbourhood coalesce spatially and thereby may form the basis for selecting a problem. Mapping may make clear the ways in which various issues are related and need to be acted on together because of their systemic nature. One example might be the identification by children of a lack of play and recreation space in an area where there is unlawful dumping of waste together with water-pollution problems. Acting on these three issues together would likely result in a more satisfactory project for the children than deciding which single problem was most important. It is because of such spatial inferences that maps are such a basic tool of ecological analysis, for children and environmental professionals alike.

Prioritizing the Issues and Selecting a Problem

How one proceeds at this point depends on the time available, the number of groups and number of children in each group, and the resources available. Another factor is the age-related intellectual and social capacity of the children to work individually or together (see Chapter 2). The best approach with older children seems to be to allow them to form spontaneously into groups around issues that most concern them. It is useful in this stage for the facilitator to remind the children of the fundamental task at hand – to prioritize issues that are important in affecting the quality of their lives and the lives of others in their community, balanced against the overall desire to maintain the ecological sustainability of the area. Because of the tendency of adults to ignore the particular perspectives of children, it is important to emphasize to children their need to think of the priorities in their own daily lives, especially if this is their first environmental project.

Literate children should write out a very clear, specific statement of their problem. This forces everyone to be explicit about collecting data on the problem. It should take the form of a question and should clearly indicate to whom the question refers – that is, which groups of people, or animals, or plants the issue affects. It is unlikely that a child will be able to write a good research question on a first attempt without adult help in defining what interests them. This question, more than anything else, will affect the clarity of the subsequent research effort.

Depending on how the problem has been prioritized, children will have either themes or specific study sites. For pre-adolescent children, having a specific study site helps them learn how to take an ecological perspective on a problem. Focusing on a specific place makes it easier to think simultaneously of many different variables to approach a phenomenon ecologically. Investigating the life of a pond or a small stream close to home, for example, is much more appropriate for most pre-adolescent children than investigating problems of water quality throughout the community. Having a single study site also makes sampling the environment easier. A systematic scheme for observing the quality of that environment over time can easily be designed with children. Young children can be introduced to the collection of scientific data but this should be done in an manner which enables them to be able to comprehend what they are doing and why. Seven-year-olds for example can analyse water quality by comparing the presence or absence of certain micro-organisms which serve as indicators of environmental quality. Because they cannot design such research however, their efforts may be reduced to simply responding to an adult-designed scheme. While this might have some educational merit it should not replace attempts at achieving a more genuine participation with its rewards of a deeper involvement. Teenagers, by comparison, have the intellectual capacity to understand complex ecological problems and to strategically design a research strategy with advisers. The reader is referred to the global programme of water quality research by secondary schools students.[7]

INVESTIGATING THE STUDY SITE OR THEME

With the action-research approach adopted here, children will usually rely on information from interviews and on simple observation. Whom to consult should be a subject of debate for the entire group of children and is best done with the help of a graphic chart. For example, the children of Hojas Anchas school in Colombia (Chapter 7) determined that, to plan the reforestation of the hill in their village, they needed to interview the elderly residents, who would be most likely to remember the types of trees that once grew there; the local nurserymen, who know which trees would grow under which microclimatic conditions; and the forester for the region, who could help with this task and also help obtain the trees.

Children need to understand that the goal of this phase of research is to maximize the diversity of

[7] Stapp and Mitchell (1995).

perspectives on an issue. They need to work hard to seek different ideas and values people will have towards a phenomenon. Classroom discussions and role playing are likely to help them think of which sources need to be investigated to maximize the diversity of their perspective.

In helping the children to think which people's perceptions need to be considered, you should remind them not only of the residents of the community but also of all those people whose decisions affect the children's community and the environment in which they live. They are likely to identify local people, whom they know have knowledge of the environment, but they will rely upon you to identify politicians, journalists, and environmental specialists.

Children should learn the importance of thinking broadly about different sources of information, including themselves. Group discussions in which children articulate experiences may be valuable, especially if amplified by skits in which they re-enact experiences related to the theme (see Chapter 11 for a discussion of skits). Depending on their degree of literacy, children can keep a notebook of articles or graphic material related to their theme from newspapers and magazines. They may also each wish to keep a simple diary if they are investigating a commonly experienced phenomenon in their daily lives, such as noise pollution or air pollution. The groups may decide to invite a resource person with particularly strong experience in the phenomenon to speak generally to the group, even though they may not yet have prepared any specific questions. Environmental professionals often will be ready to speak extemporaneously. Others, who may not have public speaking as part of their daily livelihood, may require the structure provided by a question-and-answer format.

Part III describes a number of methods that can be used in this phase of the research, including interviews, surveys, and questionnaires. Although children can be easily intimidated in interviews, these are still preferable to questionnaire surveys. Not only is the quality of information richer, but in the act of collecting the data children begin to make others aware of environmental problems, and even more important, of their own capacity to investigate such problems seriously. Surveys designed by children may simply be ignored by adults whereas interviews will not.

ANALYSING AND INTERPRETING THE DATA

Children need to get into the practice of summarizing data after each data collection trip. In this way they understand their task concretely as they proceed, rather than blindly amassing data in the hope that you will help them make sense of it all at the end. For highly literate children, this is simply a question of making a written summary of what they have learned from each interview or observation visit. For non-literate children, it may mean making a verbal report to a group, with those who have writing ability taking down the information, or it may be that the information can be summarized in the form of a drawing, which can then be reported to the larger groups. Even if children use tape recorders, there should be no delay in summarizing what they have learned each day. Simple bar charts are an excellent graphic means for large numbers of children, including those who are not literate, to see the quantitative aspects of their data take form.

Given the complex nature of all environmental problems, children need help in finding ways to express the relationship of the many relevant variables. Again, the best collective way to do this is with large wall graphics. Children can take turns pinning up symbols representing data they have collected. Gradually, a complex composite picture is created of the many factors relevant to a problem. You can help give form to this display by suggesting alternative ways of spatially arranging the variables and by drawing lines between them. Gradually, through discussion, this activity should lead to greater clarity of the important variables. Prioritizing them may involve looking back again to the data to see what various interviewees said about the relative importance of different factors. At the end of this exercise, the children should be able to summarize the important variables that are creating an environmental problem or influencing their study site. They are now ready to move on to the next stage: solutions or recommendations for change.

PLANNING ENVIRONMENTAL ACTIONS

For each problem or study site on which children have chosen to work, there are likely to be a number of alternative solutions or recommendations. Deciding which solution to act upon can become an extremely interesting and important research phase, one that can galvanize the larger community. For each alternative solution, the children are asked to make a list of likely positive and negative social and environmental impacts. To help them in this task they can re-interview the people they found most effective in the first stage of interviewing. Children can then debate which solution seems to offer the greatest degree of positive social worth with the minimum of environmental damage. So valuable is this stage of the research to an understanding of environmental problems that it would be well if it could be shared with the larger community through a presentation or exhibition.

What should be done with all that has been discovered depends upon the nature and scale of the problem. It is not necessary in all cases for the children to take action themselves to improve the environment. Having done good research they may simply need to convince others of the importance of what they have discovered. That is an action of a kind, which is discussed in Chapter 9. Making a presentation to local civic leaders or environmental planners, for example, can be an extremely satisfying experience for children if the adults seriously listen to them and ask pertinent questions. If they receive honest feedback and criticism from those in the adult world who make decisions, then they have gone a long way towards entering into the democratic process as citizens. In some instances,

the children's research efforts may become part of a larger planning effort, with their data as a source of consideration for the adult community. If this is the case, children should be allowed to follow up with this planning body to see what does or does not happen with their findings.

For children younger than ten, who have difficulty understanding complex, long-term planning processes, it is ideal if they can take some direct action emerging from their research themselves as a way of rounding out and making their experience concrete. Children are capable, however, of conducting research and drawing conclusions for actions that far exceed their abilities to carry them out, given the limitations of their political power. The challenge is to work out, with the children, an action that is achievable. PMT, the National Programme of Working Children in Ecuador, has found it best to design micro-actions first – small projects close to children's homes that can be completed in a matter of days or weeks, before joining with other children to conduct macro-actions of considerable importance to their community.

THE ACTIONS

In the following chapters, examples of actions by children are provided in a number of different domains: environmental planning and design, environmental management, public awareness, and political action.[8] If the children are led to conclude from their research that they cannot themselves do anything to improve a situation, they may decide to try to get others to do so. This may involve a public awareness campaign or it may necessitate meeting with elected officials to discuss the problem. In many countries neither of these options will be available, or there will be a pretence by decision makers of listening to children. In either case, children should follow through with a full discussion of the barriers to change, as this may be the most important part of their education in citizenship.

[8] There are a large number of books for children and young people on environmental action. While they do not give the same emphasis as this book on action based on research, they have value as resources for inspiring children and suggesting certain domains of investigation: Dee and Montez (1991); Lindsten (1990); Bronze and Brown (1993); Lewis (1991); Hopkins and Winters (1990); Fleischer (1993); Haddock and Harrison (1978). For an excellent regular series of information packs on environmental and health-related action projects for children, see United Nations Environment Programme in the Bibliography.

9 Claire received assistance with this project from Sheridan Bartlett, an environmental psychologist working with children. They can be reached at The Elementary School, Westminster West, VT 05346, USA.

Box 10: Case Study on Environmental Research by Very Young Children – an Example from Vermont

Anyone who doubts the capacity of young children to conduct research should look through the window of the little two-classroom school in Westminster West, Vermont. In different areas of the lower-age room, you will see six- to ten-year-old children intently pursuing their research goals: one gluing together a model, one making a map, one recording observations of an animal's behaviour, another referring to the dictionary, perhaps a small group in the corner planning a new project, two children at a computer printing out the data from their study of consumer behaviour.

It is hard to know where the teacher, Claire Oglesby, will be, but she's unlikely to be standing in the front of the classroom, for there is no front or back to this room. She may be sitting on the couch helping some child with a map while other children interrupt with questions like, 'Claire, I don't know how to make this rainfall data into a chart.' This is a learning community, so they are apt to get answers like: 'Try talking to Adam about the chart he made last week of electricity use in town – it was like your data – and then come and see me with a plan.'

Claire Oglesby knows that children learn best when they are interested in a phenomenon. Perhaps this is why, after 30 years of teaching in this school, she is still so enthusiastic. She is able to share in the genuine excitement of discovery of each of her children's different research questions.[9]

Admittedly, this school has some special qualities. There are about 24 children in the class, and there is a part-time teaching assistant. The community is by no means wealthy or even above average in income or education, but it does have the benefit of being small. It seems that, as long as the teaching is good, small schools often can achieve better

results and a better relationship to the community than larger schools. Also, in a small town it is easier for the school to establish a working relationship with many of the institutions and residents. By remaining in the school for so long, Claire has been able to gain respect that enables her to escape the orthodoxy of fixed lesson plans and texts that limit some teachers.

Like many good progressive schoolteachers, Claire adopts general themes for children to be working on. While individuals and small groups of children investigate their own projects, they do so within a larger context that can be shared among the children. In recent years, environmental themes have grown in importance in her classroom, and she has found that her children can engage in serious environmental research by working with the support of their parents, or sometimes with other neighbouring adults.

In some schools it would be difficult to find a willing adult to work with every child in the classroom in the way Claire Oglesby has done. I suspect that she is successful in persuading all parents to play this role, even though some might feel they really don't have the time, because of the respect she has attained in the community. For other schools in which some children do not have parental support, children can work in small groups and the teacher can find other adults in the community to work with them.

Both the general themes and the children's specific projects emerge out of the children's spontaneous interests in the classroom and sometimes through their discussions with their parents. The Westminster West Atlas Project grew out of an earlier project looking at the history of the community. It became clear to Claire that the children did not

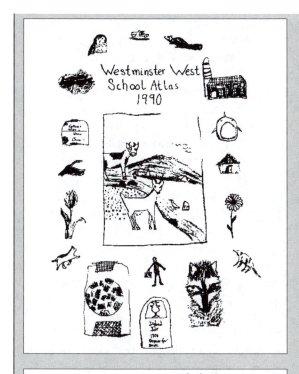

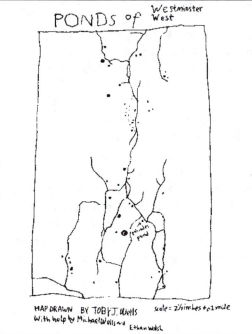

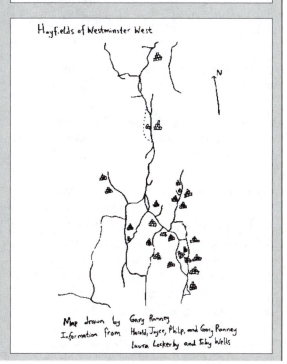

MAPS

Figure 35: Cover, table of contents, and a map from the Environmental Atlas of Westminster West, produced by six- to ten-year-old children.

know much about present-day Westminster West. This led to classroom discussions of what projects the children might do. It became clear that individual children knew a lot about particular environmental phenomena. Some enthusiastically wanted to share their knowledge of such things as horses, because they felt they knew all the horses in Westminster West. Others, proud of their knowledge of farming, knew where many of the hayfields were. After discussing how these might be mapped, one suggested that an atlas be created. In this way an exciting new project was born.

With great variation in the children's ability to map, Claire engaged them in a series of model-making and map-drawing exercises which led them to understand and be able to use outline maps of the town. The creation of a large three-dimensional model of their own was critical to developing the younger children's understanding and is strongly recommended for all elementary school teachers, although it is extremely time-consuming (see 'Mapping' in Chapter 11).

Most of the children chose to work in pairs to create a map for the atlas, although a number of them had unique interests and created a map by themselves. Once children had chosen their topic, the goal of mapping it was clear. The different routes for obtaining the information, however, posed an exciting challenge for each child. With help, children developed their own strategies for collecting information, and struggled through decision making themselves. The whole project lasted about four months, but the atlas has since remained an interesting resource for others and children periodically choose to add a new map to it. I learned that there had been no attempt to make copies of this wonderful atlas for the larger community, but that the parents would probably be very interested. Claire explained that, at this age, children are not as interested in the end product as in the process.

One of the mapping projects for the atlas was on graveyards. The children reviewed maps, visited sites, and interviewed various elder members of the community, for many of the graveyards were small, private ones conected to people's homes. Most of the field research for these projects is carried out as homework, although in this school it is possible for children to make field visits in small groups during school hours, accompanied by volunteer parents. Sadly, this flexibility does not exist in many schools. Data for the map of pets in the community were collected through the design of a survey. Children of this age cannot conduct a complete saturation survey or even a formal random sample, but a large percentage of the total community of 800 was reached by the children. The survey was carried home by the 40 children to their families and, from this beginning, carried out to relatives, neighbours, and others.

In the following year, an effort was made to deepen parental involvement in the children's learning. Before the parents were invited into the school for discussions, the children brainstormed ideas in groups. The first stage involved helping the children escape from their stereotyped ideas of 'environmental' projects. Claire finds that it is often best to separate the youngest children, from six to seven years of age, during the first brainstorming sessions in order to give their ideas free range without domination by the multitudinous ideas of the older children. The two groups then merge for a larger debate about the range of possible research topics. This discussion with all of the children lasted about one and a half hours, a clear sign of great interest in the subject. The next step was for small groups, usually three parents, to come to the school to meet with Claire and their children to discuss the design of the projects. These meetings were scheduled in such a way that every parent was able to participate.

One child came to the meeting with a clear plan

Figure 36:
Before beginning their research, the young children of Westminster West School complete a research plan in collaboration with their parents.

to study pet food, which he had not previously shared with his mother. When asked why he thought this was an important project, he said clearly, 'because pet food costs lots of money and money is paper and paper comes from trees and that must damage the rainforest.' He went on to say that he also suspected that pet food included meat from cattle that were raised in the rainforest. He hypothesized that there were probably not too many people involved in making this pet food, and they could probably easily be killed off, so there would be no more problem with the destruction of the rainforest! His mother sat with amazement through these stories but agreed it would be fine for them to work together to conduct a survey on the issue. He was able to complete the project by himself with a little help from his mother during the analysis phase.

No hard and fast rules were made about how parents should work with their children. This is necessary not only because of the different capacities of the children but also because of the different capacities of parents, their different styles of working with their children, and the different amounts of free time they have available. One young girl who had great difficulty with academic work had a chance to see that, even though her mother also had great difficulty with language, she could read and write. The daughter was empowered, it seemed, by observing her mother carrying out work that she had not previously observed. For other children it was literally a joint activity, with parent and child conducting observations and interviews together. Other parents simply gave their enthusiastic support and sometimes provided the resources for their children to conduct *their own research. In all cases the project not only succeeded in connecting the school to the community environment but also improved the connection between parents and the school curriculum.*

Another innovative feature of this project was that older siblings became involved. This was possible because, alongside the local environmental research, the children were corresponding with other children in Puerto Rico, with the intention of visiting Puerto Rico at the end of the year. Because they would be travelling as families, the older siblings became interested. One example was a book on vegetable gardening produced by a seven-year-old girl and her 11-year-old sister about the farming practices of their family's small market garden. By interviewing their parents in great detail they were able to produce a booklet worthy of publication. Through correspondence with Puerto Rico, they were able to persuade their counterparts in the Caribbean to produce similar accounts of growing crops in that part of the world.

A six-year-old and her mother chose to do a project on logging, which was the livelihood of the child's father and grandfather. The primary interview was conducted by her mother in the woods while her father was logging. The family, which still uses horses in the logging, was not involved in any way in ecological debates about forestry and forestry management. Nevertheless, through the interview and through engaging in the degree of reflection demanded by the project, the child and her mother were able to produce a document that addressed important issues in forestry management, including the value of selective felling and the use of horses

rather than machinery. The interview was videotaped and made part of the final product. As a result of this project, the family, which had never been involved in writing anything before, was offered funding by the Vermont Historical Society to produce further documentation of their logging work.

On Project Night, towards the end of the year, each of the 40 children stood up for a few minutes and made a presentation of their work to the other children and the parents. One of the unexpected benefits of this environmental research in the community was the extent to which it enabled children (and their parents) to come to understand not only the environment but also some of the relationships between livelihood and the environment. Furthermore, by looking at the work that people do in relationship to its values, children were able to escape narrow societal stereotypes of status and to find value in the work of all parents. Related to this observation, Claire told me how in a previous year children had looked specifically at the workplaces of their parents. While initially some parents resisted this idea, because of the social status issue, the project went on to have a valorizing impact, particularly on the work of those persons in what are often considered lower status positions. The father who worked in the paper mill proudly led all of the children of the school through the fascinating production process; it became the most popular project of the year. (Interestingly, the least popular site visit was to the workplace of the college professor. The children could not understand why anyone would want such a boring job!)

Box 11: Case Study on The Programme of Working Children (PMT) in Ecuador

The organization of this remarkable national programme was described in Chapter 4. What follows is an account of the processes used by dozens of groups of children operating out of Espacios Alternativas, or 'alternative spaces', throughout the country.

Phase I: Training and Social Mobilization

In each city, a local support group began training youth units to work with children already in the Espacios Alternativas. They organized street parades, panels, and conferences and even produced a video. Children were given workshops in communications, journalism, and how to achieve interviews with television, radio, and the press. They also visited schools and high schools throughout the region to invite other young people to join them. As with all phases, these social mobilization activities emphasized children as the protagonists of their own cause. The result was a high degree of creativity not possible in more formal children's programmes.

Phase II: Problem Identification and Diagnosis

The most remarkable feature of the PMT environmental programme is that although it was developed very quickly with a large number of children nationwide, it has remained true to the principle of involving children significantly in each phase of the programme, including problem identification. Critical to this phase is the existence of a well-trained group of facilitators who know how to liberate children truly to identify problems from their own experiences and from others in their community. PMT had to rely upon a small number of adult staff, trained quickly in intensive ecological workshops, who then trained

Figure 37: A sample page taken from the children's workbook entitled 'Observing the Environment that Surrounds Us'. On this page the child is asked if they live near a river and to write its name. They are then asked to describe the river banks and everything in and surrounding the river. It prompts them to say whether there is garbage or vegetation and whether or not there are fish. At the bottom of the page they are asked to draw an area of wild vegetation near their home.

small units of youth to be the promoters in each Espacio Alternativa.

The programme was able to rely upon teenagers as promoters by preparing excellent instruction material for them that was tied closely to children's workbooks. These low-cost workbooks require children to research with their own families and neighbours (see Figure 37). It is hard to teach children to take initiatives through books. No matter how well a book might stress that it is children who should identify environmental problems themselves, it must of necessity provide some examples. Not surprisingly, the examples PMT provides are the common problems of most environmental education programmes – recycling, air pollution, water pollution, noise pollution, and reforestation. As a result there is not as great a diversity in the kinds of problems identified by children in the PMT

Figure 38:
The children of San Vicente, an illegal settlement on the outskirts of Quito, chose to design a bridge as their project in the PMT Environmental Programme. It enabled those children who live on the other side of the deep ravine to attend the 'alternative space' where the programme is held.
© Roger Hart.

games, they collectively create ecological maps of their local environment. Patterns of cards expressing problems in the environment help focus their discussions about problem locations in the community, thereby leading them towards the selection of their ecological actions.

Phase III: Ecological Actions

After two months of diagnostic work in their community, the children's groups identify actions to improve their environment. The promoters are asked to limit their involvement during the choice of actions to advice on the technical, financial, and political feasibility of the proposals.

For smaller cities and towns, it was recommended that children work together in a meeting,

programme as one might like. If a community is truly identifying problems by itself, these are likely to be very different from the problems upon which other neighbourhoods choose to act. Nevertheless, there are some unique projects such as a bridge built in Quito (see Figure 38) and an ecological clubhouse in Guayaquil.

The youth instructor's book and the companion children's workbooks for the diagnostic phase of the programme begin with playful exercises in environmental awareness, using all of the senses. The children are rapidly prepared to look critically at their local environment. The authors of these materials have worked hard to create methods that by their very structure stress the importance of children as the identifiers of problems in their environments. They also emphasize the importance of interviewing the knowledgeable elders of the community. In one workbook, each child creates drawings on separate cards of elements in their environment (Figure 39). Then, through a series of sorting and mapping

using the data from the diagnostic phase, to design an action for their city. Their proposed action should not demand too many resources, but they were informed that they should submit a proposal for modest financing by the PMT headquarters in Quito. In the larger cities it was proposed that each separate group of children first carry out their own 'micro-ecological action', financed, if possible, by their own respective institution. Following this, they should meet in a conference together with children and youth from other Espacios Alternativas to design a single macro-action for their city that would be financed by PMT. These macro-actions should involve not only the Espacios Alternativas with their youth and children but also schools, colleges,

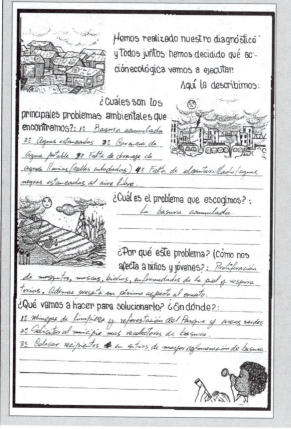

PMT design materials which stress children's individual and collective identification of problems, e.g. this series of annotated sketches. During walks of their everyday environment, children each make drawings on cards of individual features which they feel are important, both positive and negative.

The children then work together as a group to play sorting and matching games with these cards.

Next they display the cards on poster board in groupings to express their collective notion of environmental problems. With this simple exercise, the youth facilitators are able to lead young children to the production of maps which are based upon both their personal evaluations and their collective vision of their community.

community organizations, supporting environmentalists, and ideally even the municipal authorities themselves. In promoting this macro action to the larger community, PMT in each city was provided with a small budget to produce an Ecological Expo for view by community residents as well as officials. These included models, photos, and slides of the children's diagnostic phase.

Ecological Youth Patrols

In the spirit of the concept of defending children's rights, the PMT guidelines to the youth units was to try to form patrols that could work in local communities to detect and denounce those responsible for damaging the environment. These patrols are limited largely to teenage members, although some pre-

Figure 39:
A drawing and card-sorting exercise designed by PMT to enable facilitators to involve children in evaluating their environment.

Figure 40:
Page from the PMT workbook on choice of 'Ecological Actions'.

Figure 41:
The form used by children of the 'ecological patrols' to record contamination by vehicles. The first four columns record the date, type, and plate number of the vehicle. The first infraction column records a subjective evaluation of noise level, the second rates whether the horn has been blown excessively, and the third records whether or not there is visible exhaust or smoke. This information is used by the National Traffic Board to inform by public notice the responsible parties. Forty-five days are given to repair the vehicles. If after this period there is no compliance, the operating permits of the vehicles will be taken away and a sticker will be attached to the vehicle.

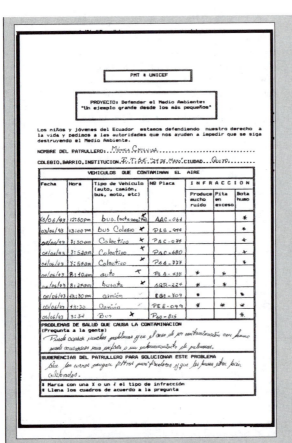

pollution, industrial air pollution, and solid waste pollution. For example, the tree forms record who damaged the trees and the nature of the damage: soil washed away, dry and broken soil, lack of plant diversity, and no wild animals. At the bottom of the forms the children are asked to record what health problems are caused by this pollution. Below this they are asked to make suggestions to the solution of the problem.

Through collaboration with the police department and the use of a local youth radio programme, the participants were able to add teeth to their programme of public awareness on the issue of automobile pollution. Whether or not such confrontation with the adult community is, in the long run, a good way to promote the idea of children as participants in community development remains a question. If the long-term goal is to have adults come to see children as capable not only of having independent ideas but also the capacity to work with the larger community to improve the environment, then the PMT projects that have dialogue as their central quality may be more appropriate. Otherwise there is a danger that a large segment of the adult population will react to the unreasonable power given to such junior citizens. The PMT staff explain that, by surrounding the actions of the Ecological Patrols with a large-scale media campaign, adults come to understand that children are merely acting to defend their rights. I was told that the polite and even jovial response of the bus and truck drivers confirms this – but it is their owners who will have to pay the bills (I wonder about the private car owners). We need comparable research on the kinds of creative initiatives undertaken by PMT if children's community participation is to become a lasting feature of community development.

adolescents do join them. The intention was to have the responsible institutions and the general public better understand existing laws and ordinances by sanctioning the guilty ones. The larger goal, of course, was to get a long-term commitment from the municipalities for children and the environment, while making the public aware of their own responsibilities as citizens.

In Quito, the youth patrols used forms to record a variety of types of damage to the environment, including air pollution and noise pollution by vehicles in the centre of the city, damage to trees, water

EVALUATION AND REPEATING THE CYCLE OF ACTION RESEARCH

If the children do engage in an action on the environment, this should be evaluated by them to determine to what extent it was successful. This may lead them to conclude that a different kind of action is required or it may lead them to a new problem. If the children concluded that they could not act on their problem they may be able to evaluate why this was, and thereby begin to identify a new problem which might be more amenable to action. Either way, they should be involved in an evaluation phase for the action research to be most beneficial as a learning experience. Basic to this process, of course, is the clear articulation of the goals of the project and the rearticulation of these goals as the project goes through different action-research cycles. This might involve children in the establishment of observable 'indicators' that could be measured before and after the actions or surveys of community residents regarding their assessment of success. At a minimum, there should be a thorough discussion by the children at the end of any action.

CHAPTER 6

Environmental Planning, Design and Construction by Children

[1] For further information, contact the Resource Centre, International Association for the Child's Right to Play, National Play Information Centre, 359–61 Euston Road, London NW1 3AL, United Kingdom. Also, there is an excellent resource for involving children with all kinds of special needs: The Handicapped Adventure Playground Association, Fulham Palace Grounds, Bishops Avenue, London, SW6.

This chapter is concerned with all aspects of transforming the environment – what in the professional world would be called planning, landscape architecture, environmental design, urban design, and architecture. Design is an inappropriate word to use for much of the world because it implies a degree of professional specialization that does not apply to them; they build their own houses and community centres and public spaces without the help of anyone trained as a designer, architect, or landscape architect and often without the involvement of an official environmental planner. The terms are used here to refer to the process anyone goes through, trained or otherwise, in creating or transforming the environment. To that extent, children are planners and designers too when they engage in construction play. The large number of examples from the United Kingdom in this chapter is a reflection of the extent to which this country has pioneered this particular kind of environmental engagement by children.

CHILDREN'S PLANNING, DESIGN, AND CONSTRUCTION OF THEIR OWN ENVIRONMENTS

Following the CRC, we should be able to 'assure to the child who is capable of forming his or her own views the right to express those views freely in all matters affecting the child' to the extent of their capacity. Children of all ages, from the third or fourth year of their lives on, can be involved in planning and design. For example, before painting a child's bedroom, a parent can choose to consult with their three-year-old

and experiment with them in the use of these colours, or they can, like most parents, just paint the room with no consultation at all. More important than the aesthetic impact on the environment from involving a child is the impact on the child. The child will develop at an early age the sense that the environment is, in part, created by people, including themselves.

Children's play in the neighbourhood close to their home can also offer opportunities for planning and design. Traditional playgrounds with fixed equipment are the most interesting to children when they are being built or dismantled. Consequently, the countries of Northern Europe have developed 'adventure playgrounds' with many materials and much participation by children in building them (see Figure 43).[1]

THE DESIGN AND CONSTRUCTION OF SCHOOL GROUNDS

In environmental design, like environmental planning projects, the purpose of the project is often determined in advance because of the larger development goals of adults or because that is what funds are available for. Nevertheless, there is often great scope for children to determine the particular nature of the design. School grounds are an excellent domain for children's involvement in all phases, including the building of the project. Before planning and design, a thorough survey of the site is necessary (see Chapter 13).

As with any good project, the design phase should begin by asking the users first to identify what activities and experiences the new environment should afford rather than beginning with preconceptions of a final design. Regrettably, this phase of 'programming' is often missing, even from adult designers' projects; for designers prefer to maintain control of the entire design process. Drawings for desired activities by individuals followed by group discussions and the charting of activities and preferences can enable children to arrive at a behavioural programme for the school ground (see Chapter 13).

For ascertaining children's own desires for activities on the schoolgrounds it may not be sufficient, however, to rely solely on their spontaneous statements of preference. My colleague and I have found that showing children a series of slides or a film is necessary to liberate their ideas.[2] I was once asked to work with the children of an elementary school in rural Vermont, in the USA, to create an adventure playground for the school grounds. I resisted being involved because it seemed to me that the children of this town already had great opportunities to construct places to play and had no need for an urban conception of a play environment. Under pressure I resolved at least to let the children decide. I simply showed them a short Danish film (with no English narration) in which a truck unloads a lot of lumber inside a fenced-off area and girls and boys begin building their own playground with support from a play leader. Without further instruction, the children of all ages understood the essential concept and began to build. I had failed to recognize that not all children in this town were encouraged or even allowed to build in the trees and bushes surrounding their homes, particularly the girls, and so they jumped at the chance inside the school grounds. Once the building was seriously underway it was possible to begin group discussions about the design of the play area and some of the problems that needed to be worked on as the playground grew. I doubt if discussion would have been as successful in getting the project rolling.

We have found modelling to be a highly effective strategy for involving children of all ages from five years

and older in the design of school grounds and playgrounds (see 'Modelling', Chapter 12).[3] The key to the success of the participatory planning and design process lies in creative negotiation among the children and between different groups. Consensus building is greatly aided by the flexibility of the modelling materials, but it also requires skilful mediation by a facilitator for some children not to walk away from the process feeling their design ideas have been rejected. Children are encouraged to reveal the reasons behind their suggestions. For example, a group of girls may insist that they have to locate the area for a skipping rope in a relatively isolated part of the site, in order to prevent interference from the boys' running games. When an outside designer or landscape architect is brought into a project to complete the final design it is valuable to document the modelling process with a videotape recorder. This allows the designers to go back to the tapes and annotate the site plan with conflicts between different users.

Towards the end of the design phase, when the conceptual design proposals are ready, it is necessary to get wider feedback from all the residents in the community. Again, modelling is valuable. In our schoolyard designs in Harlem, mobile design kiosks were manoeuvred on the sidewalks near the school entrances (see Chapter 12). Because these school grounds are also used by the whole community after school hours, everyone's opinions are relevant. Parents who came to pick up their children after school, as well as neighbours returning home from work and teenagers and young adults who use the basketball court at nighttime, were asked to comment on and to manipulate model elements of the proposed designs.

In many countries, major reconstruction of school grounds must be carried out by adult contractors, but a committed staff can do a great deal to convince education administrators to allow the children to do much of the landscaping, particularly if the parents are willing to be involved too. Figure 43 shows how much the children of Washington Elementary School in Berkeley,

[2] Iltus and Hart (1995).

[3] See Hart (1983) for a discussion of children's spontaneous architecture.

[4] Iltus and Hart (1995).

[5] Francis (1988), p. 10.

Figures 42 and 43:
Two stages in the
transformation of the
yard of the
Washington
Elementary School in
Berkeley, California,
by the children and
parents of the
community
© Robin Moore.

California, were able to achieve after a bulldozer simply removed the boring black skin which covers so many schoolyards. (Some of the exciting consequences of this act for children's research are discussed in Chapter 8.)

In addition to their value for environmental science, school grounds offer great opportunities for art activities by children. The school grounds movement in the UK has spawned dozens of original landscaping programmes across the country, with sculpture, weaving, flower gardens, and water features – settings designed for their aesthetic values as well as for the promotion of ecological understanding.[6] A fascinating example comes from a culturally diverse elementary school near the heart of the city of Manchester.[6] The project began with a creative initiative by the city planning department. They hired an artist-in-residence who then worked with the schools. The artist established a network of architects and landscape architects to work with the teachers, parents, and children of Cheetham Community Primary School. Central to the design is the use of willow saplings. These serve as a rapidly growing form of vegetation which children can plant in designs of their own making. They can then cut them down regularly for use in weaving. From their discussions with the collaborating landscape architect a design emerged

of a large willow sculpture wandering through the school grounds in the shape of an Arabic word for tree. Also related to the cultural diversity of the parents is a charcoal kiln and a Tandoor oven for Indian cooking.

The willows represent an interesting merger of the English tradition of basket-weaving, using the renewable resource of willow branches, with the basket-making knowledge of the Pakistani residents. The art activity is already benefiting the larger community. Within one year basket-weaving was being taught by two Pakistani parents to a group of 40 teachers, parents and children. The willow coppices belong to different groups of seven- and eight-year-old children, who manage them for a two-year period before handing them over to younger ones to serve as new managers. Other parents use other resources from this diverse school ground in their teaching, such as those who employ a wide range of herbs and vegetables for cooking classes. There is also a woodcraft group meeting after school hours for both parents and children. In this way the school grounds have become a resource for the entire community, re-creating some of the elements of their home countries in Vietnam, Cambodia, India, Pakistan, and Bangladesh.

[6] Adams (1990);
Titman (1994); Lucas
(1992).

Chapter 7, on environmental management, illustrates some of the ways children can be involved in school grounds on a continuous basis.

CHILDREN AS PARTICIPANTS WITH ADULTS IN COMMUNITY-BASED PLANNING

Ideally, children's experience with planning and design projects will mature to the point where they wish to work alongside adults. This should be the goal for any community, rather than keeping children's voices falsely segregated, as though adults and children lived in different communities.[7] Using the right kind of approach and materials, children can be involved from the start of a community planning process. After all, adult residents usually have as little experience as children.

Box 12 gives an early description of 'Planning for Real' by its founder, Tony Gibson.[8] Since then his Neighbourhood Initiatives Foundation in England has used his approach throughout the United Kingdom and in recent years has applied it to both rural and urban projects in Africa, India, Asia, and Latin America. The centrepiece of his method is always a model of the environment in which the people live. Planning for Real uses kits of cut-out options to the same scale which people can arrange and rearrange on a model base. This gives them a start to building a model of their own neighbourhood, and from then on scissors, coloured cardboard, and felt pens enable them to make additions (See 'Model Building', Chapter 12). Following a preliminary display of the model, a public meeting is held in which the whole model is set out and residents begin adding everything they want. From this stage, groups form to sift out the individual proposals and work through the obstacles that lie in the way of getting what is needed and identifying what major issues are in conflict. As many local professionals and government officers as can be persuaded to come to these meetings do so, but they are asked to be in attendance and offer advice only when asked, for it is critical to make sure that 'residents retain the initiative'.

Figure 44: Eight-year-old girls reading by the pond they built with parents and teachers at Wardie Primary School in Edinburgh, Scotland © Graham White, Environment Centre.

Quite often schools use the Planning for Real pack, and this becomes an entry point for the larger community: 'Gram turns up with her daughter-in-law at the public meeting centred on the community's model, quite oblivious of the leaflets publicizing the meeting that went though her letterbox'.[9] Sometimes it is possible that planners can return to the residents' meeting and use the same model to show precisely what is proposed in response to residents' proposals. In this way there is less room 'for evasion or misunderstanding'.

CHILDREN'S PARTICIPATION IN THE PLANNING OF NATURAL RESOURCE CONSERVATION PROJECTS

While teenagers are often invited to participate in tree planting and soil or beach conservation projects, these are usually large-scale social mobilization efforts on projects lying outside the home community and which rarely make an attempt to involve the young participants in research, planning, or decisions related to the phenomenon. For this reason I am including in Box 13 a detailed report by my colleague Ray Lorenzo of a project in Italy which has involved low income youth in

[7] For an introduction to participatory neighbourhood planning that involves all ages see Henter (1984).

[8] Gibson (1993).

[9] Gibson and Beane (1980) p. 14.

Box 12: Case Study on 'Planning for Real' in Scotland

Scene: A church hall in an inner-city area of multiple deprivation in Dalmarnock, Scotland. In the centre of the room five tables support a layout representing the half-mile square area surrounding the hall in which the exercise is taking place. The layout was assembled with the help of an aerial photograph, and using mainly printed outlines folded to represent tower blocks, five-storey blocks, four- and three-storey tenements, and two-storey semis. Local factories are also shown in rough 3D. Half way along one wall is the 'Advice Centre', consisting of two professional community workers equipped with several sets of card-index information – the Fact Bank. (Eventually they will issue one set to each group and keep one for their own use, together with a folder of case-history material on which they can draw to supplement their own experience.) Along one wall there are 37 bags or trays each containing token shapes, to the correct scale, to represent different utilities and amenities – access roads for rubbish vehicles, adventure playgrounds, paved areas for old people to sit on, community huts, etc.

Residents brought together by the local action group include the local district councillor, a police inspector, and a priest. They are dispersed in the four corners of the room, in groups labelled 'Mums', 'Elderly', 'Dissatisfied Youth', and 'Action Committee'. When the residents arrived they were asked to use a batch of street labels to identify every part of the layout. They found their way about it immediately, and 25 streets were labelled within a few minutes. Residents were able to identify their own houses, shops, and bars, even though these were only crudely represented.

In attendance are some 15 professional workers whose job involves them with this area. They include senior regional planners, district planners, social workers, and members of voluntary bodies. Each is available, first come first served, to be consulted by any of the groups of residents. The groups have been asked to make their own independent plans for the whole of the area represented on the model, with their own particular sections of the community in mind. They place their own shapes on the layout, first signing each shape on the back.

An hour later, each group has completed its initial plan, and groups are beginning to negotiate with each other where there are rival bids for a given area or given type of amenity. Increasing use is made of professionals, in order to check the practicability of each item in each plan. Within two hours the groups reported that the conflicts between the different sections of the community they represent have been satisfactorily resolved without the need for arbitration. The planners report that their technical advice seems to have been heeded. The Advice Centre say nobody has gone sufficiently into costing yet; fresh discussion begins on the possibilities of a combined operation on certain schemes in which the community might offset costs by voluntary efforts, e.g. in clearing the site for an adventure playground.

The residents conclude the evening with a discussion of further meetings to repeat the exercise with special reference to particular sections of the community.

Figure 45:
Alip Palayao, together with other Youth Conservation Corps members, planting pine seedlngs in the communal forest of Alapang in La Trinidad, Benguet, the Phillipines.
© PLAN International.

research, reflection, and action related to their local area of natural beauty and ecological significance.[10]

PLANNING AND DESIGN BY CHILDREN FOR ADULT 'CLIENTS'

Given the growing climate of enthusiasm for public–private partnerships in the management of environments, it is not surprising that this should have found its way into the schools. The innovative GreenIt business/school/community partnership programme, developed by the Black Country Groundwork Trust in the industrial West Midlands of England, was introduced in Chapter 4.

Pre-project preparation by the teacher is limited to logistical details; the design of the project is saved for the children. This preparatory work incorporates a visit to the site, perhaps including a video or photography to show the children in advance, locating the facilities and establishing transportation, and access to all areas of the site. This is followed by classroom work with the children, preparing them to work in the business setting. Training involves devising with the children roles and responsibilities for the project, observing, and interviewing. The groups of children treat the business as a 'client' in this relationship. Through consultation with the client a 'design brief' and budget is established. The pupils then research, design, and cost out an enhancement to some part of the landscape of the business. The project does not end with research, planning, and a proposal, but proceeds with detailed design, using computer-aided design (CAD) and input from environmental professionals of all kinds as well as suppliers of resources. These adults act on request as consultants to the pupils. Finally, the pupils have to sell their design to the business client and persuade them to put it into practice.

Figure 46:
Children surveying for a design project with the GreenIt Programme.
© Roger Hart

10 In addition to natural resource conservationthere are important opportunities for children to be involved in the conservation of the built environment. For an international review see Barthelemy and Monillereaux (1990). For a catalogue of publications for involving children in research on the historic environment, contact English Heritage Education Service, Keysign House, 429 Oxford St, London W1R 2HD.

Box 13: Case Study on Children Designing the Future in a Disadvantaged Rural Setting, Aspromonte, Italy (prepared by Ray Lorenzo)

The project described here began in the second year of the WWF 'Children's Futures Project', in 1992. The area was selected since it coincided with an important, international programme of the European Council and the International WWF entitled CADISPA (Conservation and Development in Sparsely Populated Areas). The CADISPA programme – being carried out since 1990 in poor, environmentally attractive rural areas with high emigration patterns in Spain, Portugal, Greece, Scotland, and Italy – aims at 'identifying, encouraging and activating micro-projects which permit the human communities involved to achieve economic and cultural development in harmony with the environmental characteristics and restraints of the regions in question.' The programme focuses primarily on children and youth (and, through them, their families and communities) utilizing approaches drawn from the areas of environmental education and participatory, ecological development planning. The region chosen by WWF-Italy is the mountainous Aspromonte area in the southern-most mainland region, Calabria. Aspromonte is the most 'problematic' site in the European programme, being afflicted not only by economic depression, abandonment, and cultural disintegration, but also by an ingrained criminal organization involved in the international drugs and arms trade, extortion, and kidnapping. As a result it has a severe self-image problem. The nation's mass media has contributed to the creation of the negative image. Outsiders consider it, rightfully, a dangerous area. As such, they avoid it; and the great tourist potential of the area, with many miles of sandy beaches and extraordinary, almost alpine-like mountain areas, goes untapped. Residents, and children in particular, are aware of and suffer from this image problem – a vicious circle contributing to a self fulfilling prophecy of 'worsening futures'.

Teachers in this area are for the most part demotivated and demoralized. The public education bureaucracy, typically inefficient and slow-moving in Italy, is even worse in this region – with evidence of political favouring and Mafia infiltration. Highly motivated teachers are snubbed by their colleagues and at times threatened by the 'vested interests'. Two teachers from the Bovalino middle school, which had a highly motivated, courageous headmaster, agreed to carry out the year-long curriculum proposed in the 'futures project'. Approximately half of the 25 children in the Bovalino second-year class are inhabitants of the 'infamous' mountain centre of San Luca. The 'families' involved in the flourishing criminal activities in the region are held, for the most part, to come from San Luca. San Luca possesses a middle school, but many parents prefer to send their children to Bovalino's school on the coast – a 15-mile trip, with no bus service, each way.

A central goal of the futures project approach is to overcome the often pessimistic, passive stance with regards to the future of the environment in general which develops and becomes more prevalent as children grow towards adolescence. The cause of this affirmation originates, it seems, in mass media's focus on crisis or catastrophe scenarios for the future in addition to society's commonly scarce evaluation of children and youth potentials for participation. From initial 'fantasy flights' in 'imaging the future', the project moves towards the development of concrete local problem solving and design.

In the first activities of the 'futures project' – drawing images of Aspromonte in the future and responding to and discussing the project's standard survey ('Which futures?') – it became clear that the group reflected many of the observations we had made at a national level regarding children from similar disadvantaged backgrounds. Visions of the future were consistently (with a few exceptions) pessimistic – the personal and local futures would worsen – and, even more worrisome, the children held that little or nothing could be done to change these scenarios. The problems and fears the children expressed were real and experienced in their everyday lives, and included crime and violence, unemployment, local environmental devastation (forest depletion through arson, drought, pollution of the coastal waters, etc.), and problems related specifically to children and youth (alienation, drug use, and lack of places to play, hang out and meet).

The next phase of the project – which involves various methods for evoking children's proposals for change – was carried out by the teachers without the assistance of Pasquale, the coordinator. After several weeks, Pasquale was called in by the class to discuss the children's 'proposal' – a kind of 'mega-Disneyland' to be developed in a remote mountain locality. Pasquale doubted, sincerely, that the children, alone, had actually proposed this solution to their problems. This type of project too closely resembled typical adult sponsored projects in Italy's ailing south: huge investments for infrastructure, in poorly studied contexts, usually large profits and kick-backs for investors, politicians, and planners, several years of steady employment in the building trades for some community members, followed by unemployment and, often, obsolete and inoperative facilities at the project's conclusion. In fact, at their next meeting it became clear that a theme park was not what the children desired most – in the future or at present. Instead they requested little changes which could improve their everyday lives. To begin with, the group, particularly the young girls living in San Luca, wanted to be able to 'take a stroll together down their town's main street in the evening' ... to observe the situation in the town, and to 'end up in the beautiful hills nearby'. This seemed like an easy request, so Pasquale and the group immediately made an appointment for the following week to 'take the evening stroll'. Unfortunately, on the day of the appointment their 'stroll' had to be cancelled. That day a man from the village had been gunned down in the main piazza and the town's main street would be occupied by the funeral procession ... a far cry from the peaceful stroll the children had planned.

At the next meeting in the Bovalino school, the children with Pasquale and their teacher worked hard to overcome the shock of the previous week. It was decided to focus their attention at least for the moment on Bovalino – its coast and beaches, the open space available within the city's limits – more easily accessible during school hours. The children prepared their first scored walk (Chapter 13) to observe and document with sketches, notes, and photography their likes and dislikes in the local environment. After one hour of enthusiastic data collection in this contradictory sea-side 'resort' – congruous single- and two-storey white-washed historic buildings squashed between much taller, never completed illegal condominiums; the fine sand-duned beaches interrupted by garbage dumps, polluted streams, and unfinished, vandalized beach-front promenades and bathing facilities – tragedy again struck the group of young futurologists. While photographing a litter-filled underpass which led to the beach, three children happened upon the body of a youth of approximately 20 years, hung by his neck from a lamp post. The ashen-faced, frightened children ran to Pasquale and their teacher. The police were immediately summoned. At first, the investigators and the children believed that this was just another in the long list of mob-killings. Afterwards, it was ascertained that the youth had, instead, committed suicide.

If one reflects on these two terrible incidents, it becomes clear why it is so difficult for anyone, child or adult, to have a 'positive image of the future' in the Aspromonte region. The children's teachers, in the first instance, considered abandoning the project. However, it became clear to Pasquale and the teachers in discussions with the children that the latter did not want to give up. It was also apparent that the presence of an important national organization – the WWF – with a strong 'positive image' contributed to this decision. The children felt supported by the fact that 'outsiders' – with considerable 'clout' – valued their opinions and their local environment and believed that through concerted action something could be done. In situations as difficult as this in Aspromonte local participation is not enough; action at a community level needs to be connected to national and, if possible, international efforts.

In the weeks that followed, the children and teachers worked hard to overcome the initial setbacks. They had identified an area on the coast, not far from the site of the youth's death, and had begun to develop proposals for its future use. The site measured almost 150 square feet and included an abandoned two-storey building and a citrus tree orchard. The children decided that the site was ideal for a youth hostel – with an outdoor rest and play area which could be used by both visitors and the town's children and youth. This choice seemed to demonstrate how intelligent and perceptive children can be. The children were intuitively trying to deal with one of the major problems afflicting the area – its negative image. In essays written in class explaining their choice, the children expressed the importance of bringing young outsiders to Bovalino – to introduce them to the natural beauties of Aspromonte and allow them to 'meet its inhabitants ... to understand that we're not all criminals.' From the hostel on the coast (served by a nearby railway station), visitors could be guided on bicycle and by foot into natural areas in the nearby mountains. From discussions with Pasquale, the children had acquired an understanding of the objectives of the overall CADISPA project and appreciated the capacity of WWF-Italy to attract and organize eco-tourists from its membership and through its ample information network. In theory, the children's proposal could become operational. With information concerning the characteristics of hostels and their imagination, the children began to sketch out a plan for the site and the building. They had prepared several rough sketch proposals for the hostel and had studied a trail which could link Bovalino to the inland mountain towns of San Luca and Plati, with some pleasant stops along the way.

Unfortunately, the city administration and the port authorities prefigured a more lucrative destination for this area – commercial development and new high-rise apartments – even though this was an area already saturated by unfinished housing developments. The mayor explained that 'it was too late to change the plans'. Pasquale's presence at this meeting was important, since the politicians realized that the children's connection to a national organization (and an international project) could bring their administration 'bad press'. He promised that within a week his technical staff would identify another area which the city could assign to the children.

The date of the second meeting coincided with my visit to Aspromonte. The children's spirits were high, and I later realized that my visit had much to do with this. From their teacher and Pasquale they had learned that I was the coordinator of the nation-wide 'Futures Project' which had precedents and links with many children's groups around the world. The girls and boys took turns in describing their experiences and proposals and avidly requested my comments and evaluations. In addition, they expressed interest in hearing about other groups; they wanted to know how children had resolved problems similar to the ones they were confronting. This networking between local groups is an important motivational and learning factor.

Pasquale had perceptively suggested to the children that, while awaiting the mayor's counter-offer, they keep an eye open for suitable sites for their project. Shortly afterwards, several boys had identified an interesting locality on the hilly edge of Bovalino. The local name of the site was, fittingly, 'Adam's breast'. A map of the area had been procured and our initial observations and the descriptions from children who knew the area, seemed to indicate its suitability. The mayor expressed concern over the distance (4 km) between Adam's Breast and the city. The children's teacher explained that the children had discussed this factor and, together, had come up with the idea of requesting unlimited use of the municipal school bus (not utilized during school hours) for trips to the site. She also explained that the children, together with the school principal and Pasquale, had modified their proposal/request. Since it appeared unfeasible and costly to construct ex novo an eco-tourist hostel on the site, their request was that it be 'developed' as an 'outdoor nature laboratory of the future'. The site should be entrusted not only to their class, but to the entire school-age population of Bovalino.

Once more, at this meeting, it became clear how much influence the presence of a national organization and an international expert could bear on local politics. Our description of similar projects around Italy, our explanation of the importance of this type of approach for children's and city development, and our knowledge of available funding from elsewhere convinced the mayor that the children's project should be supported. He would present the request in the City Council. He conceded the use of the city's school bus for the next day's outing.

In the months that followed, the children, with Pasquale's help, developed the details of their project. During several outings to the site, one group documented the presence of particular, in some cases 'rare', vegetation; they noted the tracks and signs of interesting birds, and in class they prepared an annotated site plan of the existing conditions. At the same time, another group studied the best path for a dirt-bike track and traced this onto their map. A third group worked on designing the furnishings (picnic tables, litter baskets, observation points, trail markers, and information panels). Some of the 'more difficult' boys in the class even began building mock-ups and scale models of these elements with the help of some local craftspersons. The teacher integrated these activities into their official school programme. In particular, the preparation of the information panels and site plan necessitated a 'full immersion' in natural science and ecology. The aid of Pasquale and other local experts and the availability of numerous WWF-Italy publications contributed greatly. The children, with their teacher's help, also prepared a list of activities which could be offered at the site and a 'code of behaviour' – both of which would serve as a guide for other classes' use of the area. One particularly 'problem' child, who had never demonstrated interest in school activities, became the class cameraman, producing useful video documentation of every phase of the project.

In early May, WWF decided that the National Educational Television Programme of the Department of Schools and Education, which was *producing a documentary on school projects involving children in local environmental or social action, should use the Bovalino project to represent the WWF's efforts. When the mayor heard of the planned arrival (in the last week of June) of the TV crew, he made every effort to move the request through the bureaucracy before that date. The proposed TV documentary also had an unexpected catalytic effect on the project. When the programme producer insisted that footage of real environmental improvement was desired, both Pasquale and I were concerned that our programme would not qualify. The children, upon hearing this, were unimpressed since, as we then learned, they had planned to skip the usual plan – city approval–working drawings – construction procedure and go right to the realization of the site modifications. Several of the boys had already engaged their fathers, uncles, and grand-dads in the construction of benches, waste baskets, birdfeeders, birdbaths and the like. The remaining tasks, which to us adults appeared insurmountable, could, according to the children, be completed easily in one month: create a pond, stake out and mark paths, make signposts and information panels, and build a dirt-bike track.*

The teacher had been able to dedicate only a small portion of class time to the project because the children had to prepare for final exams in this period, but the children managed to finish the various aspects of their project in time for the documentary filming. In addition, they had come up with the idea of organizing a city-wide sand-castle building contest to coincide with the three days of filming. It was a brilliant inauguration for an active piece of land ... the fact that there was no water at the site did not worry them in the least! Approximately 60 children from the Bovalino elementary and middle school participated in the sand castle contest; a dirt-bike exhibition race was held; and local administrators, families and children visited the nature trails. Afterwards, a traditional dinner was prepared by the children's parents in the school gymnasium. An agreement was made with the city administration to continue the project in the following year.

The positive experiences during this year of active participation all but dissipated the internal effects of the terrible events which marked the begining of the project. An alternative site for an eventual youth hostel has been offered by a native of Bovalino (presently residing in Milan). He was so favourably impressed by the CADISPA programme and, above all, by the children's efforts that he plans to donate his villa to the children of Bovalino. Additional teachers have become interested in the programme, and a proposal was written up by the school council for the financing by the local government of a permanent environmental participation workshop in the middle school.

Environmental Management

Even more important than the research, planning, and design of environments is everyday participation in responsible environmental management. All children in all types of communities should be involved in this fundamentally important activity. The need for communities to learn how to manage their own local closed-loop, non-polluting systems of food and fuel production is most obvious in poor communities, where families spend 60 to 90 per cent of their incomes and/or working effort obtaining food and fuel. But it is no less important for the children of cultures with wasteful cycles.

There are no hard and fast rules about the age at which children should be given opportunities to manage the environment. Obviously, the range of possibilities away from home will expand gradually as the children grow older (see Figure 33 on page 90). The case studies in this chapter proceed from an example of children's management of the home environment, to the school environment, and on to the larger community environment.

From the time they can walk, children want to demonstrate their competence by participating in the everyday activities of the household. In many cultures, preschool children, especially girls, manage a high proportion of the household tasks: collecting firewood, washing dishes, sharing food preparation, and watching over and feeding other children. Often they do more than they should for their healthy development because of their parents' poverty and large households. A number of development programmes around the world have observed this and have used children as catalysts for changing their household environmental management behaviours. In the best programmes, children establish a dialogue between the household and those outside interveners, such as agricultural extension workers and health workers, who think they have some improvements to suggest. Not all programmes are interactive, however, and children are often used simply as one-way message carriers.

The following are reviews of good examples of the sensitive involvement of children with their families and communities in the management of environments from the household, to the school, to the community level.

HOUSEHOLD ENVIRONMENTAL MANAGEMENT: THE HEALTH AND HAPPINESS MOBILE CIRCUS IN THE BRAZILIAN AMAZON

The concept of primary environmental care (PEC) was introduced in Chapter 1 as the environmental extension of primary health care (PHC), which is concerned with the most fundamental aspects of health maintenance.

A primary health-care project is a natural entry point for a primary environmental care project. Some PHC projects have been gradually developing the PEC concept for some time, though not under the name; Project Saude e Alegria in Brazil is an excellent example.

Project Saude e Alegria (PSA; Health and Happiness Project) is a community health project which extends its reach into sustainable development. The project was explained to me by Magnolio, the clown,

Figure 47:
Children of the 'Health and Happiness' project in the Brazilian Amazon are involved in the management of small animals as a food resource in order to reduce hunting, and in the planting of herbs in raised beds next to their homes. © Roger Hart.

who is also the programme coordinator for cultural development and education in the city of Santarem, where the project is based. It reaches 20,000 people in 17 villages along the banks of the Amazon and the Tapajoa River, a tributary reaching the Amazon River in Santarem. The strategy is to train health volunteers in the 17 villages. At the time of the interview, there were 150 volunteers. One of the major problems with the health of the villages is that people in their most active years (20 to 40 years of age) leave for the cities, resulting in an age distribution that has an uncomfortably high number of children (20 per cent) under ten years of age.

The primary strategy for animating the community is one that is used quite commonly in Brazil: the circus. It is excellent for getting the entire community to become more aware of health and community development issues. All the professional staff and volunteers of the project become performers for the evening circuses. Each village is visited for a total of approximately 60 days per year: six visits with an average of ten days per visit. Most of these visits involve two or three people, although once a year the entire team goes to the community for four days.

A creative innovation of the PSA programme is to introduce to children the concept of environmental responsibility by teaching them how much the environment has already been transformed by human action, including their own. A major vehicle for introducing these ideas is to have the children study their own ontogenesis. By beginning with the child's own birth, animators are able to emphasize that children enter the world with a responsibility because, from their first moment, they and their families are transforming the earth. Children relive the moments of their own human history by talking with their families, beginning with their birth.

The teams have a different programme for different age groups. Workshops are given for six- to 12-year-olds on issues related mostly to household management: the care of small children, hygiene, the functioning of the human body, gardening, animal husbandry, the health values of local plant materials, and water treatment and garbage issues. Thirteen- to 18-year-olds are also trained as local reporters and in newspaper and radio production, both for their inherent educational value and as a means of establishing inter-community communication. The animators also try to get the youths involved in community projects such as planting gardens or building a community sports centre.

Through these projects, the animators try to train older pre-adolescents and teenagers to become moni-tors who will then stimulate projects themselves. Ten persons in each community are trained in health, for example, and four are trained in gardening and are responsible for seed distribution. While PSA's influence on the youth seems considerable, the programme coor-dinator responded to my questions about its impact on the establishment of village democracy by explaining that the community councils have been established, and continue to be influenced, by church missionaries, which, although they have done a lot to raise commu-nity consciousness, have not tried to involve youth in these councils.

THE CHILD-TO-CHILD PROGRAMME

The child-to-child approach is undoubtedly the most widespread means of children's participation in health care in the world. While it first developed at the University of London, at the institutes of Child Health and Education, it did so with teachers, doctors, and health-care workers from all over the world.[1] This is a rare example developed from experiences of the South of an educational concept that has spread to the North. It is built upon the observation that children play a central role in the care of their younger siblings and that traditional knowledge and health practices of villages are passed on from parent to child and from child to child. Traditional knowledge alone may be inad-equate to take care of the health problems of developing communities, but the process points the way to design successful interventions that communi-ties can manage by themselves at very low cost. The child-to-child approach is founded in the belief that

health is everyone's concern, not just that of doctors or health workers. Health, as used here, does not refer just to being well in body, but also to psychological health. From its inception, the child-to-child approach has emphasized a holistic philosophy that includes not only the family but also the larger community. Furthermore, many of the training materials produced by the Child-to-Child Trust in London, and its many derivatives around the world, deal with such environ-mental health issues as community-wide water and sanitation surveys, action programmes, and solid-waste management schemes. Primary health care in many parts of the world is already becoming primary environ-mental care.

In the child-to-child model, there are four funda-mental ways children can serve as health agents for their communities. First, older children can help younger ones. This is a responsibility already shown by young people, usually girls, all over the world. Instead of just being low-cost child-minders, children can be trained to understand their siblings' development and to know how to teach them to manage their own health. Furthermore, this training can be extended to boys as well as girls. Second, children can learn from others of the same age by doing small projects together. Such child-to-child projects are particularly common in the school setting. Third, children can pass on health messages that they have learned to the larger commu-nity. This notion of children as communicators can, unfortunately, be used easily in large-scale social mobi-lization efforts, resulting in children parroting messages in a simple-minded manner rather than in the more interactive way conceived by the child-to-child programme. The fourth way the child-to-child programme works is to have children cooperate together to create health actions with their communi-ties – the form of children's participation emphasized in this handbook.

The training materials from the Child-to-Child Trust in London stress the importance of children making their own observations and drawing their own conclu-

[1] The strength of child-to-child activities varies in different countries depending on the NGO activity there. For further informa-tion contact the Child-to-Child Trust, The Institute of Education, 20 Bedford Way, London WC1H OAL, UK.

[2] Aarons and Hawes (1979).

[3] See Smith and Plecan (1989) for an excellent school garden manual.

sions before acting with their families and communities. Regrettably, because many of the health messages that have been prepared for young children are necessarily simple, this often led adult teachers and facilitators to circumvent the more participatory goals of the programme and to teach in an unimaginative, top-down way, telling children what to do and to regurgitate 'health messages'. An inevitable consequence was that the health messages remained those of the outside agencies, losing the original intention of incorporating the traditional health knowledge of the children's home area.[2] This is a danger with any successful participation programme that attempts to 'go to scale'. The Child-to-Child Trust and other agencies developing this approach could probably help stem this tendency by avoiding such phrases as 'agents for passing on health messages' and 'young people mobilize schoolchildren'. More interactive language that stresses the knowledge of outside health experts and the collective wisdom of the community would be better – 'research', 'investigate', 'share', 'collaborate'. The

Child-to-Child Trust stresses that the approach need not be used as a special alternative programme but, rather, as a component of other programmes. To this end, it has developed individual modular activity sheets that can be easily borrowed by other programmes for specific activities.

While the child-to-child approach is used in a wide variety of settings, it is most commonly employed as an active approach to health learning in elementary schools. It has had a dramatic effect on the way health education is taught, for it contrasts markedly with the normal closed-door approach of public schools all over the world. Even when the approach misses out on the important first step of problem identification by children, it is still radically different from a traditional curriculum. It links children's school learning immediately with their activities outside school, and particularly with what they do in their homes.

Ideally, projects will involve children in a community needs diagnosis, although the authors of the training manuals realistically recognize that not all teachers or facilitators are willing or will feel competent to engage in this research type of activity. They also stress that teachers most often design health activities to fit in with a predetermined curriculum of the school or school system. Therefore, they recommend that the teacher choose for the children a project that is important, doable, and fun. They suggest that the children begin to make the project their own by understanding it well in a variety of ways. Using the example of water, they propose that the children discuss the importance of water in their daily lives, learn about why it can make them ill, learn about germs and their invisibility, read stories on the subject and retell or act them out, and perhaps discuss pictures – for instance, a scene where a boy is urinating, a cow is drinking, a woman is washing, and a girl is collecting water, all at the same pond.

The manual stresses research by children and provides good examples. For instance, for the water theme, it suggests having children talk with their neighbours about what diseases they think they can get by

Figure 48:
The Six Steps Approach of the child-to-child approach.[3]

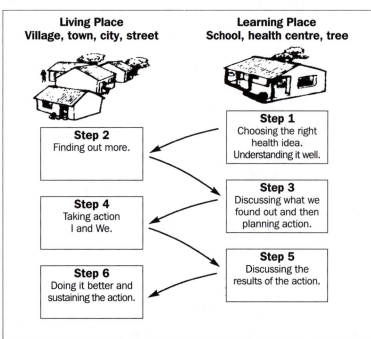

drinking dirty water, mapping out water sources in their community, investigating the sources of dirty water, checking their own homes to see how water is stored and maintained, and interviewing a health worker on the best way to get clean water into the community. In this way, the authors make it clear to teachers and facilitators that, even if it is not possible to involve children in problem identification, they should lay great stress on problem diagnosis.

The authors rightly point out that it is impossible for a person who does not know the community to suggest what child-to-child activities would be appropriate. They do, however, suggest that if the action is limited to the learning phase, as in a school clean-up campaign, the children be encouraged at least to extend programmes into the community in some way, even if it is only through an awareness drive. Their suggested activities extend all the way from teaching young children how to keep water clean by using a ladle and cover for water storage, to community water source clean-up projects, to an awareness campaign using a play to educate the community about water hygiene issues. It may be necessary during this stage to simultaneously assess people's reaction to the activities, such as by talking to the audience after a play about what they thought and learned from it, or asking their parents what the children thought of a poster they designed on the subject.

Child-to-Child stresses the need for children to engage in critical reflection on their actions. This gives them the chance to make their health messages clearer and perhaps to reinforce the message to others in certain ways so that the desired changes become a feature of everyday life rather than a short-term response to the children's programme. The authors stress that it is essential that the health messages taught at this final stage be correct and clear; wrong or unclearly modelled messages, they say, can have long-term negative effects for the children while also discrediting the programme.

THE MANAGEMENT OF SCHOOL GROUNDS

Children should have the opportunity for daily care of an environment. For many children, a family pet goes some way to providing this experience. Others may have a small home garden plot, but many parents do not allow this or do not have the resources. Schools offer an excellent opportunity for learning responsible environmental management because most children throughout the world attend them on a regular basis. Schools can establish a biodiverse landscape that can serve as a rich microcosm for children to acquire a wide range of environmental knowledge and skills. Ideally, the school will function not only as a training ground for environmental management for the children but also as a demonstration centre for the neighbourhood, beginning with the parents. The process is twofold, with children bringing home new ideas from the school in order to engage in a dialogue with their parents, and parents visiting the school to share their knowledge with children, teachers, and outside environmental agents so that they too can have a dialogue rather than a one-way transmission of information.

All over the world, the grounds surrounding schools are used primarily for children's play and recreation. In addition, many schools, particularly in the less industrialized countries, have school gardens, usually designed to provide practical education in agricultural skills. A few schools may also have a weather station for children to keep microclimatical records, but beyond these examples school grounds have rarely been used for educational purposes. With a recent growth in environmental interest and concern and the recognition of children's capacity for and interest in environmental management, many schools have begun to incorporate the outdoor environment of the school into their total approach to education. This movement has been strongest in the United Kingdom, where the British government has given it formal recognition in a variety of ways.[4]

For urban children of the Northern Hemisphere, who

[4] See Adams (1990) for a report of a large-scale study of the use, design, and management of school grounds funded by the Countryside Commission and the Department of Education and Science. Learning Through Landscapes was established in 1990 as an independent organization funded by both government and private sources. (Learning Through Landscapes, 1992; Lucas 1994). See also a study by Titman (1994) on how school grounds are viewed by children. Learning through Landscapes, 3rd Floor, Southside Offices, The Law Courts, Winchester SO23 9DL, England.

5 For further information, contact Sue Occleston or Pat King at Knowsley Health Education Resource Centre, Knowsley Community College, Rupert Road, Huyton, Merseyside L36 9TD, UK. Also see *Raised Voices*, a UNICEF film documenting children's rights issues around the world, including a report on the dog-fouling research by children in the community of Knowsley (1993).

Box 14: Case Study on Neighbourhood Health Hazard Action Research in Lancashire, England

The Knowsley Personal Social Education Team (PSE) has pioneered and adapted the child-to-child approach for use in the United Kingdom.[5] *They describe their experiences with neighbourhood health hazards researched by children in a mixed class of nine- to 11-year-olds in Knowsley, an urban community in Lancashire.*

The project began with an open discussion with the children of health hazards in the environment. Following this brainstorming, the teacher created additional visual stimuli, including pictures of cars, factories, chimneys, children in push-chairs, dogs, and so on, to enable the children to develop the discussion further in smaller groups. From these smaller groups the children developed ideas of what hazards they would like to survey in their community. The neighbourhood was divided up into sections, and small groups went out and mapped hazards. Two volunteer parents helped the teacher during this field work and throughout the length of the project. Using these mapped data, the children worked together to identify and prioritize issues that they felt were important in their community. Interest groups formed around different themes, and the children made badges to show membership in these groups. The groups then began to invite experts into the classroom for discussion, made phone calls to local council representatives, wrote letters, and collected information from books and leaflets.

One group focused on the problem of dog fouling in the community. Not only is dog excreta unpleasant to the eye and nose, it is a health hazard, especially to young children playing on the earth, in grass, and in the streets. A record was made of the number and location of mounds of excreta throughout the community. From this, the children were able to draw graphs showing the most seriously affected areas. It was clear to the children that their target group for this project was adults and that they should develop a message that made dog owners more aware of the problem and told them not to let their dogs foul the streets. In Britain, it is common for elementary schools to conduct environmental field research in relation to a number of completely different subject areas. In this case, the children designed 'pooper-scoopers' (devices for scooping up dog faeces) out of discarded plastic bottles during their science and technology class. They created posters for shops throughout the community and gave talks to adults. Adults who exercised their dogs on the school field were a particularly important target group. When dog owners were sighted on the school fields with their dogs, the children would intercept them, give them a flyer explaining the health hazard, and present them with a pooper-scooper to clean up after their dogs. At the same time, other groups of children targeted younger children and those of their own age. They designed a board game called 'Yuck' and puppets and short stories to reach these children on the dangers of dog excreta.

By thinking strategically of the target groups they wished to reach and by focusing on all the persons in their own neighbourhood, the children were able to have an impact on the problem of dog excreta in their community. This is an excellent example of how children can have a considerable impact on an issue important to their daily play lives.

Box 15: Case Study from Nicaragua

Since 1983, CISAS (Centro de Información y Servicios de Asesoría en Salud) has been promoting the child-to-child approach and methodology in Nicaragua. Annual national workshops enable children from different regions to meet and share experiences from their local community child-to-child projects. The following were recently identified by a team of children in Managua as priorities in their community: unemployment, economic problems, lack of adequate affordable schools, lack of a health centre, lack of organization in the community, dirty ditches, unclean water source, streets in need of repair, and black water in the ditches. The children were able to prioritize these and to conclude that the lack of community organization was at the heart of all the problems. As a way to begin looking at the problem of 'organization' the children decided to organize themselves and others to clear rubbish.

An excellent example of the global linking possibilities of the child-to-child approach is that a large banner created by children in Managua, with pictures drawn of some of their child-to-child activities, was sent to the children of the project described in Box 14 in Knowsley.

are increasingly restricted in their mobility by their parents' fears of traffic, crime, and negative social influences, school grounds can provide an island of safety for free exploration and play.[6] The idea is equally relevant to many children trapped in high-rise apartments of the rapidly growing cities of the South, and who commonly lack access to a toxin-free natural landscape.

School gardens and farms are already a feature of many rural areas of the South, but the emphasis often remains strictly on agricultural production skills and knowledge, rather than the school grounds serving as a resource for the total curriculum and for children's informal learning through play as well as formal learning through lessons.[7] Over the past two decades, many rural schools have extended their farming programmes into the teaching of environmental conservation practices. Some schools, like the 'New Schools' of Colombia, have also begun to involve children by analysing the best locations for certain kinds of crops and even for fish. It is but a small step further for schools to involve children in the research, transformation, and management of the entire school grounds.

An interesting aspect of the research efforts of Learning Through Landscapes has been Titman's research (1994) on the 'hidden curriculum' of school grounds. Through interviews with many children, Titman showed how children 'read' the environment. Not surprisingly, she found that children do not like the elements traditionally found in school grounds, such as tarmac, unnatural colours, lack of shelter and seating, places that are too open and boring, and dirt, pollution, or litter. They like school grounds that have different levels, trees, shady areas, wild areas, animals, and places in which to climb, hide, and explore. In short, biodiversity is valuable not only for encouraging wildlife but also for children's daily environments.[8]

The entire school population, children and staff, should be involved in the research, planning, and design of any school grounds transformations. This should be seen as a long, serious process of great educational value in itself. The school grounds need to be developed in a way that not only maximizes their value to all human users of the school, but is also a model of sustainability, guaranteeing their use by children of future generations. As an excellent example of the dangers of by-passing this stage, Bill Lucas, director of Learning Through

[6] See the special issue of *Children's Environments* on children's changing access to public spaces: 9, 2 (1992).

[7] For those schools which suffer the pressures of a traditional educational bureaucracy or doubting parents school grounds can be related not only to the study of botany and biology but also to mathematics, English, and the arts (Adams, 1990 and Lucas, 1994).

[8] See Hart (1982a, 1982b, 1993). For practical guidelines regarding wildlife in school grounds, see Learning Through Landscape Trust/Royal Society for the Protection of Birds (1992), and McKinnan and Judhee (1994).

Figure 49:
Sketch layout for
Cheetham CE
Community School,
Manchester
(Jonathan Mason,
Landscape Designer).

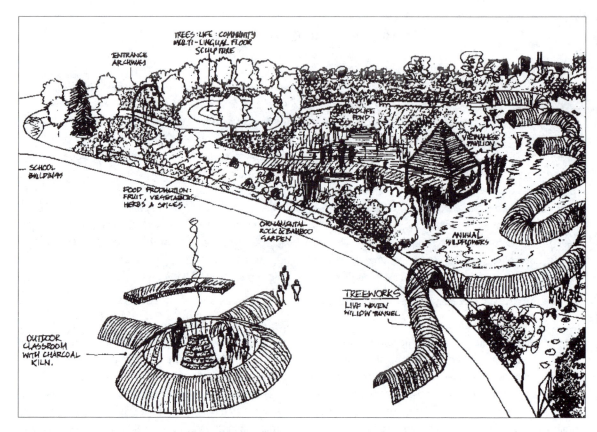

Landscapes, describes how in one school rare wildflowers were dug up so that a natural conservation area could be created! An important addendum to this chart is that there should be a final stage called 'Continuous monitoring of the site'. The monitoring of schoolyards is discussed in Chapter 8.

THE MANAGEMENT OF COMMUNITY RESOURCES BY CHILDREN

It is natural for well-managed school grounds to serve as demonstration sites for the surrounding community, and in many school gardens in rural areas of the South this has happened. But the potential for children to be involved more directly in improving the management of the surrounding community is great. Some excellent examples from South America are summarised in Boxes 16 and 17.

It may seem beyond the role of children to be responsible for the management of basic environmental resources in their communities, but examples exist. It is perhaps best to think of these as opportunities to experience such responsibility rather than as permanent positions. Colin Ward describes the example of the Pioneer Railway in Budapest, Hungary.[9] With the exception of the engine driver, this 13-mile-long narrow-gauge railway is staffed by children aged ten to 15 years. The train is used both by groups of children on field trips and by tourists, for the journey winds through beautiful wooded hills and meadows overlooking the River Danube. Apparently, there were 30 similar such ventures in the Soviet Union. Similarly, in Amsterdam in the Netherlands a restaurant is run by rotating groups of children from the schools of the city. Cooking, serving, and cleaning are all done by children,

[9] See Ward (1978).

Box 16: Case Study on Schools as Centres for Community Conservation Practices in the Peruvian Andes

For over a decade, a number of organizations have been experimenting with ways of improving the relevance of schooling to the environmental problems of the rural Andes in Peru. Initially focusing on reforestation to deal with problems of soil erosion and crop protection, the movement has recently developed a sophisticated curriculum incorporating community environmental study and participation. The larger context for this transformation of the curriculum was the inflexibility of the existing national curriculum, with its emphasis on the Spanish language and on abstract learning, divorced from the daily lives of the diverse Peruvian cultural groups, who use various Indian languages and have distinct cultural practices.

The primary issue that stimulated the incorporation of environmental learning into the school curriculum was deforestation. The steep slopes and deep valleys of the Andes present a serious challenge to farmers, who over generations, have developed a rich diversity of strategies for dealing with the dangers of soil erosion through wind and water runoff. Central to these strategies is the planting of trees. Unfortunately, the excessive cutting of trees for fuel and the importation of inappropriate foreign species of tree – notably the eucalyptus – have led to the serious deterioration of many farmlands.

The Ministry of Agriculture established the PRONOMACHS programme with a diversity of events both within and between schools to promote conservation knowledge among children and their parents. The centrepiece was an annual 'Conservation Day', when parents and children attend a festival with demonstrations and exhibitions concerning conservation. After some years with these experiments, it was concluded that children needed to be learning about environmental management in a more sustained way within their own communities. The central component of the programme that evolved was the participation of all primary schoolchildren in the production of huertas or kitchen gardens, both at school and at home. The huertas are an excellent example of how children can collaborate in environmental management from an early age.

All of the children in the PEEC (School, Ecology and Rural Community) programme have their own garden, beginning with their first year in school at the age of six.[10] In this programme they progressively learn about the diversity of crops that can be grown at the very high altitudes of their homes (some children live at a 12,000-foot elevation), the conditions needed for growth, and the nutritional

[10] Valdivia et al. (1990); Valdivia (1991).

Figure 50:
Two mountain slopes viewed from a primary school in the Andes, near Cuzco, Peru. The slopes in the foreground have been deforested and are suffering serious soil erosion. The slope on the right has benefited from a number of strategically located plantings of particular types of trees © Roger Hart.

[11] Educación Rural Andina (1993).

[12] Ward (1978).

Figure 51:
Girls at the same school in Peru, learning from a visiting parent how to build traditional housing
© Roger Hart.

desirability of different crops. Their parents are encouraged to locate a small garden at home and to bring young plants home from the propagating gardens at the school. In this way, the scene is set for children to experiment with a diversity of crops in front of their parents. Additionally, the parents are invited to help the school teacher in the garden programme at the school. In this way a modest debate is established between the children and their fathers on crops and alternative growing methods. This is not a naïve or self-righteous programme to pass on environmental information from school to children to parents in a unidirectional manner; it is recognized that the parents have a great deal of knowledge to share. In the best examples, father and child help one another, and both learn more than either knew before. In those cases where the father finds no time to assist the child with his/her own garden, he at least observes different crops and growing methods being successfully demonstrated on his own territory.

Mothers become involved via their traditional responsibility for food preparation. The programme is concerned with improving the diversity and nutritional value of food consumption in the region. Again, the learning goes in both directions. Through this programme, parents who had never even stepped into a school before find themselves teaching children, both in the classroom and in the fields. Figure 51 shows girls learning from a visiting parent how to build traditional housing.

A newly developed curriculum by Educacion Rural Andina (ERA), also in Peru, goes one step further. It recognizes that community and environmental learning is fundamentally too important to allow environmental education to be designated as a separate subject of a school curriculum.[12] As a result, a superb set of bilingual teaching and children's textbooks has been published for each of the school disciplines, building on the everyday environmental practices in the culture of the Andes. The communal biohuertos (organic gardens) at the schools include plants from which children make medicinal syrups and creams. This enables families to avoid buying foreign medicines and supplies some extra family income. Each village has a garden for children under six years of age at the Wasi Uta (children's house).

who work for a special day to produce meals for family and friends. Such experiences lie somewhere between the simulation of real-world roles in classrooms and the full responsibility of such jobs in adult society.

Children could do a great deal more than they are usually enabled to do to manage the natural environment in their communities. The community gardens found in many cities, for example, rarely involve children. City farms are also a valuable innovation in Europe, and deserve to be more generally developed in

Box 17: Case Study on Environmental Management in Hojas Anchas: a 'New School' in Colombia

The New Schools of Colombia were introduced in Chapter 3. They are an important model for review in this chapter because, rather than having special environmental projects, they make children's participation in managing the environment of the school and community integral to the basic concept of the school as a community-based centre for democratic learning. Their special qualities are best understood through the account of a single school.

I visited the Hojas Anchas school after a long ride through luxuriant mountains of Caldas, the famous coffee growing region of Colombia, with crops on every inch of land. As we drove, I noticed from time to time that children were helping their fathers spread out coffee beans to dry on the concrete patios at the side of the road alongside their homes. Knowing the flexibility of the school system in response to the working schedules of children, I expected to find a much diminished student body on my arrival. Happily, this was not the case, and most of the 115 children of the school were there to greet me. They invited me into a large classroom, where the student government and a representative from each class assembled in order to discuss the functioning of the school. As I set up my tape recorder, the 15-year-old president of the student government entered the room and, still panting, greeted me, with a gracious apology for his failure to meet me earlier. He explained in detail the work activities of his family at this time and his need to take his younger sister to the doctor for emergency treatment. This was not a schoolboy feeling guilty for being late but a responsible young adult who felt it was appropriate to explain to me his genuine regret at not being able to carry out his responsibilities. There was no prompting from any

adult supervisor. We all sat down for a long, fascinating discussion of the school, followed by a guided tour. The 'grounds' of the school seemed to be limitless, and my tour extended quite naturally out into the larger community and the hills beyond!

So well integrated is the curriculum with the life of the community that it seems as though all of it is concerned with the environment. Nevertheless, at the time of my visit to this school there were a number of environmental projects, each with its own student committee structure. These categories of projects are suggested in the students' self-guided texts, but the students explained that the particular projects emerged out of interviews with community members by the children, together with walking surveys of the entire town.

The huerta, or kitchen garden, is a common adjunct to the New Schools. Throughout the region

Figure 52:
The creative new design of the democratic community schools in Colombia, called 'New Schools', grew out of the need for the coffee growers' union to create schools that were flexible to the working schedule of children and related to their communities. Here a boy works with his father near Hojas Anchas school with their coffee bean crop.
© Roger Hart

children commonly keep small gardens at home in which a parent, usually the father, assists in preparing the bed and planting, while the mother helps with watering and harvesting. Despite these gender differences at home, the boys and girls insist that at school they all carry out the same gardening tasks. Another interesting feature of these gardens is that they are managed by all grades together, instead of separate gardens for different grades. As with all projects there is a committee, elected from all grade levels, which takes special responsibility for planning the gardens and managing the work schedule. In addition to using the food from the garden in the school restaurant, the students take produce to the market for sale. The treasurer for the garden committee handles the finances, and all the income

Figure 53: The nine-year-old president of the worm farm committee in Hojas Andean School © Roger Hart.

is used for projects in the school.

The children conduct a recycling project with the families of the entire village. While the project is overseen by the recycling committee, all children in the school participate. Recycling within the school is most sophisticated, with separation of solids and the creation of compost for the school garden in collaboration with the worm farming committee. Once per month each child collects recyclables from a number of families surrounding his or her home. The programme began with children following the education programme suggested in their self-guided workbooks: the children prepared posters to place around town and flyers to hand out to families. They then visited each family in the village to discuss the project and explain the recycling procedures. Back at the school, tin, glass, and paper are separated and sold. From the proceeds, the students pay for the administration of the project. This includes hiring an adult from the community to use a tractor to collect the non-biodegradables after they are sorted and to take them to the market in Supia, 178 kilometres from the school.

The children explained the fish farming project with great enthusiasm, for they seemed to understand clearly that they had developed a programme that had surprised both themselves and the larger community in its effectiveness as a source of income for the community and also as a way of reducing damage caused to the some of the river valleys by excessive fishing. The school is functioning very much as a test station, with children as the scientists experimenting with different altitudes for ponds and types of fish, and sharing research results with the community in order for the fish farming programme to be fully assimilated by everyone. The project is carried out in close collaboration with, and with funding from, the Junta Accion Communal (local council) of the village, and 50 per cent of the fish is made available to the community. The other 50 per cent is for school consumption – an excellent example of school and community collaboration in economic development and environmental management. The president of the fish farming committee, 14-year-old Luce Empada, explained some of the details to me as we walked. Children keep logs of the types and sizes of the fish that are caught. After five months the fish should be ready for consumption, but their size varies greatly. The critical variable is altitude, so the children were experimenting with ponds on a number of different slopes. When I asked if all this was done during class time, she explained, 'Oh no, we have to be alert with this project. The fish need to be kept fed very regularly, so we work not only after class but also on weekends.'

After discovering that the Talapia fish performed well in the first small fish pond, the students built other ponds with adult community help. The ponds higher up the slopes have not worked out well, but in the largest pond they have compared three species and again found that the Talapia performed best.

A by-product of this test has been the discovery of contamination in the ponds. The success of the students in creating clean water for this project has also benefited residents living further down the slopes. At the time of my visit the children were beginning to experiment with four different species of fish in a more distant pond.

The forest conservation project was the most ambitious of the environmental projects. The children explained that they wished to save the mountain slope next to the village by planting native species of trees. As is often the case with children's environmental projects, it was hard for me to find out where the idea had come from for this ambitious scheme. It is my sense that, while the teachers and the school's self-guided workbooks play an important catalytic role, the children become so caught up in the research phase, involving an extended diagnosis of the problem, that they truly feel ownership of the project. The children explained to me how this project poses a major challenge in educating the villagers about the problem, for they have traditionally used wood for firewood and for sale. Again, the children visited all the homes in the village to explain the project and to interview the residents about the problem. The teachers feel that the children are conscientisized about the problem through these dialogues. This concept, already introduced in Chapter 1, implies more than the word 'awareness'. Becoming aware through active dialogue with the community about the issue leads to a greater sense of ownership by the children. There is no doubt in my mind that consciensization has a much greater chance of leading to lasting environmental concern in children than does awareness. The reforestation project is still in the early stages. The children are collecting seeds from existing trees on the slope and bringing them down to the school in order to establish a nursery. The intention is to replant all the slopes with the native species in close collaboration with the adults of the community.

All of the 60 students of the upper grades of the Hojas Anchas school with whom I spoke claimed to have attended the local junta, or village government, meetings at least once. Fabiola Zapata from the seventh grade explained to me that she regularly attends and feels free to bring ideas to the meetings because she can someday imagine being on it and maybe serving as president. Similarly the junta members regularly attend meetings of all kinds at the school, including the children's elections. For example, the president of the junta sat in with the children in their meeting with me. Regrettably, such a high degree of integration between the democratic structures of the school and community is not true of most of the New Schools, but it can serve as an example of what is possible.

Figure 54:
Small, functioning
city farms offer
children the chance
to care for animals in
the heart of urban
neighbourhoods. Not
only are they enjoyed
by children as a place
to visit and be with
animals with their
friends, but they are
also managed by
children
© Roger Hart.

[13] The National
Federation of City
Farms produces a
quarterly newsletter
entitled *City Farmer*.
It is published from
The Old Vicarage, 66
Fraser Street,
Windmill Hill,
Bedminster, Bristol
B53 4LY, UK.

urban communities.[13]

A remarkable example of the management of community resources by children was provided in Chapter 4; as part of the Sarvodaya organization, children in one village were managing all of the water outlets. But while such experiences with managing the environment have obvious value for children's developing sense of competence, we cannot generally expect children to take over responsibilities for basic community environmental resources. There may, however, be a special role for children in the ongoing monitoring of environmental quality as a basis for improving community environmental awareness so that others might take action. This is considered in the following chapter.

Environmental Monitoring

Surveying can be an interesting and useful kind of research by children, at all environmental scales, from the daily records of recycling in his home kept by an eight-year-old in Westminster, Vermont (Chapter 5), through the energy monitoring of school buildings to the national surveys of ozone levels described below. Whatever the scale, it is much more engaging to a child if they are themselves involved in identifying the needs for a survey and undertaking its design. This also offers the greatest chance that the child will come to think of surveys as something they can themselves initiate in the future rather than as something always designed by others.

INVOLVING CHILDREN IN THE DEFINITION AND USE OF INDICATORS OF DEVELOPMENT AND ENVIRONMENTAL QUALITY

Research and action were described in Chapter 5 as though they were separate from environmental management. In fact, research needs to be a never-ending cyclical process. At all scales, from household to global, we need to know how the environment is changing and, particularly, how it is changing in relation to human intervention, in order to better balance development with ecological sustainability.

The idea of children's involvement in monitoring the environment is not new. In perhaps the most common example, children frequently keep regular weather records in their school – rainfall, temperature, and humidity. Teachers have found this to be a useful

strategy for teaching children to collect data and create tables and charts, for it shows them the great utility of such an exercise.

More relevant to this book's emphasis on projects designed by children is the example described in Chapter 7 of children from the fish farming committee in Colombia's Hojas Anchas school, who keep a detailed record of the number and weight of the fish in each of their experimental ponds. It is most realistic for children's ongoing monitoring efforts to be limited to the more proximate setting of their school or children's organization and to their daily living environment. But this leaves great scope for opportunity. At the building level, children can effectively monitor energy consumption or recycling efforts in their school or even in their own homes. In a fascinating action research project in Berkeley, California, third grade children (eight to nine years old) monitored their own food waste during school lunches, after first participating in the design of the research methods.[5] They found that 48 per cent of the weight of the food on children's plates was wasted, with great variation in the percentage of waste for different foods. Clearly there is great value in such research for improved management of food resources in the richer countries of the world.

MONITORING SCHOOLGROUNDS

Immediately surrounding every school there exists a wealth of opportunities to monitor the changing environment. In most instances, a school will have its own grounds, which can serve as a microcosm for intensive

[1] See Schwab, 1989.

Figure 55:
Children studying plant invasion of the exposed site in the first year after excavating the tarmac of the schoolyard, Washington Elementary School, Berkeley, California © Robin Moore.

monitoring and careful management of the environment. Unfortunately, in many cases, particularly in urban areas, school grounds look like prison yards: monotonous asphalt wastelands designed for easy maintenance, easy supervision, and easy control.

While monitoring school grounds is interesting and valuable in any school, it is particularly so when a major intervention is taking place. The dramatic example of the transformation of the grounds surrounding Washington Elementary School in Berkeley, California, was shown in photographs in Chapter 6.[2] The transition from a black asphalt yard to a green oasis with fish ponds, mature trees, and diverse wildlife provided an exciting opportunity for children to document change and to understand ecosystems by actually observing and recording them as they develop.

Before the bulldozer came in to smash the asphalt, children throughout the school were asked what they most liked about the yard as it was, what they most disliked, and what they might like to see added or changed. After two years with the asphalt removed, the land regraded, and a large open pond with dirt banks and a number of young trees and shrubs added, the children were asked to complete the survey again with the same questions. A natural invasion of plant life was already underway. Seeds that had survived beneath the asphalt somehow germinated, and the children brought found play objects and new plantings into the grounds. All these were new potential materials of interest and afforded new opportunities for play, which the children mentioned in their questionaires. An account is provided in Chapter 13 of how such surveys can be conducted by children themselves in order for them to understand the value of monitoring human use of the environment.

The teachers of the school quickly came to realize what an amazing resource they had for classroom scientific study. Strings were laid across the yard to enable the children to make detailed observations along transects, across the ecosystems. The children produced charts showing how temperatures, vegetation, and wildlife changed along the transect. Metre-square areas, again measured with string, were located along these lines so children could see how the plant and animal life differed.

With great excitement, children would report and compare what they had found in the meadow area, beside the pond, or among the trees. Bird life was observed from a mobile blind that was moved to various locations around the site.

From these studies children came to understand the intimate relationship between wildlife and the habitat. For example, in the early days of the site when a few trees had developed around a pond in the centre of the school ground, cliff swallows emerged. They dived into the pond to collect mud, which they carried to their nests beneath the eaves of the school building. As the banks of the pond developed vegetation, the mud resource disappeared, and so did the cliff swallows.

It was the lower forms of animal life that were the most accessible and regularly observable by the children. They found great pleasure and much learning opportunity at looking at the relationship between ladybirds and aphids and the seasonal changes of such animals as salamanders. Children also monitored their

Figure 56:
Monitoring water quality at the schoolyard of Washington Elementary School © Robin Moore.

own use and preferences for the environment. For example, temperatures were taken of different parts of the yard, and interviews were made by children of each other's preferences for different microclimates. From such research it was easy for teachers to build interesting lessons on such subjects as clothing in relationship to the environment and how different cultures deal with environmental differences.

Some classes of children maintained garden plots, with five or six children per plot, and kept logs of growth in their gardens each week. More interesting to the children were the monitoring of growth rates and systematic comparison of these under different conditions. In one agricultural experiment, children used soil from underneath asphalt from the school's garden beds and compost from the site in experimental seed beds in their classroom window. Beans were planted in these experimental boxes, and systematic records were kept of their growth.

While the Washington environmental yard proved an extraordinarily rich setting for children to learn the skills of environmental monitoring, it is regrettable that, as is typical of school curricula, children's monitoring records were not compared from one year to another as children moved on to a different class and a different teacher. There are few examples of such long-term monitoring by children, such as that found at the Notting Dale Urban Study Centre in London, where children from different schools have contributed to an ongoing comparative monitoring of housing and other aspects of the urban environment (Chapter 4).

COMMUNITY-BASED MONITORING IN THE PHILIPPINES

Community-based monitoring is a way of regularly monitoring the health of the community and the environment by measuring certain key physical indicators. The goal is to mobilize the entire community towards concerted action in response to any deteriorating trends that the indicators may reveal.

The Philippines has been creative in developing community-based monitoring methods with low-income communities.[3] Although to date this has not specifically involved children but, rather, volunteer adult community monitors, it is reviewed here because of the great potentials for participation by young people. Involving the community in monitoring meets a number of important objectives. First, it enables a community

[3] Ruiz (1990).

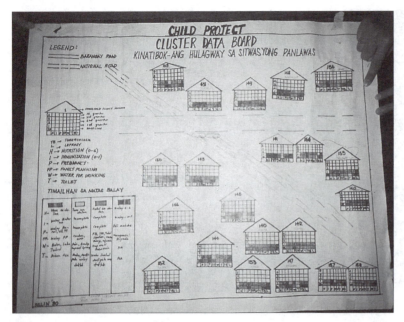

Figure 57:
Photograph of a community-based monitoring board in Little Baguio, in Olongapo, the Philippines.

minute data on every house for all residents to see. Children would greatly enjoy collecting data and mapping it on such boards (see Figure 57). This is an excellent opportunity for schoolteachers to engage children in a valuable ongoing role for their communities which has great benefits for schoolwork in literacy, mathematics, and map skills.

The successful operation of community-based monitoring in the Philippines is built on a neighbourhood clustering approach. Each neighbourhood cluster includes 15 to 25 families, who elect a leader to represent their interests in the larger community organization. This model could easily be repeated with schoolchildren. Small groups of children from distinct neighbourhoods throughout the community could become the experts for their neighbourhood cluster and even take responsibility for establishing a community-based monitoring board among their own small cluster of houses. The radical idea here is that of making the research process continuously visible to the community.

Determining what indicators a community needs to use to assess its development should be an effort involving the whole community. Where no community research, planning, and evaluation process has been established, children can, with a little help, develop their own monitoring system as a first step in convincing the community of the value of this kind of research. The critical step is for children to understand that they first need to determine what they wish to assess and then creatively identify indicators that will accurately reflect that phenomenon. Brainstorming indicators in a group and then trimming them down to a reasonable number of realistic indicators would be a fascinating exercise for schoolchildren of any age. For example, six-year-olds might decide that they wanted to improve the bird population of their school grounds. They might decide from this to count the number and variety of birds seen from the school window throughout a season. After making simple picture charts they might decide to see if they could intervene to improve the number and variety by building bird feeders. They could

to assess its interventions sensitively using indicators that the community thinks are appropriate. Also, because the research monitoring process is visible to the eyes of the entire community, there is less likelihood of error in data collection.

Furthermore, the visibility of the project increases the community's comprehension of the development goals and thereby leads to a greater mobilization of residents. Because the data from community-based monitoring are made constantly visible to the community, the periodic flow of information has the value of raising people's awareness of changes and giving them a sense that their fellow citizens are acting to do something about these changes. Ruiz states that, in community organizing, a high level of consciousness and a strong sense of belonging to a project are the two necessary elements in mobilizing collective action for change.[4]

An excellent example of community-based monitoring can be seen in the extremely poor neighbourhood of Little Baguio on the steep slopes of Olongapo in the Philippines. In the centre is a large, well-designed community-based monitoring board, with up-to-the-

[4] Ruiz (1990).

Box 18: Indicators for Community-based Monitoring Developed by Residents in Neighbourhoods of Olongapo, Pasay, and Davao in the Philippines

Health and Nutrition
  No. of children aged 0–12 months
  No. of fully immunized children
  No. of preschool children aged 0–6 years
  No. of malnourished children (2nd & 3rd)
  No. of malnourished children given food supplements
  No. of of preschool children aged 0–5 years
  No. of children aged 0–5 years with growth-monitoring charts
  No. of pregnant women
  No. of mothers given TT1–TT5
  No. of mothers breastfeeding
  No. of mothers attending mothers' classes

Water and Environmental Sanitation
  No. of families with sanitary toilets
  No. of families with safe water supply

Education
  No. of preschool children aged 3–5 years
  No. of children aged 3–5 years enrolled in DCC

Family Planning
  No. of mothers availing themselves of family planning methods

Income-Generating Project
  No. of mothers given seed capital
  Type of project
  Amount of loan

Street and Urban Working Children
  No. of street children
  No. of street children availing themselves of educational assistance
  No. of street children attending seminar/socio-cultural activities

Housing and Land Tenure
  No. of families owning a house
  No. of families owning a lot

From Ruiz (1990).

---

then monitor the effects of their intervention. Box 18 shows the categories that were developed by the residents of three cities in the Philippines for their urban neighbourhoods. Many of these are questions that children in the upper half of an elementary school could easily collect from their own families and their immediate neighbours.

Looking at Box 18, it is clear how a community can simply make an assessment of its situation as a basis for community action and how children can play a role. For example, in the realm of sanitation, they need only compare indicators 12 and 13 with the total number of families to determine whether a considerable number of families have no access to sanitary toilet facilities (indicator 12) and safe drinking water (indicator 13). As a next step, the children could map these data to determine a strategic location for any water or sanitation projects to facilitate availability to all families.

An even simpler example of community-based monitoring comes from the Programme of Working Children (PMT) in Ecuador. The children of Guayaquil produced excellent maps of garbage in their communities for this project, but these were seen by only a few adults. Had the data been mapped on very large

[5] Wildlife Watch (1992). For further information write to Wildlife Watch, The Wildlife Trusts, The Green, Witham Park, Waterside South, Lincoln LN5 7JR, UK.

Figure 58:
A map of garbage created by children of the Programme of Working Children (PMT) in a neighbourhood of Guayaquil, Ecuador
© Roger Hart.

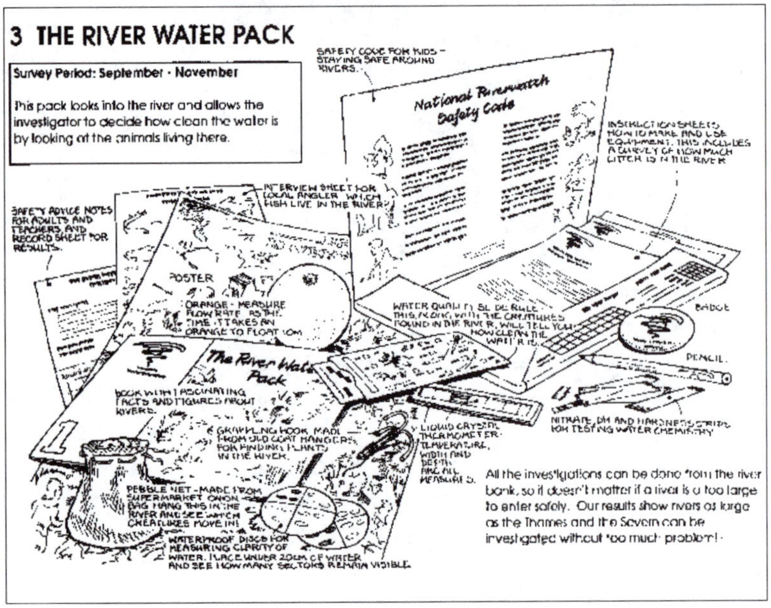

Figure 59:
The River Water Pack: illustration taken from the River Report published by Wildlife Watch, 1991.

outdoor community maps, and had they been kept up to date by the children, this would have provided a superb basis for environmental awareness efforts and political action within the community (see Figure 58).

To be truly effective, the monitoring efforts of the children need to be combined with the serious decision-making efforts of adult community members. The likelihood of this happening will vary greatly from culture to culture and community to community. Nevertheless, children and others can clearly see the benefits of monitoring if it is made visually accessible to the community. Even if adults initially fail to use it in their planning efforts, some will see what the children have done and will begin to appreciate it and come to understand that geography, mathematics, and language arts can be part of highly relevant activities for community development.

NATIONAL SURVEYS WITH ENVIRONMENTAL ORGANIZATIONS

The values of involving children in surveys were described in Chapter 3. If the information is fed back to the surveyors, this can be a valuable learning experience and a meaningful opportunity for children to participate as well as a strategy for obtaining valuable scientific data. Wildlife Watch, one of the largest environmental clubs for children in the United Kingdom, recently completed an ambitious project on water quality called the National Riverwatch, with sponsorship from a national power company and the National River Authority.[5]

As with all of the Wildlife Watch surveys, volunteers received an impressive pack of survey materials, which can be used by older children alone or by children with parents or teachers (see Figure 59). In addition to the survey instruments, the pack includes information on how the data collected can be used locally and what can be done at home and in the community about water problems. Precise instructions were provided about site selection, and the results were recorded on computer-readable data forms. Bulletins with findings were produced at regular intervals and were sent to all those who had taken part in the project. The results compared well with the scientific findings of the National River Authority's own surveys, but because National River Watch was able to involve such vast numbers of people across the country, the programme was able to improve greatly the nation's understanding of its water quality. In order to help with public under-standing of the project, staff at the local branches of the Wildlife Trusts throughout the country, together with volunteers, were available as a support network.

A particularly creative project designed by Wildlife Watch was the Watch Ozone Project.[6] The pack mailed to participants included seeds of two varieties of *Nicotiana tobaccum*, popularly known as the tobacco plant. One of these plants is particularly sensitive to ozone and becomes spotted when ozone is only a little above the normal background level experienced in the

Figure 60:
Children pond dipping with Chris Baines of Wildlife Watch
© Roger Hart.

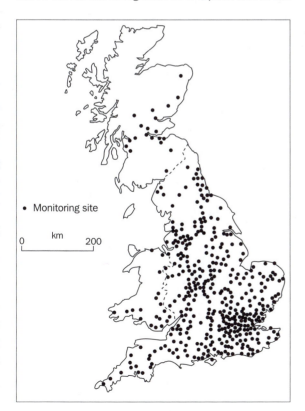

• Monitoring site

0 km 200

SPOTTING DENSITY CARD

Choose the damage category below which best describes the percentage of the leaf's surface which is covered by spots. Please choose only one of the seven categories for each leaf.

Category 1
0 spots

Category 2
1-3% spots

Category 3
4-10% spots

Category 4
11-25% spots

Category 5
26-50% spots

Category 6
51-75% spots

Category 7
DEAD!!

Figure 61:
The Wildlife Watch Ozone Monitoring Project in the United Kingdom: the spotting density card used by children to determine ozone levels by regularly monitoring the leaves of the nicotiana plants in their homes and a map showing the monitoring sites at children's homes

[6] Wildlife Watch (1992).

UK. The other is much less sensitive and begins to spot only when ozone reaches high levels. By having the participants use both plants, the project designers had a control; if the leaves on both plants spotted rapidly together, they could assume that something else was causing the spotting, such as a disease or pest attack. Participants used spotting density cards that were included in the pack to record damage once a week over a three-week period. These forms were then returned to the office of the national headquarters. Again, the project results compared well with official national scientific data, and showed that wide variations in ozone levels can occur both within and between regions of the United Kingdom. This led to the conclusion that, if the nation wishes to have a complete picture of ground level ozone, the government will need to set up more ozone-monitoring stations than currently exist. Clearly, ozone is a phenomenon that requires study over many years in order to make any useful predictions about trends, but again, this survey revealed the value of public participation and children's ability to be involved.

Children can also be involved in global monitoring of the environment. An example of this, coordinated by the US federal government with children from more than 90 nations, is described in Chapter 10. Such experiences can certainly be valuable for children's academic learning regarding scientific data but cannot satisfy the goals of including children in problem definition and the application of research to the environmental planning and management of their local communities. Children's involvement in international monitoring projects should build upon a base of local experiences with problem diagnosis.

Public Awareness and Political Action by Children

It was argued in Chapter 1 that environmental education, if honestly conducted, is inherently political. Involving children in action research is even more obviously so. Learning to deal with the political system within which one lives should of course be a basic component of all school programmes, but it is not. This is another major reason why children's community participation programmes are so valuable. The nature and extent to which one can involve children in political actions will vary enormously depending on the culture and political system. In the USA, for example, public awareness and political action seem to have become the most common types of environmental action by children.[1] Whatever the culture, children's involvement in political action should grow out of their own developing understanding of a phenomenon. At the current time, children in the USA have become noisy proponents of many policy positions on the environment, often with information which has not been critically digested by them and rarely with any direct experience with the subject. Not surprisingly, conservative politicians sometimes suspect liberal politics and media of manipulating children. Thus, there is a great danger in the USA that the genuine democratic nature of children's participation will come to be seen by the public as manipulative, or at best superficial, rather than the very essence of democratization and preparation for citizenship, as proposed in this book.

CAMPAIGNS

It is particularly risky to involve children in political campaigns. In many democratic systems political opinion is swayed by large-scale turn-outs, and children are a readily available 'army' of concern that can be easily seduced into involvement in a movement which is really not 'their own'. The measure of 'ownership', again, is the extent to which children have had access to information and to opportunities for dialogue with alternative perspectives. Ideally, children's involvement in a political campaign will emerge quite naturally out of their own research. Martin Francis, a primary school teacher in London, offers the following example:

'The Council decided to close the baths, which included a swimming pool, laundry and slipper baths, claiming that the structure was dangerous. Opponents claimed that this was an excuse, a small expenditure would make the baths safe, and the site was earmarked for development. Immediate savings and lucrative development prospects in the future were claimed as the real reason for closure. There was a big campaign in which many children took part when they realized their leisure time and school swimming was at risk. We discussed the issue at school, basing it on evidence from local newspapers and the broadsheet prepared by the S.O.B. (Save Our Baths) campaign. We did some role-playing in which pensioners and children took on the cost-cutting councillor. The children got really interested and we spent an art lesson making Save Our Baths posters, and a

[1] To exemplify how different the thinking is in the USA from most other countries, the second page of the 'warm-ups' chapter of a book for young political activists tells them how they should obtain records of US congressional committee hearings as a way of getting a larger understanding of specific issues they are working on (Schaetzel and Lesko 1992).

language lesson writing open letters to the council, arguing the case for saving the baths. We went on to discuss how these posters could be used usefully and decided to take them down to the baths for the workers to use. They were displayed outside the building when the baths were eventually occupied, by local people.

As background to this work, we investigated how many houses in the area were without baths, how many households had to share baths with others and we also looked at how expensive launderettes are in comparison with the council laundry.

All of this was an exciting and educative experience for the children. The occupation was eventually ended – a new pool has been built by the council, but it looks as though the slipper baths and the laundry have been lost. We paid a sad farewell visit to the baths when it was being demolished, and when the council's plans for a shopping complex on the site had been announced! (Francis 1982)

PUBLIC DEMONSTRATIONS

Demonstrations are a subset of 'campaigns', and so again one should beware of the manipulation of children. Children should be encouraged to parade and shout about only those things which they personally believe to be true. To do anything other than this is to prepare them for the kind of unthinking totalitarianism which is the antithesis of democratic participation. In the Sociedade Beneficente do Calabar, a non-formal school in Salvador de Bahia, Brazil, children and teenagers occasionally initiate their own projects. For example, adolescents recently started a demonstration about police harassment. The police were harassing them whenever they were looking for scapegoats, so the adolescents complained. First they discussed this problem and the problem of violence against them in school. Then they marched all over the community, dressed in white, gathering people. Following this 'peace march' around the rich community, they had a meeting with the police chief. As a result of this action, the

community managed to get its own police post in a trailer right inside the community, with full-time police staffing. A debate was held with everyone in the community about the location of the police post and the duties of the policemen, with children and teenagers centrally involved in the decision.

CONFERENCES

Conferences can be used at certain stages in a larger programme of research, planning, and action by children, but they are reviewed in this chapter because they are usually designed as awareness-raising events or, more specifically, are related to political action on the environment.

Children in Adult Conferences

For many adults, 'children's participation' conjures up an image of one or two well-groomed, verbally competent children sitting on a panel at a conference. The common result of such events is applause from the adults, who find the presentations cute and probably take a lot of photographs and even write newspaper articles about the event. No one is likely to give any of the children's ideas serious consideration. Nor should they, for these events are rarely well-prepared democratic attempts for children to represent the views of their peers. Conferences are simply the kind of thing that is done when people feel they ought to bring children into a project. More and more agencies feel the need these days to involve children in conferences, particularly when the subject of the conference is children. Furthermore, children's involvement in these events is commonly a last-minute affair that is not well thought out. The usual result is highly articulate and even moving testimony that has not emerged from the perspectives of any group of children but, rather, with a high degree of collaboration with the adults who are controlling the event. With such participation it is unlikely that any truly unique perspective will emerge from the children's commentaries. Even if it were, most of the adults would not believe it to be a representative statement, and the children themselves would know that it was not. Consequently, despite the flashing cameras, the thunderous applause, and the tears, the children's voices will have no substantial impact on the outcome of the conference. It is best thought of as a kind of therapy for the adult audience, a token event. But this need not be so.

The typical conference is not ideal for adult participation and is particularly ill-suited to pre-adolescent children. Meeting with people for extended periods of time and using words as the primary medium of communication may work for some articulate teenagers, but it is not an optimum structure for the participation of most young people, particularly pre-adolescents.

For most purposes, it is safe to use the guideline that, if children have not yet been involved in an environmental project of their own or have not thoroughly discussed environmental issues before a conference, they are not likely to feel that they have something useful to say to a larger audience and should not be asked to do so. Even when children are involved in environmental projects, adults commonly fail to have these children choose their own conference representatives. They are put on panels and are introduced as representatives of 'children' in general, with no discussion of how they were chosen or of which other children's voices they are supposed to be representing. This is classical tokenism to an adult audience, not genuine participation, no matter how moving their words.[2]

Educational or Skills Training Conferences

Some conferences are designed for young people to learn how to organize or act for the improvement of their own lives or the lives of others. This kind of conference is more suitable for older children and teenagers, who wish to seek out specific information and skills training and who find verbal presentations and workshops an appropriate format for learning. A good example of this is the annual 'We Have the Force'

conference organized by the New York City Youth Force for teenagers. The following is a title of a workshop from a recent conference:

'I Call This Place my Neighbourhood, You Call This Place a Slum!'
Examine why certain communities get dumped on more than others with sewage treatment, incinerators, lead poisoning, and other environmental hazards found most often in low-income neighbourhoods. Find out how you can stop environmental racism in your neighbourhood.

Children's Conferences

Conferences by and for children can be a valuable part of an ongoing programme of children's participation. When they are designed as single events, however, without building on current work with children and with no plans for genuine follow-up, then one should be suspicious of their value and intent. There are a number of possible reasons for holding a conference with children. It is good to be clear about them and to make them explicit to all participants when they are first invited to be involved.

Representativeness

If the conference is truly meant to include the perspectives of children, then it needs to specify clearly which children's perspectives are to be represented and, from this, how to go about selecting representatives of these children. At a minimum, it must be a process that everyone understands. If it is truly billed as a children's conference or hearing, children should elect their own representatives, but this is rarely the case. At best, conferences are self-selective; that is, children hear about a conference and apply. In these cases, at least, the children themselves volunteer, but of course it is the highly educated and well-to-do children who tend to hear about these events and can afford to travel to them.

More often, it is adults who select children to send to conferences. They may say they want to give chil-

[2] There are, of course, exceptions, as when children are making a personal account in order to provide testimony, such as a child who lives near a toxic-waste site describing to a government council on how it affected her life.

[3] The most dramatic example was the involvement of street children in the drafting of the Brazilian Constitution. At the local project level, all participating children met to discuss the draft. Some of the children then took part in state- and regional-level meetings where delegates were selected to go on to the Second National Congress. A total of 700 children came from all over Brazil, with child observers from ten other Latin American countries. The Second National Congress of Street Children in 1990 was a momentous occasion, not only for the 700 street children from Brazil and over 4,000 local child participants, but also for the politicians.

dren a voice, but they choose which children, which voices! There are many ways for the children to select from among their own ranks. One is for all the children to prepare questions they think are important to be addressed at the conference and to then compare and contrast each person's set of questions, so that the children as a whole select the person they think has the set of most relevant questions. Children may even wish to select their representatives arbitrarily through a random lottery. Whatever system is used, it is important that it is done by the children themselves and that these representatives understand that they are speaking for the larger group of children. The child representatives should be expected to report back in some form or other to the groups they represent. Again, this is an aspect of children's participation in conferences that, sadly, is not normally addressed.

In designing a community conference, children should be drawn from all of the existing children's and youth groups in that community. The age range can be wide, up to 18 years old – the upper limit of the definition of children according to the UN Convention on the Rights of the Child. Having a wide range of ages promises the possibility of much richer discussion, including some debate across the age groups themselves and between children and adults.

Fortunately, there are some valuable exceptions concerning the democratic representation of children at conferences. It is interesting that street and working children, who are commonly thought of by the public as lawless individuals, offer the best examples.[3] In the annual National Philippines Street and Working Children's Congresses, children, who have been elected by their peers in associations of street and working children at the local level and then at the island or regional level, come together to meet in Manila, the capital. For a week, children use skits, puppet shows, and song to tell one another about the problems they face in their daily lives and in their communities. Out of these performances, children discuss commonalties and identify problems that they would like to bring to the attention

of the national press and congress.

An example of a similarly democratic conference, but focused on the environment, is offered in Box 19. The first Conference of the Children and Youth of the Ecuadorian Amazon was organized in 1993 as part of the environmental programme of the National Programme of Working Children in Ecuador (PMT). Box 19 gives an excerpt from a report of the PMT Amazon Children's Conference which illustrates well some of the important principles in designing conferences for pre-adolescent children: representativeness; continuity with real environmental projects in the children's home communities; advance preparation for the children so they understand the goals of the conference and come prepared with relevant information from their own communities; opportunities for the children to generate meaningful information during the conference and a plan of action emerging from the conference with subsequent steps for them to take.

From schools and 'alternative spaces' in each of the 32 municipalities of the Amazon region, the children elected two representatives to attend the regional conference.

Continuity with a Larger Programme or Goal

Often, conferences are organized as single events with little relationship to ongoing projects in the environment and with little or no follow-up.

Organizers commonly feel the need to produce policy documents out of a conference, but there is seldom any real audience for these documents. To produce an 'action plan', with no realistic conception of who could carry out the actions or who might incorporate these actions into their own policy statement, is a waste of time. If children put together recommendations and afterwards learn that there is no one to listen to them, the exercise may actually discourage future interest in such participation. Conferences should either be thought of as part of a larger process for young people's participation, or they should not be carried out at all.

Box 19: The First Amazon Children's Conference on the Environment

In the early stages of the programme for children of the Amazon region, a conference was designed for a number of reasons: to motivate the children to study and write about their own local environment, to gain serious commitments from political leaders of the municipalities, and to serve as a demonstration and training experience for the volunteer adults of the 'alternative spaces', the centres for working children.

Low-cost workbooks were designed and distributed with pictures for children to colour in and questions for them to answer through investigation in their own communities. The goal was to have children observe their community, ask questions of the knowledgeable community residents, and reflect critically on their environment before attending the conference. In this way, the elected representatives were able to bring to the conference not only their own knowledge but also that of their peers, their communities, and the many senior residents who were interviewed by their peers.

The methodology used during the summit was designed to recognize great regional differences as well as differences in the backgrounds and knowledge of the citizens. The Amazonian region is a social mosaic including peasant farmers in an environment that they do not yet fully know; urban migrants with serious environmental and service problems; and natives from nine different ethnic groups with their own languages and cultures. For this reason, the meeting was designed as an interethnic and intercultural encounter, with exchanges of experiences and knowledge that could foster a feeling of regional belonging in the children.

It was further intended to confront the Amazonian children with their region's past, re-encountering their history and their geography. To achieve that, the oral character of the traditional cultures of the Amazon needed to be rescued. The children heard from a Secoya shaman, Don Cesario, about all the forest's secrets – the importance of each leaf, each animal – the history of their people, and their gods. The shaman encouraged the conferees to discover a new dimension of time and magic in the jungle. Doña Rebeca, a traditional Quechua pottery maker, also shared her wisdom with the children by demonstrating her ability to mould clay and, through her art, transmit the history and the mythology of their people. Finally, they heard the testimony and experiences of the earlier colonizers of the region, who revealed the long process of getting to know and adapt to the jungle.

With this information, the children re-created the past of the Amazon through drawings, stories, and dramatizations. Later, they made a great leap into the present. They used information about their own community, which they had brought to the conference, to elaborate a regional map that revealed the present situation of the environment in the Amazon. There were discussions about the contamination of rivers by oil, wastes, and mercury; about the lack of basic services in the cities; about the traffic in wild species; and about deforestation. For the first time, the children of the five Amazonian provinces had made their own environmental diagnosis. In a third phase, their task was to dream, to imagine how they wanted the Amazonian region to be, to think of desirable scenarios for a better life. From this they made an enormous collective mural over ten metres long, a dream come true in the form of a collage using flowers, seeds, branches, and leaves from the local forest.

The results of the meeting included a proclamation, signed by the president of the Consortium of Amazonian Municipalities with the children, as a commitment to improve the region's environmental conditions (see Figure 58, p. 138); the creation of environmental commissions in each of the municipal councils that would include participation from the PMT children's group of that town; an analysis of the ecological problems in the five Amazonian provinces, elaborated by the participants and leading to specific concrete action proposals; reforestation with native species; nurseries and small gardens with medicinal and ornamental plants; and educational campaigns to clean the cities and 'adopt' a river. Above all, a qualitative change was achieved in the children's perception of the Amazon region – a re-evaluation of the elders' knowledge of traditional ways of living with nature and a discovery of the possibilities of establishing a harmonic relationship with their own environment. This process, individually and collectively, will surely make the 75 children who participated into catalysts of environmental change among their peers and parents, and later into adult motors of change.

Source: Extracted from Espinosa (1994).

Alternative Media of Communication

The most obvious medium for children to use when working together with each other and with adults is the spoken word. Even when adults genuinely require the participation of children in a project, they often do not know how to go beyond the traditional adult battery of methods – conferences, panel presentations, group discussions, interviews. None of these methods should be dogmatically rejected, but it is important to recognize not only that children are commonly less sophisticated and less comfortable with speaking than adults, but panel presentations, conferences, and group discussions are not their familiar ways of working with one another. It is important to think of methods that will maximize the freedom of children of different ages and abilities to feel comfortable in exploring and expressing their own ideas. A major solution to this problem is to use other media, along with language, from the very first meeting with children. A number of alternatives are discussed in Chapter 11.

CHILDREN'S HEARINGS

As people have begun to understand the need to listen to the voices of children and youth, a new kind of event has emerged. Children's hearings involve panels or groups of children posing questions to adult panels. Some television channels in North America have recognized the value of such hearings for informing the public about youth's perspectives on pressing issues of the time, or after momentous events. After the 1992 riots in Los Angeles, for example, young people were given a national television audience in prime viewing time to talk about their concerns.

Children's hearings have been developed in Europe in the last few years as an effective alternative to some of the problems with conferences described above. Hearings are better than resolutions or letter writing because they offer the opportunity for a genuine dialogue between children and politicians. The primary characteristics that distinguish children's hearings from adult conferences with children is that the agenda is determined by children with questions that they consider to be important, thereby avoiding the common tendency of adult conferences to control the contents of the event and to patronize children and belittle their ideas. The balance of power is equalized by giving children a chance to present their views and having politicians respond with questions and comments.

The Voice of the Children organization has been active in developing hearings such as at the World Environmental Summit in Rio de Janeiro.[3] As already discussed in the 'Conferences' section, such national and international events often pose problems in terms of children's representation, travel costs, and the like. Nevertheless, these events can be effective in reaching many people through the mass media, but they suffer

[3] Voice of the Children, Norwegian People's Aid, PO Box 8844 Youngstorget, 0028 Oslo, Norway.

readily from tokenism. Their major value very often seems to be the high media profile they offer to politicians. A greater potential for children's hearings lies at the community level. Children can not only speak on issues about which they are personally well informed, but they can also, after the hearings, observe and challenge the subsequent behaviour of politicians.

The Organization of Children's Hearings

Some of the principles described for conferences are relevant to hearings for children. Additional principles are taken from a publication entitled Voice of the Children, produced by a consortium of the World Wide Fund for Nature, Save the Children, and UNICEF UK.[5]

Goals for the Hearing

The hearing should have a clear aim or a minimal set of aims. For example, the first hearing in the United Kingdom, which was held in Banbury, had the following aims:

1) to provide young people with the opportunity to discuss their own key issues
2) to provide a platform from which children could air those issues, causing the greatest concern to adults in positions of power or responsibility
3) to provide a learning experience for younger people and adults together
4) to produce a children's charter (i.e. a formal statement prepared by children clearly outlining their priorities for change).

Choosing the Adult Panel

The fundamental idea of a children's hearing is that carefully selected adults, representing the adult community, which should be responsive to children, are placed in a position of listening and responding to the questions of children. The Voice of the Children UK recommends that they be people who are influential in some way – members of parliament, local newspaper editors, local disability rights officers, religious leaders, police officers, representatives of educational authorities, environmentalists, managers of local industries. In addition, it may be important for children to consider one or two people who are particularly aware of children's needs and who may be more sensitive in responding. Even though these people may not themselves be in positions of power or great influence, they may, by responding to children's questions at the hearing, have a voice that would be important with the press and the larger public. The UK Voice of the Children booklet also advises that the panel be balanced in representation in terms of gender, culture, and social class. This requirement seems to be in conflict with the requirement that the panelists be influential – a conflict that can be an important topic of discussion for the children as they go through the difficult process of selecting the panelists.

Planning the Hearing

In the UK, the Voice of the Children has found it is necessary to allow at least three or four months to plan a hearing. One of the major reasons is to schedule the influential people who will be invited. Also, it is necessary for the children to be well prepared for this event. Some of the questions that need to be addressed in planning are as follows:

1) Who will be invited and how many can be expected to attend?
2) Will there be special invitations to the press, and will they be given special priority in seating?
3) Will a video or audio recording be made of the event, and for what purpose?
4) Will there be a panel of young children facing the adult panel, or will children from all the representative groups in the audience be allowed to address the adult panel as they wish?

The Questions

One of the advantages of having a specific panel of

[5] Save the Children (1993). UNICEF-UK/Save the Children (1990). The idea of local hearings focused specifically on the environment has since been developed by Earth Force. See also Nottingham Youth Environment Forum (1994).

children address the adult panel is that they can have sifted through a larger set of questions from the many children in the audience, and from others who may not even be represented in the audience, and can prepare these in some kind of organized sequence. Second, this approach leaves some opportunity for the spontaneous development of questions back and forth between the child panel and adult panel that would be difficult to achieve between an adult panel and a large audience of children.

Whichever strategy is used, the children who will be asking the questions should have thought about them and, ideally, discussed them among themselves well before the day of the event.

Chairing the Hearing

The Voice of the Children UK publication stresses the need to select a good chairperson. The implication is that this chair should be an adult, although I see no reason why a self-confident teenager could not handle the task. In addition to the normal chairperson tasks of making sure that things happen in a timely way and that everyone is given a chance to speak, there is a special role here of conferring a seriousness on the event by making sure that the adults do not respond in a patronizing way or otherwise act in a manner that does not give centrality to the children's questions.

ENCOUNTERS WITH POLITICIANS AND PUBLIC OFFICIALS

Numerous allusions have been made throughout this book to the dangers of tokenism, decoration, and manipulation in the contact of children with public figures, but, while there is a need to be wary of the enormous media value of children to politicians, there can be great value in children being able to meet elected officials and government agency representatives. Again, the key is honesty. The goal for the children should not be an attractive public relations or media event but an opportunity for them to express their carefully considered opinions or research or to discuss

particular community issues with a representative of the government while also learning something about the political process. If the children find that they are not taken seriously they will need help to place this within some larger context of society and political process rather than to be demoralized from their own experience. This critical awareness should also make them more effective in developing future encounters with politicians and government officials, whether as children or as adults. Here are a few examples of the ways children around the world have been contacting elected officials:

Letters

Learning to write letters when there is a reasonable hope that they will get a response from a politician is a useful way for children to enter personally into a dialogue with political decision-making. While the letters should truly be written by children, some guidance about the style is useful, such as how to structure the sequence of the ideas, how not to cloud the letter with too many overlapping concerns, how to express what groups of children they represent and where the ideas for their proposal came from, and most of all reminding them to enclose a return address!

Site Visits to Children's Projects

Children's environmental projects offer a great photo opportunity to politicians. There is of course also a benefit for the children of receiving affirmation from an elected official of the value of their work while the cameras flash. But this alone is not enough. If planned well, site visits offer children an excellent opportunity to engage in a serious dialogue with public officials, perhaps about an expansion or continuation of the project they are working on, in a setting where they feel confident because of their expertise.

Resolutions or Proclamations

The Programme of Working Children (PMT) in Ecuador makes great use of resolutions as a way of children relating to politicians. These are an effective means of taking children's voices seriously and replacing smiles and vague promises with a statement prepared with children which is clear to all – a great improvement over the normal patronizing relationship. The resolutions are presented to the mayor of the municipality with considerable pomp and a large presence of the press. Although the resolutions have no legal binding, they do capture a lot of media attention and put the politician on record with regard to community development and environmental issues. While they satisfy the politician's need for public attention, they also provide the children with a tool which they can use in subsequently reminding officials of their commitment to a cause. In combination with an active, independent press, this can be an effective strategy for children's participation in the municipal political process. Similarly, children of the Street and Working Children's Congress of the Philippines produce a proclamation at the close of their annual national conference which is presented to the National Congress. Again, these recommendations can be ignored by the politician, but at least the national press attention enables children's proposals to enter into the national policy debate, and on a number of occasions it has enabled new issues to be brought to the government and acted upon.

PUBLIC PRESENTATIONS

The most satisfying and effective kind of public and political awareness comes when children present their own work to an attentive audience. From the many good examples of survey research of the Environment and School Initiatives Project of OECD is one involving 13- and 14-year-old students in the Austrian Tyrol.[6] The students designed a questionnaire to study household energy use and then worked in pairs to collaborate with the residents of four villages to complete the data. Almost 70 per cent of the households filled in the questionnaire, making the results useful for comparison at both the household and the community level. A public meeting enabled the overall findings and recommenda-

Figure 62:
Don Cesario Piaguage with his son José, who is learning to be a Shaman, translating for him at the Amazonian Children's Conference organized by the Programme of Working Children (PMT).

tions to be fully communicated and also allowed the children to serve individual residents. Residents were able to see their own household data comparatively and, if they requested it, they were given individualized proposals for energy saving.

Examples were offered in Chapter 6 and under the discussion of local government in Chapter 4 of how effective children can be in creating plans and designs for public spaces and presenting these in public forums as a stimulus for wider debate. The example was also offered from Harlem, New York, of taking designs onto the street as a way of involving those residents who, for a variety of reasons, might not attend public meetings: the feeling that their voice would not be heard, a feeling of intimidation by those more articulate than themselves, or perhaps because they do not believe the meetings are about anything relevant to them or are just a lot of talk. By reaching out into their community in this kind of way, children can further the democratic involvement of adults as well as children.

Warnings have been given about involving the news media too soon, but a public presentation is one good time to bring them in. They can be a useful ally if

[6] Summarized in Posch (1994), p. 61–2.

handled well. They need to be prepared for the event with background material on all that the children have produced. In this way, even if the decision makers at the event are patronizing with the children's presenta-tions, the press will be able to report to the public the validity of their work rather than reinforce the normal hypocritical response to children's public presentations: applause mixed with disdain.

From Local to Global through Linking and Networks

CHAPTER
10

In Europe and North America the dominant mode of involvement for children in environmental issues is through national or international programmes exhorting them to 'save the whales' or change household consumption or recycle. I have argued that this type of massive top-down effort will not alone bring about the kind of radical reorientation of people to their own communities that is necessary for sustainable development. These large-scale programmes do sometimes help children see the connection between their small actions and global issues, but they commonly lack a critical thinking component. Whatever the merits of large-scale mobilization efforts, they do not allow for the emphasis described in this book on children as the primary constructors of their knowledge through their own research, reflection, and action. In their devotion to a single cause they are necessary top-down projects. A major challenge is for us to find ways for children to engage in locally defined research and action while also being part of global efforts.

EXCHANGE OR LINKING PROJECTS

An excellent and straightforward strategy for enabling those who are working on local projects to see their relationship to a larger regional or global situation is to have children simply exchange their learning on a regular basis with children from a very different environment. This approach is variously called exchange, linking, or twinning. It offers valuable opportunities for children to make observations and discuss similarities and differences in their own lives, their communities, and their environments, and of the development and environmental problems their communities face.

In many places, experiments with children's environmental exchanges use electronic technology, which speeds up the exchange. But one should beware of the seductive quality of such technology. It is critical that children begin with environmental issues in their local environment and that they identify these issues themselves. Also, the use of electronic technology should not obscure the importance of the multimedia nature of the exchange. Drawings, charts, photos, tape cassettes, puppets, games, and artefacts collected from their environment, not just words, should be exchanged. Finally, many of the communities we need to support in these tasks do not even have pencils and paper, let alone electronic technology.

The twinning of communities is a common phenomenon between towns and cities around the world, but most of this has been done only in the Northern Hemisphere. As part of the 'development education' movement in certain countries, classes of children have begun corresponding with one another across the Equator. Rather than learning of the problems of children in the South, as in the early days of development education, the approach now involves a genuine exchange of perspectives. Much of what follows is extracted from the work of School Links International[1] and the UK's One World Linking Association, (UKOWLA) both based in the UK. The principles of these two catalyzing and coordinating

[1] Beddes and Mares (1988); UKOWLA (1993). As with all environmental education projects in the UK at this time, there is much emphasis on how such interdisciplinary study connects to all the different subjects of the National Curriculum at each age level. In all countries this is an important question for schoolteachers and these publications might prove valuable.

[2] Hart and Perez (1981).

organizations are supplemented with reflections on my own work in organizing environmental exchange projects between city and rural children in the states of the northeastern USA.[2]

The linking approach has been limited largely to school projects, although the approach has equal merits for out-of-school programmes. Because the fundamental core of the linkage programmes emphasizes language skills, the approach has received great support from foreign-language teachers, who recognize its motivational value. Inevitably, many of the projects include an important environmental component, although it appears that the primary emphasis of linking or exchange projects is cultural awareness with a goal of counteracting prejudice and developing sympathetic attitudes towards people of other cultures with different ways of life. For example, in the United States, most linkage projects in the 1990s were between children in the USA and the former Soviet Union.

This account of linking will be limited to situations where children are already engaged in serious local research or action projects of the kind described in this book. When they are so engaged, children are most comfortable in writing to other children with pride about what they are doing and their own knowledge of their community. In those instances where the problem identification phase is carried out simultaneously in a pair of twinned communities, it is even possible for the children to decide to work on some of the same problems so that their research can be comparative.

Initiating a Linking Programme

At present, no international organization has taken upon itself to serve as a clearing-house for facilitators and teachers to obtain addresses of programmes and schools that would be interested in exchanging their work with another country. There are linkage organizations in one or two industrialized countries, but generally the linkages are established through informal networks of personal contacts rather through any official channels. The best recommendation, then, is to contact an NGO that is internationally linked, ideally one with an environmental focus. Such an NGO can serve as a speedy courier of the children's materials and may even be able to facilitate direct exchanges of children and staff from the two sites.

Some Important Principles

Although the linkage will be from programme to programme, it is also best for individual children to pair up in a 'pen-pal' exchange.

The first exchange of letters between children should be a spontaneous expression of themselves, their families, their own interests, and their priorities. We have found it extremely valuable for the children, on their first exchange, to present a drawn image of their own environment and an imagined drawing of the environment of the child with whom they are corresponding, together with an extended annotation explaining the drawing and its content. These drawings are very effective in revealing the remarkable stereotypes children often have of environments and cultural practices, and provide a superb basis for revealing to children how much they can learn from one another through correspondence.

Given the inevitable delay in correspondence, particularly when exchanges extend across the Equator, it is important that project work be sent frequently. It is frustrating for children to have long intervals before receiving responses to their own letters. Every opportunity should be taken to use non-government organizations and friends who may be visiting the other country to serve as couriers of the children's material. Use of a fax machine enables some materials to be communicated instantly, and allows them to inform their 'twins' that a package has been mailed, thereby obviating most of the frustration the children feel when relying totally upon mail.

One way of dealing with the frustration of delay in mail is for the children to link with more than one group at a time. By selecting children from a very different environment, but in their own country, as well as an international link, children can be assured of regular interaction of other children with their research. This kind of triple exchange is, of course, complex and is likely to be achieved only in a regular classroom situation where a teacher works daily with the same children.

Issues arising from differences in degrees of literacy in different countries should be discussed in pre-exchanges between teachers or facilitators before the children are involved. If a real problem is anticipated, because of dealing with children's second language or with inferior writing abilities in their own language, then one should find an appropriate medium of communication. The storyboard method, described in Chapter 11, is particularly well suited to dealing with this problem. School Links International has used tape recordings rather than written language in exchanges between Sweden and England. While the Swedish children felt comfortable speaking English, they were not always confident of their writing skills. Their tapes were linked to slides. An interesting by-product of this exchange project was that English-speaking children, who generally lack a practical motive to learn another language, enjoyed listening to tapes in the foreign language and began to try to recognize and repeat words from their corresponding partners.

Photographs, like drawings, are extremely useful, as described in Chapter 11. Children can annotate photographs in ways that express their preferences and desires for change. In poorer countries access to cameras and film may be a problem. Children in the industrialized countries have sometimes found ways to work with adults in their community to send cameras and film to their overseas partners. Rather than being a patronizing act of charity, this is a gesture that emerges out of their own desire to communicate, and the benefit is mutual.

The greatest barrier to school involvement in linking projects is teachers' fear that they will not be able to satisfy their regular curriculum if they spend too much time on an unrelated project, no matter how valuable. The solution is to build the exchange around the curriculum. If a teacher sits down for half an hour or an hour per week planning with an experienced environmental colleague it is possible to relate every part of their curriculum to local research and the corresponding exchange of that research.

It is important that children in the two groups be of approximately the same age in order to guarantee a parallel exchange of ideas.

When finances allow, correspondence exchange projects should lead to direct visits to one another's environments. The social class differences between the children involved in such exchanges should be carefully considered. There is a danger that great differences in the material wealth of children in the link can disturb the exchange, and such differences should become a matter for dialogue, not an issue of unequal power between the children. It is too easy for a project between poor and rich children in one country or between poor children in the Southern Hemisphere and rich children in the Northern Hemisphere to promote traditional benefactor/recipient relationships with a patronizing or paternalistic attitude on the part of the better-off children. Such problems should be anticipated so that they can be faced head on and not become the core of the exchange relationship. One example will suffice.

After working successfully with the exchange of 16 classes between children from New York City and children from the rural states of New Hampshire and Vermont, we were asked by a school in New England if they could join in the project.[3] We explained that we had no funds to pay for bus trips for the children to visit one another, but the rural middle-class New England community assured us that this was no problem. The result was a one-way exchange whereby low-income city children visited the New England town and stayed in private homes in the community. In contrast to our other exchange projects, where low-income children in each state stayed in dormitories and visited one another on an equal basis, this one-way exchange had an uncomfortable, patronizing quality.

[3] Hart and Perez (1981).

[4] Bennett (1993).

There are merits to having the first twinning experience be with children who do not live too far away as a kind of warm-up to an international exchange. Local twinning enables the children to receive a response to their correspondence fairly quickly. While it is possible to carry out twinning projects with children as young as six years of age, it is a good idea to have a more local link for young children, given the long international postal delays. Second, in ideal circumstances, it allows the children to visit one another at some point. This can be a powerful form of motivation. A third factor is the lower cost of correspondence when the twinning is local or regional.

Maintaining the Success of the Project

Another factor affecting the success of a project is the extent to which reliable correspondence can be established. Many projects begin with great enthusiasm but collapse after the children are sorely disappointed not to receive answers to their letters. The best solution is to address the problems of inadequate funding early on and, if necessary, for the richer country to pay for correspondence to permit a frequent exchange between the two countries. Facilitators or teachers should talk at length before a project begins to determine that they have some common aims and objectives and understand the different circumstances of one another's schools so that there are no big shocks further down the road.

For the first year of the project it is important that there be support for a teacher who has not done this kind of exchange before, otherwise they may feel a sense of isolation while waiting for correspondence and worry about the frustrations of the children. It is particularly valuable for teachers or facilitators who are working on such innovative projects to have the opportunity to meet one another to clarify the aims and methods of their project, to share experiences and frustrations, and to find solutions to practical problems.

The Norton School, a high school in Cleveland in the industrial northeast of England, had been frustrated by the inability to communicate rapidly through electronic technology with its twin school, the Lenana School in Nairobi, Kenya.[4] Finally, the Norton School sent money to Lenana to help the school purchase a computer. Mr Maneno, the Lenana principal, responded to the gift from England by explaining that he 'could not justify spending that kind of money on something that as of yet had no established place in his school curriculum, whereas the trees which the boys had planted in the school compound as part of their agricultural practice were dying through lack of water!' As a result, the money from Norton was spent on a pipeline to the garden. Communication was improved instead through the use of a fax machine at a post office in Nairobi, although this is not very close to the school.

An exchange of schoolteachers has enabled the two schools to understand each other and what resources they have to offer. While the United Kingdom had better school supplies, books, and electronic technology, Nairobi had ample land and a good stock of gardening equipment. This enables the school to focus on the kinds of environmental learning that are most relevant to the problems of this community: serious soil erosion, water supply, and fuel shortages. The priorities for work on their land are related to their survival, and this is very important for the children of the Norton School to understand. The English children will improve their four acres of rough land, previously belonging to the British Rail Authority, for wildlife and as a leisure amenity and a place of beauty for residents who live in this old industrial area.

ENVIRONMENTAL NETWORKS

Environmental networks are another way of helping children go beyond their local research and action by linking them with other parallel local efforts. Adolescents who have already been involved in their own research projects, including problem identification, can usefully be engaged in larger scientific studies, collecting the same kinds of data as young people in

Box 20: Case Study on an Urban–Rural Exchange Project in the USA

In a demonstration project with schools in New York, New Jersey, and the New England states, children living in dramatically different communities corresponded with one another for a year about their research on the environment of their community. The experiment, involving grades 4 through 8 (ages 9 to 14), served as a focus for teachers to integrate all subjects of the school curriculum. Only modest in-service support, in the form of weekly visits by graduate student environmental interns, was required to help the teachers see how to meet some of their particular curriculum goals through the project.

In the first exchange of letters about each other and about their respective environments, stereotypes were shattered. Then, in each classroom, local environmental study sites were identified by the children themselves through their own experiences and through interviews with community residents. These sites were locations that were slated to change or that the children thought should be changed. The children then spent the year studying these sites, projecting alternative futures for them, and assessing the positive and negative social and environmental impacts of their proposals. Each class created a book of their own as well as one of their twin community's study site through the correspondence. At the end of the year they visited their twin communities with enough background to tour the sites and have informed discussions without adult mediation. The classes also made presentations to community residents, environmental planners, community leaders, and local political representatives. These discussions did not often lead to physical changes. More important, through dialogue with adults, children came to understand the environmental decision-making process in their own community and the role they may play in the future. From such projects the most important changes occur in the minds of the children and in their increased sense of caring for their community.

Figure 63: Drawings and annotations from children of Harlem, New York City and Vermont, New England, before their exchange correspondences, showing their stereotyped images of one another's environments. © Roger Hart.

Figure 64: Children of Junior High School 117 in Harlem preparing materials for the regular exchange of correspondence with their peers in the small town of Reads-boro, Vermont. On the wall behind them is one of the many contributions mailed from the Vermont children: a detailed drawing of buildings on their main street. © Roger Hart.

[5] Williams, Bidlack, and Brinson (1994). For further information, contact the Rivers Curriculum Project, Southern Illinois University at Edwardsville, Box 2222, Edwardsville, IL 62026, USA. Similar water quality monitoring projects have been developed all over the world with young people. See Stapp and Mitchell (1995).

Box 21: Case Study on the Rivers Curriculum Project

The Rivers Curriculum Project began as a pilot river-sampling programme in eight high schools along the Mississippi and the lower Illinois rivers in the USA.[5] The project grew beyond water monitoring to include poetry, creative writing, songs, folklore, artwork, and research into the rivers' social and economic history, and of course it has inspired a great deal of activism on water quality by students. High schools which choose to join the Rivers Project send an interdisciplinary team of science, social studies, and English teachers to a training session, where they learn how to collect data and to use the project's computer network. Students conduct nine kinds of water-quality tests. They also collect small insects and aquatic animals as indicators of the water's quality as a habitat. The data are transformed into a water quality index and entered on the electronic network. Students can then share data with students from other schools as well as transmit data to a national centre run by the US Fish and Wildlife Service.

What distinguishes this project from others in this book is its regional networking quality, which allows children to collaborate with one another over great distances on a project of scientific and human importance. The children were able to be pioneers in tracking the spread of the zebra mussel. This animal, introduced into North American waters in 1985, *reproduces itself so quickly and attaches itself so thickly to pipes, boats, and the habitat of native mussels that it poses an ecological and economic threat. By mapping data on the zebra mussel, children have been able to watch river history in the making and to help control the spread of a troublesome invader.*

Each spring, children are able to meet their peers from different schools throughout the region at an annual student congress. In the 1993 congress more than 500 students from 52 schools in three states made 90 presentations concerning rivers. The presentations ranged from scientific reports and exhibits to slide shows of local history, original music, plays, puppet shows, and readings.

There have been many examples of spontaneous activism in the schools. Students from Jerseyville High School in Illinois, for example, found a level of faecal coliform in a nearby local creek which was unsafe for swimming and body contact by children playing in the creek. Through an intense campaign of letter writing, attending public meetings, further investigating the history of the city's sewage programmes, developing a specific survey on the issue, and working with journalists they have been able to motivate the town to search for finance for a new sewage system.

other locales and sharing it with them. This is where electronic communication can really make a difference in children's research and action. But no matter how good an electronic or any other kind of network actually is, its value will still depend on the quality and relevance of the data being transferred. While there is great excitement in the USA over the importance of electronic networking for children's environmental initiatives, it does not yet appear to be inspiring children to identify their own community issues and collect their own data. Networking needs to be linked to serious work by children on the ground as in the case study in Box 21.

6 The GLOBE Program, 744 Jackson Place, Washington, DC 20503. Email: info@globe.gov

Box 22: Case Study on Global Learning and Observations to Benefit the Environment (GLOBE)

For years, many schoolchildren in the industrialized nations have been electronically connected to global environmental databases for extreme geophysical events (earthquakes, volcanoes, hurricanes, etc.) in order to map out data as a learning exercise in schools. It is of much greater interest, however, for children to collect as well as map global data. In 1995 the National Oceanic and Atmospheric Administration of the US federal government embarked on an ambitious global programme to involve children from over 90 nations in environmental monitoring with scientists in a worldwide network. The students report their data to a GLOBE processing centre, receive and use global images created from their own data, and study related environmental topics.[6] The children are provided with scientific instruments for this research and all participating schools have a personal computer with the capacity to be linked to the GLOBE processing centre through an Internet telephone connection.

Measurements are taken in atmospheres (climate), water chemistry, biology, and geology. For children from kindergarten through fifth grade (five to 11 years old) the programme initially involves measuring maximum and minimum air temperature, precipitation and cloud cover, water temperature,

and the acidity level of precipitation. In the biology and geology domain they record biometrics, identify species, and document land cover. Older children (12–18 years of age), using more advanced equipment, note the acidity levels of precipitation, soil moisture, and phenology or seasonal change, and make accurate records of the site locations at which their physical measurements are taken.

This programme offers an exciting opportunity for children to become involved in an important scientific research endeavour and to make a rare link between global and local research. Its three goals are: 1) to enhance the environmental awareness of individuals worldwide, 2) to increase scientific understanding of the earth, and 3) to help all students reach higher levels of understanding in science and mathematics. It is not yet clear how the programme designers intend the children to work with their local environment and community. The programme, ideally, would guide teachers and children in the use of the local data by the local community, and would also encourage children to identify and collect other data that may be useful to their community or subregion but may not be part of the global monitoring goals of the US federal government.

PART
3
METHODS

Introduction

Many of the methods described below are relevant to each of the chapters of Part II: environmental research, planning, design management, education, and political action. To avoid duplication, the different applications of each method to these different domains are described here together. Additional published resources are referred to in footnotes.[1] No attempt has been made here to discuss the many approaches to 'warm up' that can increase the proportion of children who might be made to feel comfortable to participate in any session and improve the functioning of the group as a whole. This is because there are so many of these methods and their appropriateness varies so much according to culture that the reader is encouraged to refer to a local source. Much emphasis is given in this section to visual methods, for they can so dramatically improve the degree of community participation by people of all ages.[2] Nevertheless, most of the growing literature on methodologies for participation ignores children.[3]

© Ray Lorenzo.

[1] Some books offering different approaches and methods for children's participation are Brobze and Brown (1993); Scanlan (1978); Schaetzel Lesko (1992); Hopkins and Winters (1990); Fleisher (1993); Nelson (1977, 1984).

[2] The International Institute for Environment and Development in London publishes a valuable Participatory Methodology Series. Contact the International Institute for Environment and Development, 3 Endsleigh Street, London WC1H 0DD, UK.

[3] A valuable recent exception is a study of participatory rural appraisal in Uganda. See Guijt et al. (1995).

CHAPTER 11

Drawings and Collages

[1] Some methodological guides to the use of visual methods with adults are also relevant to work with children. In particular, see Bradley (1995) and UNICEF Bangladesh (1993).

[2] Adams (1982); Scoffham (1980).

[3] Nelson (1995).

The medium that first comes to the minds of most adults for allowing young children to express themselves is that of drawing. It is familiar, enjoyable for most young children, and inexpensive.[1] But drawing has its pitfalls. Some of them are reviewed here, together with some alternative forms of collective visual expression that enable all children to be involved.

INDIVIDUAL DRAWINGS

Some problems with drawing as a method stem from the fact that it is a medium used so frequently by children. They may employ stereotyped images that relate to what they have learned to draw, which in turn is often an expression of a limited range of objects emphasized by the particular culture or subculture (e.g. for an English child, a stereotypical house with four windows, a door, a path, smoke from a chimney, some flowers, and a sun).

Another problem is that most children have had a history of adults pretending to be interested in their drawings while actually paying only token attention to their content. Unless special efforts are made by the adult facilitator, children sometimes do not consider this medium a serious opportunity to express their ideas. Furthermore, children who have been in school for a few years commonly conclude that they have no artistic talent and begin to feel intimidated when asked to draw.

Properly introduced, however, drawing can be used effectively as a warm-up exercise for children under ten, or as a stimulus for further discussion or expression. It is also valuable as a method for getting children to become aware of the visual qualities of the environment and of possibilities for improvement.[2] But projects using their drawings as the primary method of giving children a voice should be viewed with suspicion, for this leaves a great deal of room for the pre-emption of children's ideas by adult interpreters. An exhibition of children's art, for example, would have greater legitimacy as part of a more interactive communication with children or if it were designed with children and included commentaries or guides by them.

Ideally, one should try to maximize free expression at the beginning of an activity by using a medium which is readily available so that children feel free to make 'mistakes'. This may be a problem in poor communities, though chalkboards and slates are realistic alternatives to pens and paper. Later, drawings may be made using better quality, more expensive materials. If the activity reminds children of school drawing exercises, your serious interest may help them believe in its importance.

STORYBOARDS

Most children are very familiar with comics. For young children with restricted writing abilities, the use of a sequence of annotated drawings (called 'storyboards' by the film industry) offers great potential (see Figure 65). While children in the early school years are limited in their capacity to construct and especially to communicate concepts, from as young as the age of three children can describe 'scripts' of common events in their lives.[3] It is possible for preschool children to use this method to communicate with one another or with adults as soon as they can draw on events in pictures. All one needs to do is provide them with a sequence of open boxes on a sheet of paper and one or two examples of storyboards previously produced by other children.

With the youngest children, it is also necessary to offer oneself as an annotator of their drawings. Children who have difficulty writing often gladly accept this assistance, for, rather than taking away from the significance of their own work, it adds to it as long as one simply writes what they tell in a slavelike fashion. This method can be a very useful way of convincing children that you take what they have to say very seriously. If you attend to them word by word and enable them to complete a storyboard, they are able to exhibit it proudly, use it in a publication with their peers, or mail it to children in another community.

To make a collective statement during a project, children can first make individual storyboards and then be led to select elements from each storyboard to create a collective script. Inevitably, one of the 'artists' of the group will become the final executor of this collective storyboard, but as long as the artist is responding to the instructions of the group and using the details which the group wishes to express, this seems to be a satisfactory collective solution.

COLLECTIVE DRAWING

This is an excellent 'warm-up' activity for any group, but it also has the potential of being a central technique in allowing a group to move towards a unified expression of its desires. Again, the material resources are inexpensive: a piece of cardboard or large sheet of thick paper or canvas on a wall, and paint or markers. Each participant can make some kind of graphic addition to the whole. The subject of the creative expression can either be left open, stressing its warm-up nature, or it can be focused. Stanley King, an architect from Vancouver, British Columbia, has been extremely successful in using giant wall drawings for 'design-ins' involving people of all ages.

Figure 65:
The use of the storyboard method by a group of eight- and nine-year-olds from the Earth School in Manhattan, New York, to describe how their garden was developed (reprinted with permission from Zuzu, a young people's newspaper produced in New York City).

COLLAGE MAKING[4]

Drawings, especially after several years of schooling, are generally less spontaneous or original than the collage approach. In collage, images are often chosen by intuition or pleasure with colour and forms. Collage making seems to increase the visualizing capabilities. Also, the possibility of contrasts of scale – for example, a sheep as large as a public housing tower – can have symbolic and metaphoric potential that children often do not feel free to express in drawing. A mixture of expressive forms – photos, colours, words, and drawings – is almost always richer in content than only one means of expression. Children who do not usually write can create word collages elaborated from letters that they cut out of magazines. Finally, collage making is more easily done in a group than are drawings. Thus, the process of choosing images, cutting, pasting, and positioning can contribute to the goal of collaborative work.

[4] Multi-media collage making has been used successfully as a technique with children aged seven to 11 in a large number of Futures projects in Italy, the United Kingdom, and the USA by Ray Lorenzo, and the guidelines in this section have been prepared by him.

Figure 66:
Children in Red Hook,
Brooklyn, New York,
making a collage.
© Ray Lorenzo.

The collage made in 'reality' (a photograph of a neighbourhood) is not an abstraction. It is an engaging tool for enabling children to reveal their own interpretations of the meaning of places, structures, and situations, to identify neighbourhood problems and resources, or to evoke ideas and proposals for neighbourhood change. It often concretizes the desire to transform a specific site or elicits the evaluation of the site in a stronger manner than neighbourhood drawings.

For collage making, the following materials are suggested: a wide array of sources of images (colour magazines, comic books, unwanted brochures, reports, photographs, photocopies of pictures of the neighbourhood, newspapers); fine and wide-tip coloured markers; coloured washes (watercolours); scissors; glue (glue sticks are more expensive, but cleaner); and loose 3D parts (industrial remnants – plastic, wood, glitter, cloth pieces, leather pieces, etc.) that are relatively flat. Readers can contribute their own ideas for expanding the visual potential of the project.

Several questions have been raised about the range of types of magazines used in the collage-making process. In a multicultural/multiracial context such as New York City, the magazines often do not represent the types of people, in terms of race, sex, or class, with whom the children identify; the children have often thus not selected images of this type or have been turned off the activity entirely. It remains an issue as to whether one should look for specific publications (e.g. women in non-traditional roles) or whether the children should discover the absence of certain images from the mass media and transform the media themselves.

There is also a problem of sexism or violence in magazine images. The solution is to try to make a range of images available and let the activity become part of a critical evaluation on the part of the children. In the best instances, children have transformed the images through colouring faces or collaging heads from other places, such as their own photos and so on.

If possible, environmental magazines – natural history, wildlife, architecture, and landscape magazines – should be made available as sources of collage materials. These items expand the range of possible available environmental ideas beyond what one usually finds in the mass media, but they should not be the only source. They should be supplemented with an array of non-expert built environments. Travel brochures are one possibility.

DRAWINGS ON SLIDES

Young children are also able to make drawings for presentation in slide/tape shows. Technical requirements are modest, especially if the visuals are made by drawing directly onto blank film in slide mounts. Alternatively, black film, similarly mounted, can be scratched on with a pin. This is a low-cost method of introducing children to media production. Equipment requirements are a light table, slide projector, and cassette tape recorder – much less costly than the equipment needed for video production. Ideally, of course, these shows also include photographic slides, discussed later.

Mapping and Modelling

Mapping is a basic method in all ecological research because maps provide the means of expressing spatially the relationship of organisms to their habitat, or living environment. This is as true for mapping children's worlds as it is for describing the habitat of baboons or spotted owls. Mapping is also a method that children, including non-literate children, greatly enjoy using, as long as it is introduced in an unintimidating way with appropriate materials.[1] Twenty years ago I had all the children aged between four and ten in a small New England town build for me, individually, a model of their own known world, which they then transformed into a map.[2] When I meet them today, as adults, they spontaneously recall the importance of that event, even remembering elements they forgot to express in their maps!

Whether or not a community map exists, there is great value in having children begin a project by making their own map. This is a fascinating task that will give each participant a personal basis for arguing what should be shown on a collective community base map. The ability of a child to draw maps varies greatly according to their age and culture, but as long as you are accepting of very different styles and degrees of ability, most children over five will enjoy the activity and will produce some elements that can subsequently be included on the collective community base map. Figure 67 summarizes children's intellectual development and their map-making and map-using abilities.[3]

CHILD-MADE MAPS

For children under about eight years of age, it is best to allow them first to build a model of the places they know well using wooden blocks, cardboard cutout houses and roads, and moss to serve as trees and bushes. Only after they have finished do I mention the word 'map', because sometimes this can intimidate them. In fact, all four-year-old children I have worked with are able to produce a recognizable map in this way.[4] This can be done in the dirt or in sand, but at some point should be executed on paper so that the children can trace around their models, create symbols for them, and make a legend or key. The models are then removed, leaving behind their first map!

Making a map may initially intimidate children who have had little or no schooling with paper and pencil, but, once they begin, it is clear to them how much they know of their environment. The method can be particularly liberating for non-literate children, for it enables them to reveal to themselves and others that they have knowledge. Thus empowered through this informal method, they will be more likely to believe that they have other knowledge worthy of expression. The method can provide valuable insight for others into children's everyday environment because it is based on features that they consider important, and hence can lead to good discussion about aspects of their lives that might not so easily emerge in words.

For most children over about eight years of age, you can provide a large sheet of paper (at least 0.5 metres square) and a pencil with an eraser. Unless children have

[1] For an excellent introduction to mapping with young children, see the classic book by Sprague-Mitchell (1934).

[2] Hart (1978).

[3] For further understanding of th development of children's understanding of spatial relationships and the use of maps see Hart and Moore (1976), Hart (1978), and Liben and Downs (1986 and 1992).

[4] Hart (1978).

Figure 67:
The development of children's capacity to make and use maps.

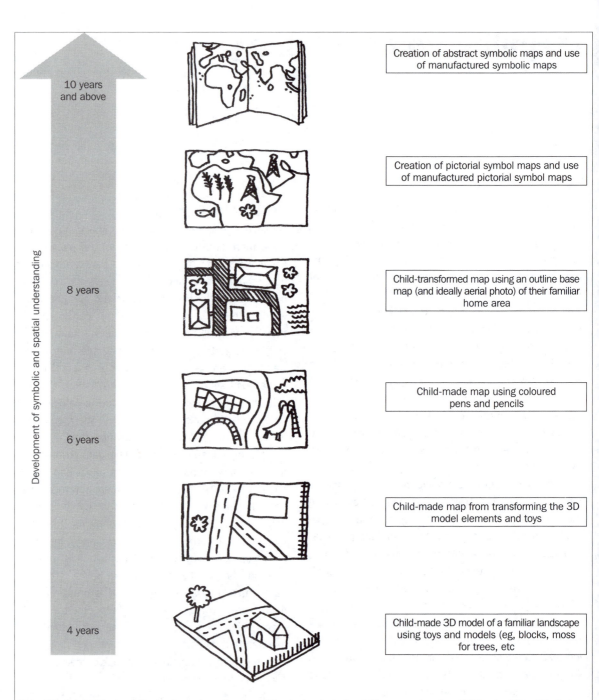

Development of symbolic and spatial understanding

10 years and above — Creation of abstract symbolic maps and use of manufactured symbolic maps

Creation of pictorial symbol maps and use of manufactured pictorial symbol maps

8 years — Child-transformed map using an outline base map (and ideally aerial photo) of their familiar home area

Child-made map using coloured pens and pencils

6 years — Child-made map from transforming the 3D model elements and toys

4 years — Child-made 3D model of a familiar landscape using toys and models (eg, blocks, moss for trees, etc

Note: This is a highly generalised scheme based upon children's developing cognitive competencies. Children's skills will in fact vary greatly depending upon their degree of experience with maps and with the particular media and map symbol conventions used by their culture.

Figure 68:
Building miniature worlds in their play with toys, milk cartons, dirt, sand or sticks and stones is common for children all over the world. It is a small step to build on this in order to introduce mapping to children as young as four years of age (Hart, 1978).
© Roger Hart.

had experience with map drawing, their initial attempts will be tentative. They will wish to make frequent changes, and mistakes are frustrating. After the major elements of the map are drawn, you can suggest that they go over the pencil lines with coloured pens.

Once having mastered mapping it can be used as a tool for environmental projects at all scales, from sampling square metre experimental agricultural plots to making a plan of a garden to the layout of a re-afforestation plan.[5]

MAPPING PERSONAL WORLDS

For children who will be making maps for community research purposes, personal maps are useful as a first step. For children living in difficult circumstances, who need to investigate more and act upon the conditions of their own life, such 'personal worlds' maps are fundamental. By mapping their use and evaluation of their daily environment, they can build a more ecological account of their world than if this information were collected by adults though an interview. In the case of street and working children, for example, such a map will include their social supports, activities, workplaces, and sleeping and eating places.

For children living or working on the streets, mapping is a useful way to express the history and current status of the spatial characteristics of their social world. Some of the problems in children's lives will relate directly to the spatial properties of this data, such as prohibitive transportation distances between home and workplace. Other spatial problems may be less obvious until one takes a close look at the maps with a child – for example, the conclusion that children are working in locations with the highest concentrations of carbon monoxide.

The materials required are few and simple: a map

[5] Wentworth et al (1976) is a very valuable resource for working with children.

Figure 69:
Children drawing a grid on their school-yard in Harlem, New York City, which they used in order to map the daily patterns of shade on the yard. This enabled them to design the locations of the planting areas. © Roger Hart.

of the entire area children use in order to locate all the places visited, and coloured pencils and pens. For children who work on the street, this may mean a map of a whole city. If possible, it is good for children to use a camera to photograph the most significant people, places, and activities to glue onto the map.

Children enjoy this method, which can be extended over a number of sessions on different days to enable them to reflect more upon their daily environment during their work and play and to bring this additional information back to record on their maps. It provides much more valid accounts of the children's environments than is possible through traditional interview techniques. It is a liberating method, for each child is in the position of being a leader. This is the opposite of most interviews, where the investigator has the ques-

tions and hence controls the exchange. The method is particularly useful for children who are illiterate, since it enables them to express efficiently much that would otherwise go unrecorded.

MAKING A COMMUNITY BASE MAP

A basic tool for any community development or environmental project is a base map of the community. Ideally, this should be large enough to enable the children to identify their own homes. If the community has no such map, often there will be one in the hands of a government agency for water, sanitation, housing, or city planning that can be updated and have more detail added by working with the children and their parents. In many instances, the map will be at too small a scale for children to be able to draw the details they know from their daily activities. For very young children to be able to use a map, personally meaningful places should be located with self-evident symbols that they themselves have created. Enlarging a map is a relatively easy and enjoyable task for children over nine years of age.

Very young children can read aerial photographs. In work with teachers of eight- and nine-year-old children, I have found that, as long as one begins with large-scale aerial photographs, children can easily identify specific features of their neighbourhoods.[6] They enjoy inventing and designing map symbols by choosing colours, colouring in the aerial photos, and making legends. As an end product each child has a sophisticated map of the same area. These individual maps can be readily contrasted and discussed and the data transferred to a larger outline map, if desired, to produce a group expression of the children's perceptions, preferences, and planning ideas.

Maps are a valuable means for allowing children and adults to express their individual preferences, dislikes, and ideas for places or parts of the environment and to compare and synthesize these with those of others to achieve a more collective expression. A good way to get children started on an environmental planning project is to ask them to make an inventory of

[6] Hart (1971); see also Blaut, McCleary and Blaut (1972).

positive and negative places in the target environment by drawing or photographing features and then marking the features on a standard printed base map. Air photographs can also be used as a base. The collage method, described earlier by Ray Lorenzo, can be used with these maps – for example, gluing children's photos or drawings of places onto the appropriate location on the base maps. Individuals can then share their evaluations in groups of five or six. If the project truly involves different interest groups, these sessions can include a representative mix of the different ages. These groups can synthesize their evaluations and plot them on a base map, which can then be displayed before everyone works in a large group to combine perspectives on a single map.

A highly motivating method to use with young children is a walk-on map. A large, cheap decorator's canvas can be used (approximately $10 for a 12' x 12' canvas). Outlines of well-known fixed features can be drawn in first, leaving the children (and adults) to use coloured markers to fill in changes they would like to see. This method is best used when the children have already developed clear ideas of what they want to express on the map through such activities as scored walks and interviews. It is also valuable to have a large base map for such projects as redesigning school grounds (see Figure 70).

Often one needs a flexible kind of map on which the symbols can be erased or removed. Superb no-cost maps can be build in dirt or sand if the need is short-term. A rather more expensive method is to stretch Mylar tightly across a baseboard and use washable felt marker pens (permanent markers can be used for any basic outline parts of the map). A cheap but effective method that the Children's Environments Research Group has used for community planning with children from nine or ten years of age and up is the use of cardboard templates. These can either be highly representative, such as benches, tables, or trees drawn to scale, or they can simply be map symbols on discs. Some of these can be left blank, of course, for the chil-

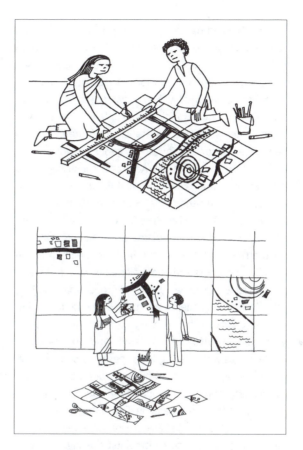

dren to develop their own symbols. This method is described below under 'Small-scale Modelling'.

One of the major values of drawing large maps is that, when completed, they can be hung in a prominent place for members of a larger community to see, comment on, and even add to. The Escuelas Nuevas of Colombia reveal their community emphasis by having community maps at a grand scale on the outside as well as the inside walls of their buildings.

SMALL-SCALE MODELLING

It is surprising that planners and designers have not made more attempts to work with children using toys and models, for toys are the tools of language between children in their everyday play with each other. Children are most familiar with this medium and most eager to

Figures 70 and 71: The process of enlarging a community base map. The task begins with children drawing a grid system over the map, then drawing a large grid over the blank piece of paper that the map will be copied onto. the squares on each map are then numbered and each child can select a square of the map which they will copy onto the larger map. A smaller version of the community base map should also be made, which can be duplicated for use by individuals or small groups working in the field. Each of the grids of the map could also be duplicated at the large scale for first research use.

use it.[7] Children as young as four can manipulate toys to express their design preferences. Furthermore, older children, teenagers, and adults have also been willing to work with such models for the design of play and recreation areas in New York City.[8] Models, then, are an ideal tool for communication on planning and design projects across a wide age range. Unfortunately, it is very time-consuming for all the model making to be done by the participants. Adults are less willing to devote such time, so some prefabrication is required.

Sidney Brower of the Baltimore City Planning Department has used models in conjunction with role-playing to produce interesting and valuable data on children's use of open space in an inner-city housing area.[9] The housing and street elements were fixed, and the movable pieces were dolls representing children, their friends, and their parents. With these dolls, children re-created their everyday play behaviours with a vividness, an attention to detail, and an emotional content that was missing from the more conventional observational and interview methods of urban planners. In this case, the relationship of the adults to the children was of the more traditional social science variety: where the children's behaviour was recorded by video camera and interpreted by the adult investigators. One can easily imagine, however, how this technique could be used effectively in more participatory situations, where the children would be fully aware of the purposes of the study and directly involved in the interpretation of the data following the enactment of such dramas with one another.

The Children's Environments Research Group has found it effective to use mobile design carts on the sidewalks of New York, but with a realistic base model of a neighbourhood site that the community wishes to redesign. Residents of all ages who do not normally attend community meetings are animated to become immediately involved. By manipulating cardboard templates representing trees, shrubs, seats, basketball courts, and so on, even the most cynical of teenagers have been persuaded to get involved in the planning

and design process and to argue their point of view fervently. Children can be effective animators of adults with this method. Figure 72 shows children of the Young People's Harlem Resource Centre displaying their alternative designs for a play area on the sidewalk next to the site for discussion with other residents.

For children to take the exercise seriously, models should be as realistic as possible or should be made by children themselves. The materials should, of course, be appropriate to a particular culture and setting. In community gardens in New York City, children like to work in soil with natural elements – sticks, flower petals, and stones – to design alternative garden layouts (see Figure 73). The materials should be diverse, and some should allow great flexibility in their meaning so children can discuss a range of themes. With a little extra time, children can build everything themselves with clay, and many features can be added with paper or cardboard.

Different modelling techniques and tools can be adopted for different groups and ages. A common denominator is the size of the overall model. The scale should be large enough to manipulate the design elements. A scale of 1 to 50 usually works well in the design of outdoor environments. The participatory design workshops can be carried out by one or two facilitators and a group of children around the base map. The size of the group should not be very big, ideally no more than ten children, in order to give each child enough opportunity to participate. Different modelling techniques and tools can be adopted for different groups and ages. An important principle is for the scale to be large enough to manipulate the design elements.

FULL-SIZE SIMULATIONS

It is difficult for children under eight to project themselves mentally into the model of an environment in order to imagine the full-sized version and to coordinate mentally with others in design discussions. It is even difficult for adults to imagine their behaviour in such mentally transformed spaces. With young chil-

[7] Hart (1978).

[8] Hart (1987); Iltus and Hart (1995). See also Nelson (1977 and 1984) for discussion of the use of models for simulating city planning decision-making with children.

[9] Brower et al (1977).

dren, one should try to simulate a full-sized version when possible. If the goal is to modify a school classroom, for example, then, rather than relying only upon the use of a small-scale model of the classroom, one might experiment with the actual classroom using temporary materials to see how it looks and feels. Similarly, if one is adding a greenhouse onto the school and is interested in letting the first-grade children (age six) take part in the design, one might build with them a full-sized cardboard greenhouse in the classroom and let them conduct some of the critical greenhouse functions, such as reaching over benches to lift or water plant pots. One can use these experiences as the basis for design discussions with the children. Strong cardboard from cardboard boxes or, ideally, 'tri-wall' (i.e. sturdy three-ply cardboard) is good for this simulation purpose. It can easily be cut by young children using saws and readily taped together.

In Habitat, the United Nations Human Settlements Conference of 1976, 35 elementary schoolchildren, who had never been together, before built their own human settlement. Using cardboard, tape, and large felt-tip pens, the children, all under the age of 12, built a 'city' in a couple of days that filled the school's gymnasium. With no specific direction from adults, the children formed themselves into small groups of three to six and built 'homes'. Quickly, problems arose over some of the classic issues found in human settlements: crowding, privacy, rights of way, definition of open space, and shared services. As these issues arose, the children met in a large group to discuss them. By discussing alternative solutions to these problems and making parallels to the same problems in the real world, this Junior Habitat workshop was able to make a contribution to the larger conference that suited the ages of the children concerned.

Figure 72:
Models used by children for the design of community play spaces in Harlem, New York City, being displayed in the street for discussion with the community.
© Roger Hart.

Figure 73:
The design of a community garden in Long Island City by young children using dirt, stones, sticks, and flower petals: it took them only two hours but led to very good negotiations with the adults over the design and how the children would be included in the garden.
© Roger Hart.

Interviewing and Surveys

INTERVIEWS

Interviewing is extremely valuable for helping young children to understand that different people can have very different ideas about the same environment or issue. It is a basic technique for any community environmental research project. It may not, however, seem to many readers to be a particularly appropriate technique for children. Young children are commonly intimidated by the idea of interviewing adults, and many adults, particularly in certain cultures, find the idea of a child interviewing them strange. A successful interview, however, can dramatically change an adult's opinion of

Figure 74:
Children are familiar with interviewing from the mass media: these children, from the Ivory Coast, in Africa, have constructed their own toy tape recorder and microphone.
© Chantal Lombard.

the capacities of a young child. Therefore, if a child is well prepared for interviewing, the act itself can be an important step in changing the perception of children's competencies and potential value to the community. It is a method with which children are extremely familiar from television and radio news programmes, and one that can often serve to empower children quickly with the realization that they can themselves become the collectors and purveyors of information.

One way to avoid a sense of intimidation is for children to conduct their interviews in groups of two or three. They can clearly share different roles: one actually conducting the interview, the second taking notes, a third managing the tape recorder. In the ERA project in the Andes of Peru described in Chapter 7 the teachers found it effective for the class as a whole to interview knowledgeable community elders. The farmers were invited into the classroom to speak about their knowledge of the environment, its resources, and its problems. After a number of embarrassing situations where the farmers remained largely silent, the teacher discovered that turning the event into an interview process, with the questions carefully prepared in advance by the children, resulted in lengthy, valuable exchanges between the children and the senior residents of their community. The programme coordinator reports that from this experience the elders come to see their knowledge as useful and the children recover confidence in their own culture.

A good way to achieve confidence in interviewing is to have small groups of children design questions and practise asking them of other children. Very young children can do the interviewing; the problem lies more in recording the answers than in asking the questions. Portable tape recorders are useful, but someone must transcribe the answers. One useful trick is to help the children design relatively 'closed' interviews, including some 'yes' or 'no' and fixed-choice questions. It is important, however, for the children to learn that such interviews do not give the respondents full freedom of expression. A good compromise is to ask the children each first to do some 'open' interviewing with each other on the topic under question, and then to work out together with all participants a suitable range of more particular questions for a standardized interview. With this kind of approach, interviewing can work well with many children of nine years of age or even younger.

It is useful to work out with children a standard way of introducing themselves. This can be helpful in reducing intimidation by some very official-looking adults. We have had great success in this way with novice 11-year-old journalists doing telephone interviews in New York. It is important to remember to have some debriefing group sessions with the children, because interviewing is a skill that benefits a great deal from reflection after the excitement of the event; a tape recording is, of course, particularly valuable for this. These debriefing sessions will help the children discover things they are forgetting to say and learn that how one asks the question greatly influences the answer. Even if they have a tape recorder, it is useful for children to carry a clipboard with the interview schedule and space for them to write in the answers, or at least to check off the questions as they ask them. This clipboard also seems to give children a sense of their own credentials as interviewers!

This method might seem suitable only for older, literate children, but there are a variety of ways to use interviewing with children of many ages, including those who are not literate. For children with limited writing abilities, using a tape recorder in the interview enables them to obtain a complete record. Analysing the information from this record can subsequently be valuable

in developing their literacy skills, and the information may be recorded in graphic form onto charts, maps, or tables. Interview questions should be prepared in advance and written down or, in the case of non-literate children, committed to memory. There should not be too many questions. There should be alternative ways of asking the same question in case the adult fails to understand the intentions of the child. Ideally, there would be time for children to ask some spontaneous questions, although this is a skill that is likely to develop gradually.

Having practised with one another, children might wish to try out the interview with their parents, who in many instances will also be an important source of information for the research. In some cultures, where there is an authoritarian relationship between parent and child, the parent may not be the ideal person to interview first. The facilitator should identify in advance some people in the community who are supportive of the idea of children's participation and would welcome an interview by them. With time, children will become more confident in introducing themselves to doubting adults and explaining why children need to do this research. It helps for children to have something to hold onto as a symbol of their legitimacy as researchers. A large microphone, attached to even the smallest tape recorder, seems to have an empowering effect on a young child. Similarly, a T-shirt or badge indicating

Figure 75:
The pages from the interview booklet reproduced here were prepared by the Ecuadorian Working Children's Programme (PMT) for use during the problem-identification phase of children's research. It is a good design for a form for pre-adolescent children because the content of the questions makes clear to both children and adults why the interview exchange is taking place. Second, the form is designed to have a minimum number of questions yet still reveal useful information to get children started on the identification of problems in the community. Third, its appealing graphics, which can be coloured in by children, makes it an attractive yet inexpensive document.
© Roger Hart.

membership in a research group can be valuable.

Perhaps the greatest weakness in interviewing by children is that they may be hesitant to ask an adult to repeat an answer or to speak more slowly or clearly. The facilitator can play the role of the interviewee as well as the interviewer to help children develop this skill. The interview should close with a question about what additional information the interviewee might offer on the general subject, followed by an open commentary on how the interviewee felt about being interviewed by children, and whether any of the questions could have been asked differently or in a better way.

Analysis of the interviews will depend upon the nature of the questions. If children have been interested primarily in gaining people's yes/no responses to specific questions, or degrees to which people like/dislike something, then the data can be summarized easily. If, on the other hand, the interview is designed largely to reveal people's perspectives on a problem, the children will need assistance in learning how to go though an interview to pull out categories of ideas and evaluations made by the respondent. This kind of analysis, of course, would be extremely difficult for children who lack literacy skills. For this reason, it is preferable for non-literate children to conduct interviews with a minimum number of closed questions, perhaps even with graphic reminders of each of these questions.

Once children have become familiar with interviewing as a method, they are in a position to design and use questionnaires for surveying larger numbers of people. Questionnaires are commonly useful later in the research process, once the children have identified a problem and have specific questions related to that problem, such as: Which of these do you think is the most important problem in your community? or In which of the following ways do you usually dispose of your garbage? Unfortunately, while few adults are likely to fill out a questionnaire by children, many more are likely to be willing to be interviewed by them, depending upon the culture.

[1] Johnson et al (1995).

SURVEYS

Surveys are a straightforward and satisfying kind of research activity for facilitators and teachers to use in any culture, with children of all ages. Examples of their use have already been offered in Chapters 7 and 8, but their importance requires some special comment. Surveys build upon the great fascination children have with collecting and mapping and, if designed well, can excite them by providing opportunities for detective work. With remarkably little effort, children in any community can collect information and express it in map and graphic forms that the residents have never seen before. In this way, adults can clearly see that children can play a role in their community, one that is not discordant with parents' traditional notions of the kinds of skills that should be learned in school. Thus, they are a good way to begin a new programme in schools that do not have a record of community research.

Personal Environmental Inventories

An excellent project to help children to understand how to use research in planning a project is for them to conduct a survey on their own everyday behaviour. For example, a creative study of working children in Nepal includes a 'time allocation exercise', which was carried out with all the members of the sample household being studied.[1] One of the major goals of the participatory research with these communities was to understand the work patterns of children and how they varied by age and by gender. This was important information for the community in their development planning and in considering the possibilities for schooling versus income-producing work in their children's development. To help children and their families further in evaluating their work patterns, they were also involved in ranking their preferences for different work activities. Figure 76 shows how this could be done with children from any culture. The categories would of course be generated uniquely for each community by the children as the first step of this project. To avoid confusion, when working with a group, it would be best to carry out each step of the process separately and completely before proceeding to the next one. Following this principle, and using pictorial symbols, one could work with children who have the most rudimentary understanding of arithmetic.

Surveys of Environmental Values

Another valuable kind of survey emerged out of the 'Children, Peace, and Nature' conference held with children from many countries in Assisi, Italy, in 1991. During a workshop, nine children, from almost as many countries, found themselves in a passionate argument over the insects and animals they had each killed and what was acceptable and not acceptable. This led to the design of a survey to be conducted with the entire plenary conference audience of 350 children. The children excited their peers by first recording on a large survey sheet how many children in the audience had killed different categories of wildlife and then asking questions about the data, such as why so many spiders and why no ladybirds had been killed. There are many similar environmental value surveys that children could conduct with their peers and their communities that would lead to important debates.

Mapping of Environmental Problems

The community base map described in Chapter 12 is a basic tool that enables children to collect, by interviewing or observation, a wide range of types of data that a community is unlikely to have mapped before. In Part II examples were given of children's maps of local jobs, pets, and dog-fouling of an urban neighbourhood. A wheelchair survey showing parts of the city that are accessible for people with a particular disability is something all cities could use but few have.[2] Such surveys should, of course, be designed in close consultation with the groups they claim to be serving. For their wheelchair survey, 80 high school girls in Swansea divided up the entire city into districts so that small teams of girls could conduct research street by street. Conducting such a survey can lead children into a criti-

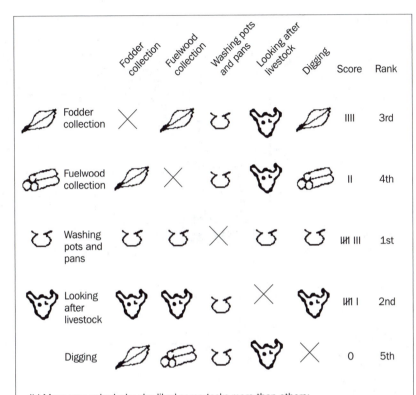

Jiri Maya was asked why she liked some tasks more than others:

1st: Washing pots and pans: it is easy work and gives me a chance to stay at home.
2nd: Looking after livestock: it is easier than other work.
3rd: Fodder collection: it is better than firewood collection (4th).
5th: Digging: it is very difficult work.

cal analysis of existing conditions and actions towards improving them. A well-produced map of accessibility and inaccessibility can be a powerful tool for change by children for any group with special needs.

Surveys of Animal and Human Behaviour

Knowledge of the existing use of an environment is important for any project where children hope to improve an area, such as a small leftover wild space that they wish to improve as a wildlife habitat or a park or playground that they wish to redesign. Also, observational surveys and mapping of the data are useful for introducing children to ecological concepts – to the relationship

Figure 76:

A ranking of the work preferences of Jiri Maya Low, aged 13, in Nepal (extracted with permission from Johnson et al., 1995).

[2] Thomas (1970)

Figure 77: Children at the 'Children, Peace and Nature' Conference in Assisi, Italy, conducting a survey on the killing of wildlife with the 350 participants of the conference.

WHY DO WE KILL CREATURES? PERCHÉ SI UCCIDE CREATURE? HAVE YOU EVER KILLED CREATURES? DLACZEGO MY ZABIŁAMY TE ZWIERZETA?	ANTS Formiche	LADYBUG Coccinelle	FLIES + MOSQUITOS Moscho+ Zanzane	SPIDERS Ragno	SNAKES Serpenti	FISH Pesci	BIRDS Uccelli	MICE Topi	BIGGER ANIMALS Piu grande	PLANTS Pianti
A HANDFUL (under ten)		✓			✓		✓		✓	
LESS THAN ¼ OF AUDIENCE						✓				
LESS THAN ½ OF AUDIENCE								✓		
LESS THAN ¾ OF AUDIENCE										
EVERYONE	✓		✓	✓						✓

[3] For further information, including the school survey instrument write to Learning Through Landscapes, 3rd Floor, South Side Offices, The Law Courts, Winchester, Hampshire SO23 9DL, UK. The survey has already been used by a large percentage of schools in the United Kingdom, thereby providing not only a valuable resource for each school in its planning, design, and management efforts, but also a comprehensive overview of the ways in which school grounds are currently being used. The hope is to computerize this so that children's survey work can be part of a national programme of environmental monitoring.

of organisms to their habitat. Children develop valuable skills of observation and record making.

Recording is best done in pairs as part of a total group effort that can be of almost any size, provided supervision is adequate. The time spent can range from quickie thirty-minute introductory awareness exercises to surveys for major projects extending over several weeks. Materials can be simple – coloured pencils and maps on clipboards – or they can include still cameras or video cameras. As an introductory exercise, records can easily be made by observing through a window birds visiting a feeder. Another valuable way of helping young children understand the value of observation is to set up a blind in the group's own space, like those used by bird watchers; this blind seems to emphasize the importance of observing in a quiet and concentrated manner.

Landscape Surveys

One kind of survey suitable for every schoolchild in the world is a detailed inventory of the landscape and its resources surrounding their school building. Considerable emphasis has already been given to the importance of establishing around primary schools a diverse natural environment through which children can learn in their informal play, and can develop responsibility through monitoring and managing the environment. Learning Through Landscapes, a national organization in the United Kingdom that has devoted itself to transforming the country's school grounds, developed a survey to be used by all primary and secondary schools.[3]

Before begining the survey, you will need a large-scale site plan (see Chapter 12). Learning Through Landscapes then suggests the following headings for a comprehensive survey of the school grounds:

- history of the school and its site
- microclimate
- land use in the area surrounding the school and school grounds, in order to understand surrounding wildlife or environmental factors that might affect the quality of the site
- boundaries – walls, fences, and hedges, and the 'messages' they give to others
- soil
- other surfaces, and their suitability for different activities
- trees, shrubs, and other plants
- footpaths, formal and informal
- access for those with special needs and for those using wheelchairs or other devices
- use of the ground for play, recreation, classwork, scientific monitoring of the site, gardening, livestock management, the study of wildlife, and the extent of other activities such as vandalism
- the programme of site maintenance.

Large-Scale Scientific Surveys

Occasionally, environmental professionals realize the enormous potential of involving children and teenagers in large-scale scientific surveys (see Wildlife Watch in Chapter 8). The challenge is to make such surveys more interactive, instead of having children simply following instructions. Wildlife Watch, in the United Kingdom, has an interesting package called 'Enviroscope' designed to help children conduct surveys in their own community.[4] From a large choice of survey forms and information sheets, children can select which surveys they wish to conduct for use in their own community. This information can then be sent into the national computer centre, thereby enabling Wildlife Watch to collate data that concern children on a national scale. The primary intention is to encourage children to use Enviroscope to help them design their own projects as part of school programmes or scout projects or with their own neighbours. For this reason, the survey sheets are interspersed with information

sheets suggesting possible follow-ups related to the different subjects. Survey sheets are small enough to be easily manageable by children and not to make them obvious in the field as surveyors. As a reflection of the extreme fears for children's safety that have overtaken parents in many of the Northern industrialized countries and are affecting children's relationship to the environment, the outside of the Enviroscope package is a general safety code for children which stresses avoiding strangers as well as physical dangers.

TRAILS OR 'SCORED' WALKS

The best way to raise awareness about local environmental issues is to experience them directly with all of one's senses while walking. Pathways through the environment allow for that experience. Trails can be designed by adults as a way of introducing children to environmental issues, or they can be designed by or

Figure 78:
A sample page from the Enviroscope survey package produced by Wildlife Watch in the United Kingdom: this page deals with roadside verges and wildlife. It is a good example of the multiple value of survey research by children: the children become aware of the problem through using the survey, the residents they interview come to understand the problem through answering the questions, the data the children collect has value in enabling them to design their own interventions in the community, and finally the data are submitted to the National Wildlife Watch Centre, where they provide useful information for the ongoing monitoring of environments and environmental behaviour in the country. It is essential that children receive the results of their survey work.

[4] Wildlife Watch (1994).

Figure 79:
An example of an environmental appraisal sheet for use in an urban area.

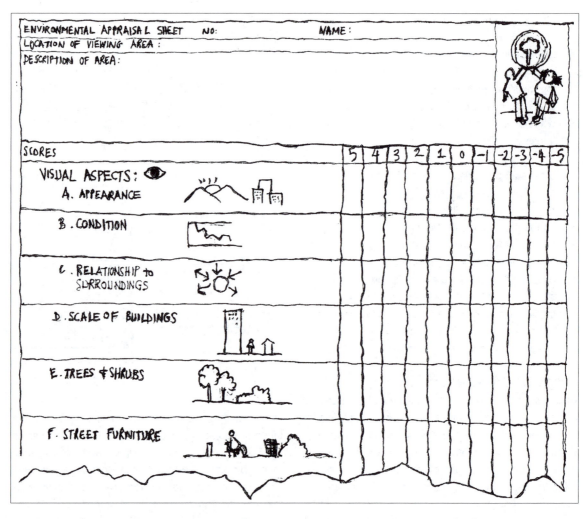

[5] See, for example, Kaplan's (1991) use of trails by children and senior citizens together.

[6] Wheeler and Waites (1972); Ward and Fyson (1976); Ranger (1991); Tracey (1991).

with children for use by other members of the community. The range extends from permanent trails, to 'scored' walks serving more specific shorter-term ends, to one-off trips to investigate the local environment. These techniques provide excellent vehicles for joint participation by different age groups.[5]

The reader may associate the word trail with 'nature trail', a unidirectional approach to learning, which takes the viewer from point to point in order to identify discrete objects in the landscape that the nature conservation expert thinks are important to be

seen. Town trails, developed by teachers and environmental planners in urban environmental education in the United Kingdom, are quite different.[6] They are more active: the viewer is expected to play the role of detective rather than that of passive observer. Even when a trail is designed by adults for children, the 'trackers' should receive a set of questions and clues to guide them rather than a specific set of facts about what to look for and its significance. The trail is not meant to leave trackers feeling that they have learned what they were supposed to have learned; rather, it should stimulate the desire to investigate further. It is, in fact, an excellent introduction for children who have previously been exposed only to formal environmental education; it lets them know that the environment is perceived differently by different people and that their own perspective is important. In such instances, an environmental appraisal sheet may be useful (Figure 79).

The following description of how to make a town trail and some of the important qualities of trails are drawn largely from work in the United Kingdom. Following this is a specific account of how to involve children in designing trails. With so much to see in any environment, the selection of phenomena to look at will inevitably reflect a particular theme, such as 'economic development potentials' or 'environmental pollution' or 'sites for alternative plans'. The appraisal sheet shown here reflects the particular bias of much of the work of the town trail movement in the UK towards the visual qualities of the urban environment.

Wheeler and Waites (1972) tell us that the length of trails should depend on the number and variety of visual experiences to be included, but of course the age and physical abilities of your children are an even more important consideration. Contrast, juxtapositions, and surprises are essential to the success of the trail, they say. Certainly, do not take the trail along an obvious route or a beaten path, but rather travel through controversial areas where people may be in conflict with developers or planners over a particular use of a site. The following extract from a town trail guide in Leicester describes a stop at a shopping arcade. It illustrates that, while directive, trails also offer much opportunity for both personal commentary and research:

Compare the type of shops and style of architecture found here with that in the village arcade (you may have to go back to take another look!). Which do you prefer? Look upwards at the various balcony levels. Make a sketch of the interior. Note the building materials used. Find the stairs in the arcade and walk

along the balconies. Make 'spot interviews' with any of the shoppers or shopkeepers. Find out how they regard this building. What would you do with the arcade? Pull it down or conserve it?

One should aim to focus the attention of trackers on each of the senses – listening for noises, smelling the pleasant and unpleasant parts of the environment, and even reaching out to touch aesthetically pleasing objects in the built environment. One warning here: designers of nature trails complain that the desire to touch leads to a desire to take, and so, after a period of use, a trail can become a remarkably deserted pathway through an otherwise rich environment!

A good trail is designed for versatility, enabling trackers to use it at their own level of interest and in their own time. Nevertheless, there will be sections of the trail that are rich and interesting and others which are relatively uninteresting for most users. To help you understand the existing knowledge and the areas of potentially greater interest for trackers, you may wish to precede the design of the trail with an investigation of the 'mental maps' held by children of the age range you will be working with. The route of the trail should be depicted clearly on an outline map of the area. This map should not have too much extraneous information; it is your annotations about the trail that should be highlighted. It will be necessary, however, to include landmarks that all the children know (again, 'mental mapping' is useful here). It is important to have at least one outlook point in a trail: a hill from which a panorama can be offered or, in the case of a town, a tall building. This offers a vantage point for new kinds of information and helps place the trail in a larger context.

The use of an environmental appraisal form is not meant to turn this activity into a quantitative survey. The purpose of the appraisal sheet is rather to focus children on certain aspects of the environment in order to have them make subjective discriminations that will be useful in subsequent discussion. To stress further that

[7] Wheeler and Waites (1972).

[8] For more resources on trails and scored walks, see Scanlan (1978); Ward and Fyson (1976).

[9] Childhood City Newsletter (1980).

this is not a competition or quantitative exercise, trackers can work in groups of two or three to fill out these sheets. Although the sheet includes a scale, this is simply meant to aid trackers in a relative comparison of their evaluations of different parts of the environment and in a comparison with the perspectives of others during the subsequent discussion. Children can work together to transform their individual appraisals into a very large version on the wall. Doing this collectively obviously leads children to reflect on the differences between one another's evaluations. These differences in perspective and the discussions that ensue can be the roots of future projects by children. Ideally, the teacher or facilitator will have experimented in using the trail themselves and will have assembled resources related to the issues on the trail in anticipation of these discussion periods. Particularly valuable are photographs or colour slides of certain sections of the trail.

One way of guaranteeing failure is to have large groups of children all move along the trail at the same time, much as coach loads of tourists do. Ideally, trackers should be briefed on the route beforehand and introduced to symbols used on the map, but then should be allowed to travel independently, either alone or in small groups. You may decide to lead a larger group over a small section of the trail simply to demonstrate use of the environmental appraisal form, but to continue to operate in a large group would lead trackers to retreat into a more orthodox, passive learning role. Very small groups or individuals are also more likely to be successful in moving though a natural environment with minimal disturbance of the animal life, or through an urban environment with minimal disturbance to the regular activities of the resident populations. As a result of the discussions, children may wish to redesign or supplement the trail for future use by other children or adults in their community. They may also be inspired to design their own trails.

Trails Designed by Children[8]

The clearest way to introduce children to how to make

a trail is to have them focus on the environment they know and use every day, with a view to sharing it with other children or adults. This is best explained through an example. 'Our City and the Places We Play' was a special event planned as part of the 'Children, Nature and the Urban Environment' conference in Washington, DC.[9] The aim was to increase adult understanding of children's daily use and evaluation of the environment. The event consisted of a neighbourhood walking tour for participants in the conference designed by ten-year-old children at Stevens Elementary School. The students produced a booklet of the tour for use by visiting children and adults.

Before the conference, adult facilitators met with the students at Stevens School to plan the 'Our City' tour. Drawings of favourite places and exploratory walks enabled the children collectively to identify preferred places in their neighbourhood. A final 'scored walk' prepared by the children included a photocopied booklet of collage elements of each place on the walk and a map showing the location of the nine favourite places. These were handed out to visiting children and to the conference participants in their registration materials.

On the first day of the conference, Stevens School children and symposium visitors met at the school for a child-led tour. The group was joined by visiting children from a rural school in Vermont. Unfortunately, a horde of press also came along – the idea of children being able to say something to adults sounded more interesting to them than the many famous adult speakers that were scheduled. The walk was extremely successful in revealing the kinds of neighbourhood places valued by the Washington children, including such 'undesigned' places as the 'Scary Dairy', an abandoned dairy building near their school.

Scored walks designed by children can help open up a dialogue with planners so that children's ideas become more integral to neighbourhood plans. A scored walk was developed by the 'Time for a Change' team at the Longfellow School, Berkeley, California, to help direct the attention of students, parents, teachers, administrators, and people from the surrounding neighbourhood towards opportunities to improve the school site. Robin Moore describes the process they used.[10] Based on survey work that had been done with the students and suggestions from the planning committee, a scored walk of the school site was designed with some 30 stations. The walk was used as the opening segment of a three-hour community-planning workshop. At each station, participants noted likes and dislikes and listed comments about the physical conditions. It took about an hour to complete the circuit. Most of the 35 participants worked in pairs, discussing their opinions as they moved from station to station, although each individual made his or her own record. Back at the workshop meeting, the results of the walk were discussed in small groups and on a wall graphic, which was used as the basis for group discussion. Sticky notes with ideas for change were added to the scored walk maps, and by the end of the workshop consensus was reached on a ranked list of high-priority projects that subsequently formed the core of the improvement programme.

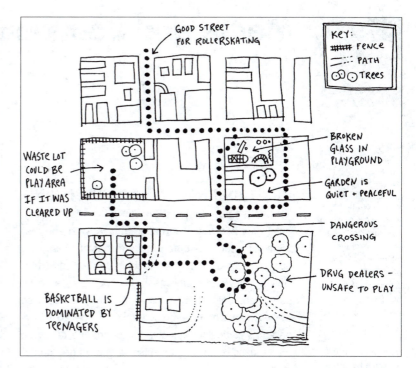

Figure 80:
A simple map by children can serve as a trail guide to problems in their everyday environment.

[10] Moore (1980).

Media and Communication

[1] This section is drawn from the experiences of Alison King and Kim Sabo, facilitators of the international Voices of Children in Journalism Project, and their global network of children's news bureaus at the Children's Environments Research Group at the City University of New York Graduate School. See also Granfield (1993), Brigham (1982) and Guthrie et al. (1994).

PRINT JOURNALISM AND PUBLISHING

For adults who doubt that children have much to say, publishing is a way of revealing that they do and that their perspective is different from that of those who normally write for them. Publishing is a logical extension of many of the projects in this book and can even be the end point of research – the goal being to raise the awareness of others to action.[1] Young people's journalism is particularly valuable for turning the tables on the tendencies towards tokenism with children's participation. For children to appear with a microphone, tape recorder, or video camera at a conference, for example, is a very different expression of children's role in society than when they are simply allowed to speak for a few minutes, in the maner of an entertainment break, within the serious discourses of the adults.

Journalism is also an excellent training ground for children who wish to be seriously involved in changing the world. With guidance, it enables them to see the value of learning the many sides of a story. Encouraged to ask about perspectives other than their own and those of their peers, they become able to probe deeper into the complexity of environmental issues. This encourages them to investigate such issues with a healthy dose of scepticism in order to distinguish the facts from the values and interpretations of different actors in a story. It also sensitizes children to the larger political issues surrounding their cause.

Newsletters and magazines are particularly well suited to production by young children because they can be done on photocopying or mimeograph machines that are broadly, if not universally, accessible. Books demand much more involvement from adults because of the need to obtain funds, work with printers and binders, and find ways of marketing the finished product. Whatever the nature of the publication, it is advisable to have a clear demarcation of roles for such a challenging task. The roles may, of course, be rotated from time to time to give everyone opportunities to learn. There are benefits to having older children take greater responsibility for the editing and possibly for the final layout because of their competencies in these areas, but if one adopts a mixed-age-group approach, the younger children can still be involved in these tasks in the draft stage and serve as apprentices with the teenagers to the end. The layout format can also be developed collectively, with everyone sharing in the draft stages of this process. This should come after a highly participatory period of both collecting information and selecting pieces to include. The task is not unlike that of producing a collage. With younger children, one may even decide to do the initial rough layout of the publication in a large, wall-mounted version.

A bureau of young journalists, called the GRAPEs, have also found it valuable to keep an ongoing collection of pages torn from their favourite magazines and newspapers. In design parlance, this is called a 'morgue' or 'idea file'. The children keep their eyes open for graphic design elements (headlines, storyboards, sidebars) that they like and paste these into a large blank sketchbook. A short note on each page explains why they liked the graphic. When the members of the graphic design team run out of ideas or have trouble articulating a graphic style, they refer to the morgue for inspiration. Similar books or files may also be kept by the reporters and copywriters for collecting new story topic ideas from other publications. Ultimately, the morgues expand the way children think of their roles: writers can contribute to the design process, and artists can help direct the written content of the publication.[2]

There are a variety of different kinds of publishing ventures in which children can engage, and each is briefly summarized below.

Publications for Children, with Children's Material

This is the most common kind of publishing by children, produced by schools and children's organizations for internal distribution to their membership. In most instances it is also probably the most authentic kind because of the tendency towards adult overcontrol when children's news publications are produced for adult audiences. Journalism can be used to give coherence to any project by having some children document and consistently inform the group of what is happening day by day. Such daily journals can also be used to unify and inform children within a conference. For example, during the United Nations Conference on the Sustainable Development of Small Island Ecosystems, held in Barbados in 1994, children produced a daily broadsheet by listening to and interviewing speakers from islands from all over the world. This broadsheet was then carried by child messengers on bicycles to schools across the island. A group of correspondents from *New Moon*, 'the Magazine for Girls and their Dreams', based in Minnesota in the USA, went to the Beijing International Conference on Women's Rights in 1995. Using the World Wide Web, an international electronic network, the girls posted daily logs of their experiences at the conference. Girls around the world were encouraged to respond to these logs though *New Moon's* direct link electronic mail on the Web page. The

daily logs were also syndicated in US newspapers and provided material for *New Moon's* special magazine issue about the rights of girls.

Most adult-produced magazines for children do not involve children in the editing. Although this seems an unfortunate missed opportunity, there is nothing inherently wrong about such magazines as long as they are clear about who the editors are and what the editorial process is. Many superb publications with children's material are produced in this way, such as the one issued by the Mazingira in Kenya, described in Chapter 3. No doubt, the thinking of editors of children's magazines is that children would not be able to edit a coherent or interesting magazine, but surely there is a place for some involvement by children or teenagers in the editorial process.

Electronic Publishing

Print journalism is changing drastically in this age of electronic publishing. At the time of writing there is an enormous explosion in national and even international communication by children using the World Wide Web for communicating their ideas. It is difficult at this time to see any positive outcomes for the development of children's local knowledge and involvement in community development. Also, there is a great danger that electronic communication will help establish a new class division between the rich and the poor, for many children have no hope of obtaining direct access to electronic communication.

The positive qualities of electronic communication seem to be that it eliminates the need for paper, broadens the reach of children's voices, and allows for instant feedback. Those who use the Web, however, need to remember that, rather than creating some kind of new social order, they may be contributing to a new kind of elitism. Children should be aware of the bias in communicating only with young people that use electronic networks. One exception is a global student news network on the Web that acts as a free clearing-house for student-written articles which can then be down-

[2] The Bureau of Young GRAPES (which stands for Global Reporters, Artists, Producers, and Editors) is an international project. Teenagers and children are preparing booklets to guide other budding young journalists in print, radio, video, and electronic journalism. For the first book in the series, *We're in Print: The Whole Story by Kids for Kids*, and for further information, contact the Bureau of Young GRAPEs, Children's Environments Research Group, City University of New York, 33 West 42nd Street, New York, NY 10036, USA.

[3] Peace Child International (1994).

loaded and republished in any newspaper, student or otherwise, in the world. Also, at the time of writing a group of children and teenagers called the Bureau of Young GRAPEs is working with groups of child journalists around the world to produce a series of written guidelines to foster networks of young journalists that are not exclusive and that engage in both local and global communication.

Contributions to Adult Newspapers and Magazines

Even if children produce their own magazine, there is value in also sending material to the editors of local newspapers for adults, where children's voices can have an impact on the larger community. In newspapers in some countries there is a growing trend to include children's pages, where children are encouraged to send in articles, book reviews, and opinion. Regrettably, these pages rarely have child editorial boards to review the material submitted, and it is even less common for children or youth to work as regular correspondents alongside adults.

Books by Children for Children and Adults

Sometimes there is cause for children to produce a publication on a particular theme for a general audience that requires their perspective. Peace Child International, an NGO in the United Kingdom, recently issued a children's version of Agenda 21, the Rio Declaration on Sustainable Development.[3] This highly professional publication uses the drawings and stories of children and teenagers from all over the world to introduce Agenda 21 to both children and adults in an effective, appealing way; simultaneously it promotes the general idea of children having a voice. The layout was produced with older teenagers working with some professional guidance, although the editorial process is not discussed. This is a problem with all children's publications: as part of the desire to emphasize that a publication is produced by children with minimum inter-

ference by adults, adults seem to find it necessary to avoid discussing how children and adults worked together.

From our work at the Children's Environments Research Group with the Bureau of Young GRAPEs we know that the relationship between children, youth, and adults is a complex and changing one and that the process of learning to work together is worthy of documentation and sharing with others. We encourage all adults who work with children to improve their self-documentation and to share in a preface to their publications the nature of their working relationship with children and a summary of the production process. The Young GRAPEs have found it valuable for both children and adults to keep their own logs and to hold frequent meetings to discuss the process and the relationships among members of the group.

PHOTOGRAPHY

Photo documentation is an effective means of getting small groups to focus on specific positive and negative aspects of their surroundings. They are also particularly useful for the documentation by children of difficult sites along trails they have designed. Quick results are possible with instant print cameras, although the film for these is prohibitively expensive. There are many inexpensive, fully automatic cameras available, and children as young as eight can safely develop and print their own film.

Involvement in the developing and printing process improves the artistic dimension of photography and can thereby further sensitize children to the beauty of the environment. If funds are available, children can take colour slides, which have the value of being able to be presented to a larger audience. Furthermore, as described in Chapter 11, children can draw on blank slides, which can be mixed with slide photographs. Both black and white photography and slides are particularly useful for documentation of trails.

Shooting Back was founded in 1989 as a non-profit organization to coordinate workshops in photography, writing, and other media with homeless and at-risk children living in the metropolitan area of Washington, DC.[4] The project subsequently spread to Minneapolis, Minnesota, and to Native American reservations in Arizona. The programme received massive media coverage and has grown dramatically as a result of public exposure resulting from exhibits of the children's work. The idea developed as a means to increase self-esteem among children who live in extremely difficult circumstances – hence the term 'shooting back'.

Shooting Back provides weekly photography workshops for children aged eight to 12 years of age. These workshops offer both photography and photographic developing and printing. Volunteer photographers and artists become mentors to the children, working with them both in the streets and in the laboratories. The result of this programme has been not only to empower at-risk children by teaching them how to express themselves in new creative ways, but also to educate the public about poverty and its impact on young people in America through exhibitions of the children's photographs, informational events, and massive media exposure. From such a base of improved self-esteem it is easy to see how children who might not previously have been interested in engaging in community projects would now be willing to use their new skills for the community's improvement.

In 1991 Shooting Back photographers joined forces with child reporters from Children's Express (a children's journalism group) to produce the 1991 Annual Report for the Prudential Foundation. The Prudential Foundation claims that 'it is the first Annual Report for a corporate philanthropic organization created entirely by children'.

VIDEO AND TELEVISION

The idea of making television is seductive to young people because it offers an instant finished product. But a high-quality finished product takes a lot of work. The problem with the ease of operation of video is that many young people use it without help or encourage-ment and then never use it again because it failed to meet their expectations. There are some useful guides to using video with children, and the following notes are designed to offer a few warnings and to outline some of the different uses of the technology.[5]

Children should be told from the beginning that there are many different degrees of technical understanding and skill training, and they should be assisted in a manner suited to the particular goals of a project. None of the lightweight machines are too difficult for children to operate, but some are more straightforward, with fewer things that can be forgotten or left unplugged. Nothing is more frustrating for children than to return after a day's work to find, when they play back, that their recording is not there! A straightforward checklist of parts and procedures should be distilled from the usually overwhelming technical manuals that come with a newly purchased machine. Fortunately, principles of camera use can be learned through experience, because videotape can be reused, but be ready to comment on two annoying tendencies of most new users: panning and zooming. These techniques should be reserved for rare occasions.

It is difficult, but not impossible, to have children under eight working with video, especially if simple, lightweight, 8mm machines are used. If young children find the camera too heavy, a supermarket trolley can be adapted to serve as a moving tripod (called a 'dolly' in the film world). The age of the children also affects how many can work on a project. With children older than ten it is easier to have them plan a whole project and invent many separate tasks in addition to handling the camera and recorder. But, to complete a product, one should avoid the temptation of having these exciting tasks shared by too many persons. Even with a small group, it is best for each to take a defined role – director, cameraman, sound recorder, scenery and props manager, and so on.

The following are just a few of the possibilities for using video with children and teenagers.

[4] Shooting Back, 1901 Eighteenth Street, NW, Washington, DC 20009, USA.

[5] Dowmunt (1969)

[6] Dowmunt (1969)

[7] Roberts (1994).

Attracting and Animating Children

Video is a powerful attraction to children. Once they have been attracted and allowed to see its potential, ideas for projects that they could do might emerge. Tony Dowmunt gives the example of a youth worker in England who attracted a group of young people by simply walking onto a housing estate with a camera in hand.[6] The youths then produced a videotape on the lack of recreation space in the area. This was shown to the local government representatives, with the end result that the youths were given a room in which to meet on the estate.

Interviewing

Interviewing may seem an obvious and unexciting way of using video, but if interviewing is a part of a project, video can be a valuable tool in helping children understand and practise their role. They have seen people interviewing others dozens of times on the TV. The experience of holding a microphone and having a cameraman seems simultaneously to enlighten them about the process, empower them to feel competent, and allow them to gain expertise by doing it and then reviewing the product.

Aiding Group Process

Children can use video to see how they and their colleagues interact in a group. Such a use of video equipment must be handled sensitively. The facilitators must be prepared to hear critical commentary on their own behaviour. This use of video also offers children a chance to address problems of self-consciousness and to become comfortable with themselves before speaking in front of an audience. Giving all children a chance to operate the equipment helps them discover how the video provides a selective view of reality, with the story told through the lens depending upon how the camera is used and how the tape is edited.

Practice Presentations

When a formal presentation must be prepared, such as participating in a panel at a conference with adults, a simulation of the event can be set up and videotaped. By playing this back, children can learn how to improve their performance and can gain confidence for the real event.

Expressing Personal Evaluations

In the hands of an individual child, video can be a powerful tool for expressing feelings about an environment or event. An example is a tape produced by an 11-year-old boy in an unpublished project by Simon Nicholson. The tape was a straightforward re-creation by the boy of his experience on the first day in his new secondary school. It served as an evocative critique of the inhumane scale of some schools and the lack of thought or care about welcoming a child into such an environment. Such a tape can be used for presentation to one's peers or as part of a presentation to others, such as a school board in the preceding example, or the need to improve an environment.

Making a Presentation

With a little training and assistance in editing, children as young as eight or nine can successfully edit a programme of value for community-planning purposes.[7] Inter-Action in London worked with a group of youths to create a video on the 'city farm' concept for their own housing area. The teenagers simply mixed scenes of the farm with scenes of their own housing estate. By showing this tape to the tenants, the young people were able to introduce them effectively to a new idea for their community.

RADIO PRODUCTION

While it is difficult for children to convince television stations to broadcast their videotapes, many groups have had considerable success in producing radio programmes. The other major advantage of radio is the

Box 23: Project Paranoa – a Public School Community development Programme in Brasilia

A variety of creative projects concerned with community development have been conducted through the arts curriculum of a public school for children aged 12 to 17 in a poor favela called Paranoa in Brasilia. Nelson Ramos Filho and Marcia Selva de Oliviera are art teachers, but the nature of their work calls for a much broader description. The children in their art classes are free to choose from a broad range of media: music, painting, drawing, ceramics, dance, and video (funded by UNICEF). Using all these different media, the children focus on different themes related to their community. Students use video to document the projects so that they can continue to have an impact on the community after the project is finished. Some videos are made on specific topics that the children consider important. For example, one video by pregnant and parent teenagers in the group for other children and teenagers in the country dealt with how it feels to be pregnant and give birth and the problems of having children when one is so young.

Figure 81:
At the time of my visit, the residents of Paranoa were to be moved from their land to a new site. They decided to make a video about the experience called 'Mia Terre' (My Land). This would describe their experience of the move and the process of improving one block of their new community, both physically and visually.
© Correio Braziliense Brasilia D. F., Brazil.

relatively low cost and ease of access to tape recorders compared to video recorders. Yet another advantage for many poor communities around the world is that more people have radios than television. Most of what is reported here is from 'We are on the Radio', an excellent publication from the Child-to-Child Trust.[8] The book comes with a tape cassette on the subject of children on the radio which can itself be broadcast. The flipside contains different examples of children's health broadcasts from a variety of countries.

Most of the child-to-child radio programmes have been related to health, although, as Chapter 7 revealed, primary health care is becoming primary environmental care. One example is *Hatemalo*, meaning 'Hand in

8 Hanbury and McCrum (1994).

Hand'. It is a weekly ten-minute radio programme for children which has been broadcast for the past five years by Radio Nepal in Kathmandu. Children produce radio plays, sometimes with several episodes, on health topics and helping children with disabilities. The producer conducts a quiz every two months to see to what extent children have understood information given in previous programmes, a reminder of the heavy educational component of the child-to-child programmes, and their strong association with the schools.

Children can quite freely use tape recorders to collect material from a variety of sources. These recordings are usually not good enough quality for radio broadcast and so the content may have to be repeated on studio standard equipment at a later date. Ideally, there may also be a studio to allow different parts to be mixed, music or sound effects to be added, short excerpts placed together in a rapid montage to make a broadcast flow more quickly, and fades to enable a smoother link between sections. However, none of these studio requirements are necessary for children to participate in radio. By linking up with other children and with radio stations, children can themselves produce tapes which can be sent in and broadcast as part of a larger programme.

Hanbury and McCrum (1994) recommend that, before making broadcasts of their own, children spend time listening and critically discussing what they hear. From this they will be able to determine collectively what they like and why. They further suggest that, even if the material they produce will be sent as a contribution to a larger programme, the children should be encouraged to produce an entire programme themselves. This will help them understand why broadcasts are made and why it may be necessary for professional involvement in production on account of technical limitations. Children can be made more conscious of sound by carrying out games such as closing their eyes and listening for three minutes before sharing with a partner all the sounds they hear. From such experiences children become aware of how much background noise

and echo can affect the way things sound, and thereby they might be more selective in using or rejecting such natural sounds in their own productions.

On many community radio stations around the world, community development and environmental care are fundamental parts of the regular programme scheduling, and so they may have time to include programmes or spots by children. Alternatively, on a commercial radio station, children may have to approach businesses to underwrite their programme. Hanbury and McCrum recommend approaching manufacturers of children's products such as medicines, publications, or clothes and voluntary organizations who work on children's development issues.

As with all of the child-to-child programmes, this manual recommends that children evaluate their radio productions. They suggest having people listen to the programme and then interview them about their reactions. The kinds of questions that might be included would go beyond whether they found it interesting or not to include such questions as: Was it too long or short? Were the voices clear? Was it confusing with too many different kinds of material or did it cohere as a whole? Ideally the evaluation would address the three major aims of programming according to the authors: Did it catch the listener's attention? Did it hold the listener's attention? and Will it change what they do? For the latter part to be achieved it is important to provide clearly and repeatedly information such as a contact phone number or address in order for listeners to follow up on the inspiring messages of the children.

Try to avoid talks by people. Interviews, discussions, and especially stories are much more lively and interesting to the listener. Interviews should avoid being too stilted. It is much more pleasant to be listening to something that sounds like a conversation than a structured interview. This may take some practice before children feel comfortable. Interviews should not be limited to children but should include all the actors in a community issue, including politicians if possible. Finally, if children are able to achieve a regular weekly spot on a radio station, they could consider having a news report. This would enable them to describe in some degree all initiatives being taken by children and youth in the community as well as other news items that the adult news has not deemed to be important. To this end, there is great value in helping children exchange their radio programmes as part of a correspondence exchange programme. Inserting commentaries by children from other countries into one's own radio programmes is another way of bringing out the global significance of children's local actions.

PERFORMANCE

Music and Dance

Singing, dancing, and acting are all wonderful ways for children to express their concern for the environment and their communities. Song and dance lend themselves to simple, straightforward messages, but they may be valuable components of a larger communication. They can serve as a festive introduction or summary or can be used to punctuate and emphasize the important dimensions of a message. When children present simple messages in song or dance without any other involvement, this constitutes 'social mobilization' rather than authentic participation. But this need not be so. In recent years, adolescents in the United States have revealed how powerful they can be in communicating their own sophisticated messages through music. Actionaid found songs to be a valuable means of enabling girls in Nepal to recount views about daily work beyond that which could be learned from interviews.[9]

Music and dance have great value for helping children develop a sense of camaraderie and solidarity in a group. In visiting organizations working with very low income children in Brazil, I learned that music and dance were considered essential first steps in empowering children with low self-esteem and a poor sense of cultural identity. This reflected not only the importance of music and dance to all Brazilians, but also a conscious policy programme of preparing children to contribute to the development of their communities by first strengthening their sense of themselves and their sense of membership in a larger group and community.

Drama and Puppetry

Drama and puppetry with children have many values. They are particularly valuable therapeutically for enabling children to share difficult personal experiences, and street workers often use theatre for this purpose. They can also be very useful as a way for children collectively to identify from their daily lives important themes for them to address through community research and action. There is also a great value in using children's theatre to communicate ideas to others. The child-to-child programme stresses the use of drama for enabling children to communicate health messages to other children. Other groups have gone one step further and used theatre as a central vehicle for sharing ideas with the larger community. The children of the Sarvodaya movement in Sri Lanka regularly use song, dance, puppetry, and theatre to communicate health and environment messages to adults in the village communities. By employing the traditional art forms of Buddhist culture children play a critical role in enabling the Sarvodaya movement to spread rapidly to serve hundreds of villages throughout the country. The children's groups, usually managed by two young women in each village, develop performances around simple themes and, following the principles of social mobilization, carry these to all the members of the community. With the village priest and village elders present, it is difficult for parents to stay away from a performance by their children, so the message reaches an extremely large audience.

Many organizations for street and working children scattered throughout the islands of the Philippines use both skits (mini-dramas) and puppet shows as a way for children to communicate to one another about their daily lives. These provide the children with valuable therapeutic experiences as they share painful aspects of their lives with others who have had similar experi-

[9] Johnson et al. (1995).

ences. This also enables them to find common areas of concern on which they would like to work collectively. Theatre is also used by representative children from the local groups in regional workshops and national congresses. In this way, local issues are carried forth all the way to presentation to other children throughout the Philippines at the National Congress of Street and Working Children.

In the Philippines, a great source of stimulus and advice for theatre in the country has been the Philippine Educational Theatre Association (PETA). PETA offers some valuable pointers in group dynamics to consider.[10] In its children's theatre teacher's manual, PETA stresses the development of self-esteem and the fostering of social skills between children. Theatre has great value for enabling children to express their ideas to one another and, through this, to learn the skills of social interaction and cooperation. In preparing for performances, children learn to lead, to follow instructions, and to give and receive feedback.

PETA emphasizes the importance of physical arrangements in their children's theatre workshops. Ideally, at first, children should be seated comfortably on the floor in a circle, with the teachers or facilitators sitting as members of that circle. PETA stresses that, while one should be trying to avoid authority, there is a need for the facilitator to be in control of the workshop situation. The difficult balance between an atmosphere of free expression and spontaneity and one of order and discipline is, they believe, best achieved through advance planning and a clear structure for the activity. The facilitator helps clarify ideas, suggests new material or procedures, and assists the children when they run into problems. Before children can be expected to write or produce their own skit or play, PETA tells us they will need some experiences to make them feel comfortable in performance. The best approach is to create a situation where children are at ease, interested, happy, and active – in short, a playful situation. To help children move into an imaginary frame of mind, they are asked to lie down and close their eyes, and

are then told a story with them as a central figure, which takes them through many different spaces, sensations, and even self-transformations. Other exercises involve taking children to dramatically different environments and asking them to draw or write about how they felt and what they saw in these different settings. The exercises enable the children to identify their own feelings and share them with one another. Clearly these experiences are valuable to any group wishing to improve environmental awareness and communication whether or not they choose to go on to develop dramatic productions.

RITUALS AND SPECIAL EVENTS: FESTIVALS, PARADES, AND PLANT-INS

Regrettably, many adults seem to be more interested in getting children involved in single large-scale events than in finding ways to support them in lasting genuine participatory projects. I have already used the term social mobilization to describe this kind of animation. But many of the same kinds of methods – festivals, parades, demonstrations, and tree plant-ins – can also be used as introductions to long-term opportunities for children to participate in environmental programmes. Also, all environmental programmes need moments of pause in order to celebrate their existence, mark their success, help change their direction, or remind a larger community of their presence.

Festivals are an excellent way to launch an environmental project or move it to another stage. Kaplan found in his Neighbourhoods 2000 intergenerational programme that mural-making can be an effective way of bringing a wide range of ages out into a neighbourhood to work together. By creating a mural of what they would like to see in their neighbourhood in the future during an all-day event in the streets of Long Island City, New York, Kaplan was able to kick off a successful year-long activity in which senior citizens volunteered to work with teenagers and children to develop planning proposals for the neighbourhood's controversial water-

[10] Philippine Educational Theatre Association (1994).

Figure 82:
A parade through the streets of a poor neighbourhood of Sao Paulo designed by children and two streetworkers from the Secretaria di Minor (Ministry of Childhood).

front areas.[11] A few months later, the Neighbourhoods 2000 organizer was able to attract over 300 community residents into the local senior citizen's centre for a Futures Festival. Sixteen different participating organizations from the neighbourhood attended and presented their ideas in the form of models, skits, and songs. The goal was twofold: to provide recognition to the momentum of the effort of the young and older persons working on the project and to inform the wider community of some important planning decisions that needed to be faced.

Parades can also be used to focus community energy on achieving a particular goal in a short period of time, or to launch a programme of action. The 'Eco-caravanas' or ecological theme parades of the National Programme of Working Children (PMT) in Ecuador were effective invitations for hundreds of children to become involved in their environmental programmes. Children of all ages can participate in the event itself, but they may need adult involvement in planning and management because of the complexity of the logistics, coordination, and interaction with government bureaucracies.

'Plant-ins' are good examples of special events for all age groups. Over the past three decades, tree plantings have become an effective introduction to environmental action for tens of thousands of children in dozens of countries. Unfortunately, many of these projects miss the opportunity to build upon the momentum of such events and to offer some continuity by establishing ongoing tree management programmes.

[11] Kaplan (1990, 1991, 1994).

CHAPTER 15

Conclusions: Communities for Sustainable Development in the Twenty-First Century

As tomorrow's adult citizens, children must be able to create and manage sustainable communities. In writing this book, I have often been daunted by the thought of the enormous barriers to moving society towards community sustainable development, but I have also learned that millions of people are already groping for new kinds of relationships to the environment. I have documented many examples of children working together in new ways, with a different vision of the environment. Beneath the headlong growth of consumerism, more and more people are feeling the need for a deeper meaning to life. They are showing a willingness to work and even make sacrifices for the sake of the environment. There is still no general public recognition, however, that the loss of the sense of community, which is growing in the industrialized world, is part of the same trend towards globalism, and that local environmental action can also be a way of reconnecting people with one another. In many countries, however, there is a growing disenchantment with the rationalism of science, technology, and environmental planning, and a turning towards the spiritual, the intuitive, and even the magical for insights to the meaning of life.

The central theme of this book is that children need to understand the right of all persons to have a voice in establishing a healthy and meaningful life for themselves on this planet, in accordance with principles of ecological sustainability and in balance with the needs of all others, including future human generations and other living things. It has been argued that this can be

achieved only through frequent experiences with direct democratic participation in institutional settings: children's organizations, community organizations, and most notably schools. In this way, children can come gradually to construct authentic participatory democracies as adults. They can help transform the tired systems of representative democracy, driven by marketplace forces, which work against community building and local sustainability, towards a society in which direct democratic participation is part of daily life. For global sustainable development, the world needs local community sustainable development.

Already, the forces of globalism are destroying a sense of community in many parts of the world as people lose the capacity to use their local resources in familiar ways to produce a livelihood for themselves. More and more decisions about development are made by distant persons who know nothing about the uniqueness of places or of local cultural practices. To establish local sustainable development, communities will need to engage in a kind of 'cultural resistance' to the forces of globalism. They will need to build upon and develop local knowledge through research, dialogue, and reflection on how they should act to make best use of their resources. Cultural continuity will be maintained in using the environment, but, in most instances, there will now also be a more self-conscious approach to preserving the environment for future generations and other living things with greater equality for all.

An important by-product of local sustainable development will be a reversal of the trend towards cultural homogeneity. Through their efforts, children will help maintain, and even rescue, the identity, the uniqueness, of places.

Fostering a sense of place and an affection for the local environment and community in childhood seems an overwhelming task when one thinks of the enormous and expanding power of technology and the mass media to seduce children into desiring all that they do not currently have. Cultural resistance will necessarily involve resistance to this rampant consumerism. Children in the 1990s have already begun to understand from an early age the importance of not using up some of the earth's more fragile natural resources, such as the rainforests. A more challenging step is for them to begin to criticize the failure of their own communities to be sustainable. This task is only just beginning, and so this book has not been able to point to any communities that are yet successfully working with a large proportion of their residents to assess critically and to foster their communities' sustainability. There is an urgent need to establish new kinds of organizations and ways of working with children that will enable them to play a central role at the local level in this revolutionary way of thinking about development.

The education of children in familiar ways will not give us a solution to this new kind of development. It is oriented to a world beyond the local, it stresses competition rather than cooperation, it is about success rather than fulfilment, and it is abstract and unconnected to practical resourcefulness. The practice of sustainable development needs to be brought to all institutions in every community. But for purposes of mobilizing for change it seems necessary to establish in all communities, whether they be villages or urban neighbourhoods, spaces in which people can engage in regular dialogue on sustainable development. Public schools may seem obvious locations because they exist in most communities of the world, but it is unlikely that they will take a lead in becoming places to reflect on social change, given their traditional role as preservers of the status quo. More likely, communities will need to establish

Figure 83:
A girl from the Environmental Exchange Programme in rural Vermont using a microphone as part of a video-documentation of the visit by the 'twin' school from Harlem, New York City.

new centres lying somewhere between school, home, and workplace – the modern equivalent of a town hall or community meeting house.

We can imagine what some of the fundamental qualities of children's developing relationship to their community and environment will need to be, though the specific mechanisms to be created will vary according to culture. Children will have opportunities from the earliest possible age to develop an affection for the natural world through informal play and learning in biodiverse settings. From such experiences in early childhood, they will have progressively expanding opportunities to manage the environment with caring adults in their homes. Even before entering school, children will gradually and naturally come to assume that they have a right and responsibility to be involved with others in caring for any setting in which they play and work. They will have opportunities to participate in community decision making with people of all ages at increasing scales according to their growing range of experience. To this end, each community would have a community environmental centre, perhaps based at the local elementary school, but certainly designed to be used by all residents of all ages. With this new emphasis on community, parochialism would be avoided for the environmental centres would work in collaboration with each other in bioregional associations. There would also be regular exchanges between children of different cultures, social classes, and environments, both regionally and internationally, sharing the work they are conducting in their communities.

With this new emphasis on community, parochialism would be avoided for the environmental centres would work in collaboration with each other in bioregional associations. There would also be regular exchanges between children of different cultures, social classes, and environment, both regionally and internationally, sharing the work they are conducting in their communities.

This book has argued that sustainable development in the 21st century will need to be achieved locally by thinking citizens. Along with greater equity in the distribution of resources, we will need greater participation in decision-making regarding those resources. Children will need to help us go beyond the environmental dictum coined in the 1970s, to 'think globally, act locally'. The new call will be for citizens to think and act, both locally and globally.

Bibliography

Aarons, A., & Hawes, H. (1979). Child-to-Child. London: Macmillan.

Adams, E. (1982). Art and the Built Environment. Harlow: Longman.

Adams, E. (1990). Learning Through Landscapes: The Final Report. Winchester, UK: Learning Through Landscapes Trust.

Alcoff, & Potter (Eds.). (1993). Feminist methodologies. London: Routledge.

Alston, P. (Ed.). (1994). The Best Interests of the Child: Reconciling Culture and Human Rights. Florence, Italy: International Child Development Centre, UNICEF and Oxford: Clarendon Press.

Ariyaratne, A. T. (1978). A Struggle to Awaken. Sri Lanka: Sarvodaya Research Institute, 148 Galle Road, Dehiwala, Sri Lanka.

Ariyaratne, A. T. (1980). Collected Works–Volumes 1 and 2. Sarvodaya Research Institute, 148 Galle Road, Dehiwala, Sri Lanka.

Armstrong, A. (1979). Planning and Environmental Education. London: Centre for Environmental Studies.

Armstrong, A. (1980). Plan Away A Day. Bulletin of Environmental Education, 105(Jan, 1980), 9–19.

Arnstein, S. R. (1979). Eight Rungs on the Ladder of Citizen Participation. Journal of the American Institute of Planners.

Aronowitz, S., & Dhaliwal, A. (1994). Radical Democracy. Socialist Review, 93(3).

Bajracharya, D. (1994). Primary Environmental Care for Sustainable Livelihood: A UNICEF Perspective. Childhood, 2, 41–55.

Bajracharya, D. (1995). UNICEF and the Challenge of Sustainable Development: An Overview. New York: UNICEF.

Ball, C., & Ball, M. (1973). Education for a Change. Harmondsworth, Middlesex: Penguin.

Bandura, A., & Walters, R. H. (1963). Social Learning and Personality Development. New York: Holt, Rinehart & Winston.

Barber, B. (1995) Strong Democracy: Participatory Politics for a New Age. Boulder, Colorado: University of Colorado Press

Baumrind, D. (1971). Current patterns of parental authority. Developmental Psychology Monograph, 4 (1, Pt.2).

Beddes, R., & Mares, C. (1988). A New Approach to Primary School Linking Around the World. Avon: Avon County Council, Education Department.

Benjamin, J. (1976). Grounds for Play. London: Belford Square Press/The National Council for Social Service.

Berry, W. (1987). The Landscape of Harmony: Two Essays on Wildness and Community. Madley, Hereford, England: Five Seasons Press.

Berry, W. (1990). A Remarkable Man. In W. Berry (Ed.), What are People for: Essays by Wendell Berry (pp. 17–29). San Francisco: North Point Press.

Bishop, J., Kean, J., & Adams, E. (1992). Children, Environment and Education: Personal Views of Urban Environmental Education in Britain. Children's Environments, 9(1), 49–67.

Bjorklid, P. (1994). Children - Traffic - Environment. Architecture and Behaviour, 10 (4), 399–406.

Blanc, C. S., & Contributors (1994). Urban Children in Distress: Global Predicaments and Innovative Strategies. Florence, Italy: International Child Development Centre of UNICEF & London: Gordon and Breach.

Blaut, McCleary and Blaut (1972). Environmental Mapping in Young Children. Environment and Behaviour, 2, 335–349.

Boulding, E. (1987). Children's Rights and the Wheel of Life. New Brunswick, New Jersey: Transaction Books.

Boyden, J., & Holden, P. (1991). Children of the Cities. London: Zed Books.

Bradley, S. M. (1995). How People Use Pictures: An Annotated Bibliography. London: International Institute for Environment and Development.

Brigham, N. (1982). How to Do Leaflets, Newsletters and Newspapers. New York: Hastings House.

Brobze, L., & Brown, P. (1993). The Blue Peter Action Book. London: BBC Books.

Brower, S., Gray, L., & Stough, R. (1977). Doll Play as a Tool for Urban Designers. Baltimore, Maryland: Baltimore City Planning Commission.

Carson, R. (1984). The Sense of Wonder. New York: Harper & Row.

Chandler, M. J. (1977). Social cognition: A selective review of current research. In W. F. Overton & J. Gallagher (Eds.), Knowledge and Development (pp. 93–147). New York: Plenum.

Chawla, L. (1986). Ecology of Environmental Memory. Children's Environments Quarterly, 3(4), 34–42.

Chawla, L., & Hart, R. (1988). The Roots of Environmental Concern. In Proceedings of the 19th Annual Conference of the Environmental Design Research Association. Oklahoma City: Environmental Design Research Association.

Chawla, L. (1994). In the First Country of Places: Nature, Poetry, and Childhood Memory. State University of New York Press.

Child-to-Child Trust (1995). The Child-to-Child Training Manual. London: The Child-to-Child Trust.

Childhood City Newsletter (1980). Special Issue on Participation Methods. New York: Children's Environments Research Group, City University of New York.

Children's Environments (Journal). London: Chapman & Hall. Back Issues may be purchased from the Children's Environments Research Group, 33 West 42nd Street, New York, NY 10036 USA.

City Farmer. National Federation of City Farms, The Old Vicarage, 66 Fraser Street, Windmill Hill, Bedminster, Bristol, B534LY, United Kingdom.

Clay, G. (1969). Remembered Landscapes. In P. Shepard & D. McKinley (Eds.), The Subversive Science: Essays Toward an Ecology of Man. Boston: Houghton Mifflin.

Cobb, E. (1977). The Ecology of Imagination in Childhood. New York: Columbia University Press.

Cockett, M. (1993). Art and the Built Environment. Manchester: Manchester City Council Education Department.

Coggin, P. A. (1968). Wiltshire Schools' M4 Motorway Project. Town and Country Planning (Oct./Nov.), 494–496.

Coggin, P. A. (Ed.). (1974). The Birth of a Road. London: Rupert Hart-Davis.

Coles, R. (1986). The Political Life of Children. Boston: Houghton Mifflin Company.

Council for Environmental Education (1990). Earth Works Action Pack. In Council for Environmental Education, University of Reading, London Road, Reading, RG1 5AQ, United Kingdom.

Cox, T. H., Lobel, S. A., & McLeod, P. L. (1991). Effects of Ethnic Group Cultural Differences on Cooperative and Competitive Behavior on a Group Task. Academy of Management Journal, 34(4), 827–847.

Daiute, C. and Griffin, T. M. In ???

Daiute, C. (Ed.). (1993). The Development of Literacy Through Social Interaction. San Francisco: Jossey-Bass Publishers.

Dallape, F. (1987). An Experience with Street

Children. Nairobi, Kenya: Undugu Society.

Dallape, F., & Gilbert, C. (1994). Children's Participation in Action Research. Harare, Zimbabwe: ENDA, PO Box 3492, Harare, Zimbabwe.

Dawes, R. M., van de Kragt, A. J. C., & Orbell, J. M. (1990). Cooperation for the Benefit of Us–Not Me, or My Conscience. In J. J. Mansbridge (Ed.), Beyond Self-Interest. Chicago and London: The University of Chicago Press.

De Vries, R., & Zan, B. (1993). Moral classrooms, moral children. New York: Teachers College Press.

DEA Monthly Bulletin. Development Education Association, 29–31 Cowper Street, London EC2A 4AP, United Kingdom.

Development Education Journal. Development Education Association, 29–31 Cowper Street, London EC2A 4AP, United Kingdom.

Dewey, J. (1900). The School and Society. Chicago: University of Chicago Press.

Doise, W., & Mugny, G. (1984). The Social Development of the Intellect. Oxford: Pergamon Press.

Dowmunt, T. (1969). Children and Video. London: Interaction.

EDEV (Education for Development) News. New York and Geneva: Education for Development Section, UNICEF.

Educación Rural Andina (ERA) (1993). Estructura Curricular Diversificada. Cuzco, Peru: Educacion Rural Andina. Oswaldo Baca 402, Urb. Magisterio, Cuzco.

Educators for Social Responsibility (1992(a)). ESR Journal: Educating for Democracy. Cambridge, Mass, USA: Educators for Social Responsibility.

Educators for Social Responsibility (1992(b)). Taking Part: An Elementary Curriculum in the Participation Series. Cambridge, Mass, USA: Educators for Social Responsibility.

Elkind, D. (1967). Egocentrism in adolescence. Child Development, 38, 1025–1034.

Elliott, J. (1991). Action Research for Educational Change. Milton Keynes, UK: Open Press University.

Environment and Urbanization (Journal). International Institute for Environment and Development, 3 Endsleigh Street, London, WC1 0DD, United Kingdom. Published twice yearly.

Erikson, E. (1950). Childhood and Society In New York. New York: Norton.

Erikson, E. (1980). Identity and the Life Cycle. New York: Norton.

Escobar, A. (1995). Encountering Development: The Making and Unmaking of the Third World. Princeton, New Jersey: Princeton University Press.

Espinosa, M. F. (1994). The First Amazonian Children's Conference on the Environment. Children's Environments, 11(3), 212–220.

Fiviush, R. (1994). The Remembering of Self: Construction and Accuracy in the Self-Narrative. Cambridge, UK: Cambridge University Press.

Fleisher, P. (1993). Changing Our World: A Handbook for Young Advocates. Tucson, Arizona: Zephyr Press.

Fountain, S. (1994). Learning Together: Global Education 4 to 7. Cheltenham, England: Stanley Thomas.

Fountain, S. (1995). It's Only Right!: A Practical Guide to Learning About the Convention on the Rights of the Child. New York: Education for Development Section, UNICEF.

Fox, W. (1990). Toward a Transpersonal Ecology: Developing New Foundations for Environmentalism. Boston: Shambhala.

Francis, M. (1982). Community, Conflict and the Classroom. Bulletin for Environmental Education (June).

Francis, M. (1988). Negotiating Between Child and Adult Design Values. Design Studies, 9(2), 67–75.

Freire, P. (1970). Pedagogy of the Oppressed. Harmondsworth, Middlesex: Penguin Books.

Freire, P. (1974). Education: The Practice of Freedom. London: Writers & Readers Publishing Cooperative.

Freire, P. (1975). Cultural Action for Freedom.

Harmondsworth, Middlesex: Penguin Education.

Gardner, H. (1993). Frames of Mind: The Theory of Multiple Intelligences. London: Paladin.

Gibson, T. (1993). Making it Happen: A User's Guide to the Neighborhood Action Packs. Lightmoor: Neighbourhood Initiatives Foundation, The Poplars, Lightmoor, Telford, TF43QN, United Kingdom.

Gilligan, C. (1982). In a Different Voice. Cambridge: Harvard University Press.

Godwin, N. (1993) Education for Development: An Educational Concept for Global Citizenship. In UNICEF (1992) Preparing Children to Participate in their Future: Report of the Education for Development Seminar for Eastern and Southern Africa. New York: UNICEF.

Goodman, P. (1957). Growing Up Absurd. New York: Random House.

Granfield, L. (1993). Extra! Extra! The Who, What, Where, When and Why of Newspapers. New York: Orchard Books.

GRAPEs (Global Reporters, Artists, Producers and Editors), (1996). We're in Print: The Whole Story by Kids for Kids. New York: Children's Environments Research Group, City University of New York Graduate School, 33 West 42nd Street, New York, NY 10036, USA.

Guijt, I., Fugelsand, A., & Kisadha, T. (1995). It is the Young Trees that Make a Thick Forest: A Report on Redd Barna's Learning Experiences with Participatory Rural Appraisal. London: International Institute for Environment and Development.

Guthrie, D., Bentley, N., & Keck, A. K. (1994). The Young Author's Do-It-Yourself Book: How to Write, Illustrate and Produce Your Own Book. Brookfield: The Millbrook Press.

Hanbury, C., & McCrum, S. (1994). We Are On the Radio. London: Child-to-Child Trust.

Hardoy, J. E., Mitlin, D., & Satterthwaite, D. (1992). Environmental Problems in Third World Cities. London: Earthscan.

Hart, R. A. (1971) Aerial Geography: An Experiment in Elementary Education. Graduate School of Geography, Clark University, Place Perception – Worcester, MA.

Hart, R., & Moore, G. T. (1976). The Development of Spatial Cognition: A Review. In W. Ittelson, H. Proshansky, & L. Rivlin (Eds.), Environmental Psychology: People and their Physical Settings New York: Holt, Rinehart and Winston.

Hart, R. A. (1978). Children's Experience of Place: A Developmental Study. New York: Irvington Publishers, Inc.

Hart, R., & Perez, C. (1981). The Environmental Exchange Program. Bulletin of Environmental Education.

Hart, R., & Chawla, L. (1982). The Development of Children's Concern for the Environment. Zeitschrift für Umelweltpolitik.

Hart, R. A. (1982). Wildlands for Children: A Consideration of the Values of Natural Environments in Landscape Planning. Landschaft und Stadt, 14(1), 33–40.

Hart, R. (1983). Children's Spontaneous Architecture. In C. Moore (Ed.), Home Sweet Home: American Vernacular Domestic Architecture. New York: Rizzoli.

Hart, R. (1987) The Changing City of Childhood. Publication of the Annual Catherine T. Maloney Memorial Scholarship Lecture, City College of New York.

Hart, R. (1987). Children's Participation in Planning and Design: Theory, Research and Practice. In C. Weinstein & T. David (Eds.), Spaces for Children. New York: Plenum.

Hart, R. (1992). Children's Participation: From Tokenism to Citizenship. Florence: International Child Development Centre, UNICEF.

Hart, R., Daiute, C., Iltus, S., Sabo, K., Kritt, D., & Rome, M. (1996). Child and Youth Development Through Community Participation and Children's Developing Capacity to Participate. Report to the Children and the Environment Project of The California Wellness Foundation, Berkeley, California.

Hart, R. (1993). Affection for Nature and the Promotion of Earth Stewardship. New York: Children's Environments Research Group, City University of New York, Graduate School.

Heath, S. B., & McLaughlin, M. W. (Eds.). (1993). Identity and Inner-City Youth: Beyond Ethnicity and Gender. New York: Teachers College Press.

Hester Jr., R. T. (1984). Planning Neighborhood Space with People. New York: Van Nostrand Reinhold Company.

Hopkins, S., & Winters, J. (1990). Discover the World: Empowering Children to Value Themselves and Others. Gabrioloa Island, BC, Canada: New Society Publishers.

Hungerford, H., Litherland, R. A., Peyton, R. B., Ramsey, J. M., & Volk, T. L. (1990). Investigating and Evaluating Environmental Issues and Actions: Skill Development Modules. Champaign, IL: Stipes Publishing.

Iltus, S., & Hart, R. (1995). Participatory Planning and Design of Recreational Spaces with Children. Architecture & Behaviour, 10(4), 361–370.

International Children's Play Journal (3 issues per year). London: Chapman & Hall.

Isaacs, S. (1930). Intellectual Growth in Young Children. New York: Harcourt Brace.

IUCN (1991). Walia: The Approach Practical Guide. Gland, Switzerland: International Union for the Conservation of Nature.

Johnson, K. (1977) Do as the Land Bids: A Study of Okomi Resource Use on the Eve of Irrigation. Ph.D. Dissertation, Clark University, Worcester, Massachusetts.

Johnson, V., Hill, J., & Ivan-Smith, E. (1995). Listening to Smaller Voices: Children in an Environment of Change. Chard, Somerset, United Kingdom: Actionaid.

Jones, S. (1979). The Houses Game. Bulletin of Environmental Education, 99.

Kaplan, M. (1990). Designing Community Participation Special Events that Cross Generational Boundaries.

In R. Selby, K. Anthony, J. Choi, & B. Orland (Eds.), Proceedings of the 21st Annual Conference of the Environmental Design Research Association (pp. 120–128). Oklahoma City, OK: Environmental Design Research Association.

Kaplan, M. (1991). Neighborhoods 2000: An Intergenerational Urban Studies Curriculum (Guidebook for Teachers). New York: Center for Human Environments, City University of New York Graduate School.

Kaplan, M. (1994). Promoting Community Education and Action Through Intergenerational Programming. Children's Environments, 11(1), 48–60.

Kassam, Y., & Mustafa, K. (Eds.). (1982). Participatory Research: An Emerging Alternative Methodology in Social Science Research. Society for Participatory Research in Asia, 45 Sainik Farm, Khanpur, New Delhi-110 062.

Katz, C. (1986a) If There Weren't Kids There Wouldn't be Fields: Children's Environmental Learning, Knowledge and Interactions in a Changing Socio-Economic Context in Rural Sudan. Ph.D. Dissertation, Clark University, Worcester, Massachusetts.

Katz, C. (1986b). Children and the Environment: Work, Play and Learning in Rural Sudan. Children's Environments, 3(4), 43–51.

Kean, J. and Adams, E. (1991) Local Environmental Resource Centers. Newcastle: The Newcastle Architecture Workshop.

Keating, M. (1994). The Earth Summit's Agenda for Change: A plain language version of Agenda 21 and the other Rio Agreements. Centre for Our Common Future.

Kellert, S., & Wilson, E. O. (Eds.). (1993). The Biophilia Hypothesis. Washington DC: Island Press.

Korten, D. C. (1990). Getting to the 21st Century: Voluntary Action and the Global Agenda. West Hartford: Kumarian Press.

Kritt, D. (1993). Authenticity, Reflection and Self-evaluation in Alternative Assessment. Middle

School Journal, 25 (2), 43–44.

L'Anacej (National Association for Children and Youth Boards) (1995). Children and Young People's City Councils: An Evaluation. In G. H. Bell (Eds.), Educating European Citizens (pp. 35–45).

Learning Through Landscapes and the Royal Society for the Protection of Birds (1992). Wildlife and the School Environment. Winchester, UK: Learning Through Landscapes Trust.

Lee-Smith, D., & Chauwdry, T. (1990). Environmental Information for and from Children. Environment and Urbanization, 2(2), 27–32.

Leopold, A. (1966). A Sand County Almanac. Oxford University Press.

Liben, L., & Downs, R. (1986) Children's Production and Comprehension of Maps: Increasing Graphic Literacy. Department of Psychology and Geography, Pennsylvania State University, University Park, PA, 16802.

Liben, L. & Downs, R. (1992). Developing an Understanding of Graphic Representations in Children and Adults: The Case of Geo-Graphics. Cognitive Development, 7, 331–349.

Living Earth Foundation (1994). The Living Earth: A Resource for Learning. London: Hodder and Stoughton.

Lorenzo, R. (1988). Let's Discover the Urban Environment. Rome, Italy: World Wide Fund for Nature.

Lorenzo, R. (1990). Gruppo Futuro: Children Designing the Neighborhood Futures. In Architecture Multiple and Complex. Florence, Italy: Sansoni Editor.

Lorenzo, R. (1991). Imaginare Il Futuro. Panda Junior (WWF Italy), 25(9).

Lucas, B. (1994). Learning Through Landscapes: An Organization's Attempt to Move School Grounds to the Top of the Educational Agenda. Children's Environments, 12(2), 233–244.

Maccoby, E. E., & Martin, J. A. (1983). Socialization in the Context of the Family: Parent-Child Interaction. In P. Mussen (Ed.), Manual of Child Psychology Volume 1 (pp. 1–102). New York: Wiley.

Marcus, H., & Kityama, S. (1991). Cultural and the self: Implications for cognition, emotion, and motivation. Psychological Review, 98, 224–253.

Matthews, G. B. (1994). The Philosophy of Childhood. Cambridge: Harvard University Press.

Mazingira (Journal). Contact The Mazingira Institute, Box 14550, Nairobi, Kenya.

McKibben, B. (1995). Human and Wild: True Stories of Living Lightly on the Earth. Boston: Little Brown.

McKinnon, G., & Sudheer, C. (1994). Wee Green School Pack: Introduction to Creating Wildlife Projects Within Schoolgrounds for Nursery and Primary School Age Children. In High School Yards Nursery School, High School Yards, Off Infirmary Street, Edinburgh, EH1 1LZ, Scotland.

Mitchell, M. S., Stapp, M. K., & William, B. (1994). Field Manual for Water Quality Monitoring: An Environmental Education Program for Schools. Dexture, Michigan: Thomson-Shore.

Moore, R. C. (1980). Learning form the Yard. In P. F. Wilkinson (Ed.), Innovation in Play Environments London: Croom Helm.

Moore, R. C. (in press). Natural Learning. Berkeley: Mig Communications.

Nabhan, G. P., & Trimble, S. (1994). The Geography of Childhood: Why Children Need Wild Places. Boston: Beacon Press.

Nelson, K. (1995). Making Sense: The Acquisition of Shared Meaning. New York: Academic.

Nelson, D. (1977). City Building: A Way to Learn. Social Studies Review, 16(3).

Nelson, D. (1984) Transformations: Process and Theory. Santa Monica, CA: Center for City Building Education Programs.

N. G. O. Committee of UNICEF

Nicholson, S. (19??). How Not to Cheat Children: The Theory of Loose Parts. Landscape Architecture.

Nottingham Youth Environment Forum (1994). Plan It: The Essential Guide to Saving the Planet. Contact Andy Rothery, Environment Officer: Nottinghamshire

County Council, Trent Bridge House, Fox Road, West Bridgford, Nottingham, NG2 6BJ, United Kingdom.

Oakley, M., & Russel, G. (1979). Planners and Teachers. The Planner, July, 106–110.

Oakley, P., & Marsden, D. (1990). Approaches to Participation in Rural Development. Geneva: International Labour Office/ACC Task Force on Rural Development.

Orr, D. W. (1992). Ecological Literacy: Education and the Transition to a Postmodern World. Albany, New York: State University of New York.

Outreach Information Packs. (1994). United Nations Environment Program, PO Box 30552, Nairobi, Kenya.

Pacheco, M. (1992). Recycling in Bogota: Developing a Culture for Urban Sustainability. Environment and Urbanization, 4(No. 2), 74–79.

Participatory Research Network (1982). Participatory Research: An Introduction. New Delhi: Society for Participatory Research in Asia, 45 Sainik Farm, Khanpur, New Delhi, 110062.

Peace Child International (1994). Rescue Mission Planet Earth: A Children's Edition of Agenda 21. London: Kingfisher Books.

Philippine Educational Theatre Association (1984). Children's Theatre Teacher's Manual. Manila: Philippine Educational Theatre Association.

Piaget, J. (1954). The Construction of Reality in the Child. New York: Basic Books.

Piaget, J. (1960). The Child's Conception of Physical Causality. Totowa, New Jersey: Littlefield, Adams, Patterson.

Piaget, J. (1963, orig. French 1947). The Psychology of Intelligence. Tokowa, New Jersey: Littlefield Adams.

Piaget, J. (1965). The Moral Development of the Child. New York: Free Press.

Play Rights (quarterly newsletter). IPA Resources, National Play Information Centre, 359–361 Euston Road, London, NW1 3AL, United Kingdom.

Posch, P. (1994). Networking in Environmental Education. In Evaluating Innovation in Environmental Education. Paris: OECD.

Purdy, L. M. (1992). In Their Best Interest?: The Case against Equal Rights for Children. Ithaca, NY: Cornell University Press.

Ranger, G. (1991). Town Trails and Learning Outcomes. Streetwise(6), 30–31.

Redclift, M. (1987). Sustainable Development: Exploring the Contradictions. London and New York: Methuen.

Reiff, J. C. (1992). Learning styles: What research says to the teacher. Washington, DC: National Education Association.

Riger, S. (1993). What's Wrong with Empowerment. American Journal of Community Psychology, 21(3), 279–292.

Robottom, I. (1985). Evaluation in Environmental Education: Time for a Change in Perspective. The Journal of Environmental Education, 17(1), 31–36.

Rogoff, B., Sellers, J., Pirolta, S., Fox, N., & White, S. H. (1976). Age of Assignment of Roles and Responsibilities to Children: A Cross Cultural Survey. Human Development, 19.

Ruiz, H. R. (1990). A Manual on Community-Based Monitoring. Manila, The Philippines: UNICEF.

Sabo, K., Hart, R. A. and Iltus, S. (1996). Children's Participation in the Evaluation of Projects and Programmes. Report to the Children and the Environment Project of the California Wellness Foundation. New York: Children's Environmental Research Group, City University Graduate School.

Salomon, G. (1979). Interaction of Media, Cognition, and Learning: An Exploration of How Symbolic Forms Cultivate Mental Skills and Affect Knowledge Acquisition (First ed.). San Francisco: Jossey-Bass, Inc., Publishers.

Sarbin, T. & Allen, V. (1968). Role Enactment. In G. Lindzey & E. Aronson (Eds.) Handbook of Social Psychology (pp. 488–567). Cambridge: MA: Addison-Wesley.

Satterthwaite, D., Hart, R., Levy, C., Mitlin, D., Ross, D., Smit, J., & Stephens, C. (1996). An Environment for Children: Understanding and acting on the environmental hazards that threaten infants and children and their parents. London: Earthscan.

Scanlan, T. (1978). Neighborhood Geography: A Research Manual for Teachers. Toronto, Ontario: Is Five Foundation.

Schaetzel Lesko, W. (1992). No Kidding Around: America's Young Activists are Changing Our World and You Can Too. Kensington, Maryland: Information, USA.

Schiefelbein, E. (1991). In Search of the School of the 21st Century: Is the Colombian Escuela Nueva the Right Pathfinder? Santiago, Chile: UNESCO Regional Office for Education in Latin America and the Caribbean, Santiago, Chile.

Schwab, M. G. (1989). Participatory Research with Children: A New Approach to Nutrition Education. Journal of Nutrition Education, 21(184B).

Scoffham, S. (1980). Using the School Surroundings. London: Ward Lock.

Selman, R. L. (1980). The Growth of Interpersonal Understanding: Development and Clinical Analysis. New York: Academic Press.

Smith, M., & Plecan, J. (1989). School Garden Manual. Westport, CT: Save the Children.

Smith, P. K., Boulton, M. J., & Cowie, H. (1993). The Impact of Cooperative Group Work on Ethnic Relations in Middle School. Sage (School Psychology International), 14, 21–42.

Society for Participatory Research in Asia (1982). Participatory Research: An Introduction. New Delhi: Society for Participatory Research in Asia, 45 Sainik Farm, Khanpur, New Delhi-110062.

Sprague-Mitchell, L. (1934). Young Geographers. New York: Bank Street College of Education.

Stapp, W. B. & Mitchell, M. K. (1995). Field Manual for Global Low-Cost Water Quality Monitoring. Dexter, Michigan: Thomson-Shore, Inc..

Strayer, F. F. (1989). Co-adaptation within the early peer group: A psychobiological study of social competence. In B. H. Schneider, G. Attili, J. Nadel, & R. Weissberg (Eds.), Social Competence in Developmental Perspective (pp. 145–174). Dordrecht, Netherlands: Kluwer.

Streetwise (Journal, formerly the Bulletin of Environmental Education). Lewis Cohen Urban Studies Centre, University of Brighton, 68 Grand Parade, Brighton BN2 2JY, United Kingdom.

Stuart, J. S. (1991). Classroom Action Research in Africa: a Lesotho Case Study of Curriculum and Professional Development. In K. M. Lewin (Ed.), Educational Innovation in Developing Countries: Case-Studies of Changemakers. London: Macmillan.

Sugarman, S. (1987). Piaget's Construction of the Child's Reality. Cambridge: Cambridge University Press.

Tanner, T. (1980). Significant Life Experiences. Journal of Environmental Education, 11(4), 20–24.

Tay, A. K. B. (Ed.). Child-to-Child in Africa: Towards an Open Learning Strategy. UNESCO Digest 29. Paris: UNESCO, 1989.

Taylor-Ide, D., & Taylor, C. E. (1995). Community Based Sustainable Human Development. New York: UNICEF.

Thomas, L. (1970). Access for the Disabled (Project No. 71). London: Community Service Volunteers.

Titman, W. (1994). Special Places, Special People: The Hidden Curriculum of Schoolgrounds. Godalming, Surrey: World Wide Fund for Nature.

Torres, R. M. (1991). Escuela Nueva: Una Innovacion Desde El Estado. Quito, Ecuador:

Tracey, J. (1991). Adapting Town Trails for the National Curriculum. Streetwise(6), 20–23.

Triandis, H. C. (1989). Cross-Cultural Studies of Individualism-Collectivism. In J. J. Berman (Ed.), Nebraska Symposium on Motivation: Cross-Cultural Perspectives (pp. 41–133). Lincoln: University of Nebraska Press.

UKOWLA (UK One World Linking Association) (1993).

School Linking and The Curriculum. Chesterfield: UKOWLA, Town Hall, Chesterfield, S40 1LP, United Kingdom.

UNICEF (1987). Paulo Friere And The Street Educators: An Analytical Approach. Bogota: UNICEF, TACRO–The Americas and Caribbean Regional Office.

UNICEF (1992). Children and Agenda 21: A Guide to UNICEF issues in the Earth Summit's Blueprint for Development into the 21st Century. Geneva: UNICEF.

UNICEF (1993). Children, Environment and Sustainable Development: UNICEF Response to Agenda 21. In UNICEF Executive Board 1993 Session Summary: New York: Urban Section of UNICEF.

UNICEF (Bangladesh), (1993). Visualization in Participatory Programs: A Manual for Facilitators and Trainers in Participation Groups Events. Dhaka, Bangladesh: UNICEF.

UNICEF UK (1989). Clean Water – A Right For All. London, England: UNICEF.

UNICEF UK/Save the Children (1990). A four volume series on children's rights: It's Our Right, The Whole Child, Keep Us Safe, and Teacher's Handbook. London: UNICEF UK/Save the Children.

Valdivia, M., Jaegher, C., Cahuana, E., & Furman, R. (1990). Naturaleza y Communidad: Guia Metodológia Tercer Grado. Lima: Proyecto Escuela Ecologia y Communidad Campesina, Apdo. 140016, Lima 14, Peru.

Valdivia, M. (1991). Kay Pacha: Escuela Ecologia y Communidad Campesina. Lima: Proyecto Escuela Ecologia y Communidad Campesina, Apdo. 140016, Lima 14, Peru.

Van Matre, S. (1979). Sunship Earth: An Acclimatization Program for Outdoor Learning. Martinsville, Indiana: American Camping Association.

Van Matre, S. (1990). Earth Education: A New Beginning. Greenville, West Virginia: The Institute for Earth Education.

Ward, C., & Fyson, A. (1976). Streetwork: The Exploding School. London: Routledge & Kegan Paul.

Ward, C. (1978). The Child in the City. New York: Pantheon Books.

Ward, C. (1988). The Child in the Country. London: Robert Hale.

Wentworth, D. F., Couchman, J. K., MacBean, J. C., & Stecher, A. (1976). Mapping Small Places: Examining Your Environment. Toronto, Ontario: Holt, Rinehart & Winston.

Wheeler, K., & Waites, B. (1972). How to Make a Town Trail. A Special Double Issue of the Bulletin of Environmental Education (now Streetwise), November, 16 and 17.

Wigginton, E. (Ed.). (1973). Foxfire 2. Garden City, New York: Doubleday.

Wigginton, E., & and his students (Ed.). (1991). Foxfire: 25 Years. New York: Doubleday.

Wildlife Watch (1991). The River Report. Slough, United Kingdom: Richmond Publishing Co.

Wildlife Watch (1992). The Ozone Project. Slough, United Kingdom: Richmond Publishing Co.

Wildlife Watch (1994). Enviroscope: The Results Book. Slough, United Kingdom: Richmond Publishing Co.

Williams, R., Bidlack, C., & Brinson, B. (1994). The Rivers Curriculum Project: A Cooperative Interdisciplinary Model. Children's Environments, 11(3), 251–254.

Williamson, D. A., Williamson, S. H., Watkins, P. C., & Hughes, H. H. (1992). Increasing Cooperation Among Children Using Dependent Group-Oriented Reinforcement Contingencies. Behavior Modification, 16(3), 414–425.

Wilson, E. O. (1984). The Human Bond With Other Species. Cambridge: Harvard University Press.

World Commission on Environment and Development (1987). Our Common Future. Oxford: Oxford University Press.

Youniss, J. (1980). Parents and Peers in Social Development. Chicago: The University of Chicago Press.

Index

Page numbers in **bold** refer to figures and boxes